Just Between Us

Just Between Us

Pat & Jill Williams

WITH JERRY JENKINS

Fleming H. Revell Company
Tarrytown, New York

Scripture quotations in this publication are from The New King James Version. Copyright © 1979, 1980, 1982 Thomas Nelson, Inc., Publishers.

Library of Congress Cataloging-in-Publication Data
Williams, Pat.
    Just between us / Pat and Jill Williams with Jerry Jenkins.
        p.   cm.
    ISBN 0-8007-1663-9
    1. Parents—Prayer-books and devotions—English.
    2. Devotional calendars. I. Williams, Jill (Jill M. P.) II. Jenkins, Jerry B.
    III. Title.
    BV4845.W55   1991
    242'.2—dc20   91-15127
                                                          CIP

Published by the Fleming H. Revell Company
Tarrytown, New York 10591
Printed in the United States of America

TO busy parents who care

Why a Devotional Companion?

We are not pretending this book is all you need in your devotional life. First, of course, you need your Bible. When you have time for nothing else, read Scripture.

We also recommend lots of Christian books, not just devotionals. Some people decry the deluge of Christian books flooding the market, but if you have ever been to Eastern Europe or a Third World country, you know what a privilege we enjoy with so much Christian literature to choose from. It is not all first-rate, but enough of it is that we usually find ourselves in the middle of reading one of the latest offerings.

Few books purport to be total devotionals in themselves. Even those that do often recommend Scripture readings, so you need a Bible with those too. Many have recommended passages, a memory verse, thoughts for the day, summary questions, and the devotional thought or commentary. Ours, however, is not that. Ours is an a la carte selection for your devotional smorgasbord.

You should be in the Word every day, of course, but don't feel bad if you miss a day, or a week, or even two weeks in this book. If you misplace it or forget about it (ouch), or even get tired of it (OUCH!), just come back to it when you want to and fast forward to the appropriate date. This is not a book to be read in one sitting, nor is it one you *must* read every day for a year.

It is simply a devotional companion, something to think about each day in addition to your Scripture reading, praying, singing, journalizing, or whatever it is you do to maintain your walk with Christ. We won't always be profound or deep or theological. We will certainly try to be biblical, and though you won't find memory verses or recommended reading here, we're all for that. We are Scripture memorizers ourselves, and we even see value in reading through the Bible in a year. There are good guides for both of those disciplines.

Consider this a nonfattening, sugar-free dessert. It will take a minute or two to read each time, and we hope it tops off your meal of meaty spiritual food.

Throughout you will see references to us and our kids. Pat is the husband and the dad. He is president and general manager of the Orlando Magic professional basketball team and the Orlando SunRays professional baseball team. He's a busy executive, promoter, and speaker (speaking many times a year in all kinds of venues).

Jill is the wife and mother. She's a speaker, a vocalist, a violinist, chairperson of the board of The Adoption Centre in Maitland, Florida, and was named Mother of the Year in 1990 by Mom International of West Virginia (the birthplace of Mother's Day).

Our homegrown children are:

Jim (born in May 1974)
Bob (June 1977)
Karyn (July 1979)
Michael (June 1984)

Our adopted children are:

David, a Filipino (September 1979)
Peter, a Filipino (April 1980)
Stephen and Thomas (T. J.), twin Koreans (July 1981)

Brian, a Filipino (July 1981)
Sarah, a Korean (July 1980)
Andrea, a Korean (July 1981)
Samuel, a Filipino (May 1984)
Gabriela, a Romanian (November 1984)

That's thirteen in all, and except for Mom (January, never mind), David, and Gabriela, all the birthdays fall between April and July.

We know what it means to be busy parents, and we also know how important it is to keep carving out time for our walks with the Lord. Give us a minute or two a day, and let's enjoy the year together.

PAT AND JILL WILLIAMS

Just Between Us

❧January 1❧

The other day we heard a girl say her New Year's resolution was to gain twenty pounds. There's one you don't hear very often!

But she had a reason: last year she vowed to lose ten pounds and gained ten. So, by this time next year, if she has broken her resolution, will she have lost twenty?

Today is a good day to resolve to improve relationships. We are constantly trying to make smooth the male-female relationship in our home, partly because we have learned and are learning this marriage business the hard way (*see* our previous books, particularly *Rekindled*) and partly because we believe the adage that the best thing a father can do for his children is love their mother (and vice versa).

Here are a few admonitions for the new year:

Women, seldom tell a man he has no idea how difficult it is to be a woman. Don't feel compelled to start looking your age or your mother's age. Pretend you are still dating, and remember how important it is to look good. Try to remember what it was you liked about your husband in the first place.

Men, don't expect a ticker-tape parade every time you put something away. Don't believe your wife when she says she wants nothing for her birthday, Valentine's Day, anniversary, or Christmas. Call home when you are running late; she may have a romantic dinner planned. Try to remember what it was you liked about her in the first place.

✎§ January 2 ℈❧

Kids need occasional pushes.

Bobby got an unusual opportunity when he was very young. The baseball coach at nearby Rollins College said he could work out with the baseball team whenever he wanted. The coach, Boyd Coffee, said he would treat Bob, only eleven at the time, just like one of his catchers.

What a break! Bob, though small for his age, has always been a natural athlete and a good catcher (just like his dad, who played in the Phillies farm system). Bob would learn the finer points of the game, get into terrific shape, and enjoy a privilege unique to someone his age.

After the first day, though, when he suffered through drills, getting into shape, and being treated like everyone else, he cried and said he wasn't going back. Of course, we insisted. Now he can't wait to get there every chance he gets.

When Jim was fourteen, Pat took him to his first surfing competition. Jim was eager and confident until they arrived. He had become quite a proficient neighborhood surfer since coming to Florida, but now he saw all the tall, broad, bronzed sixteen-to-eighteen-year-olds, and he panicked.

"Dad, can't I just surf at the condo by myself?"

Pat would have none of it. Jim competed, and though he did not do well, he's a better surfer and will be a better man because he tried.

✎§ January 3 ℈❧

A few years ago, Pat got a letter from his old friend Landey Patton, the original Chicago Bulls mascot. Landey is an outspoken Christian who shared what he called "random thoughts that have captured my imagination in recent weeks and months," in the hope Pat might find "something of value in them."

Pat sure did, and maybe you will too:

1. Jesus Christ is the only Person in all of history to come to earth by His own choice. Everyone else is here because of the choices of other people.

2. Jesus came with the full knowledge that He was to give His life for others. No wonder He was called "a man of sorrows and acquainted with grief" (Isaiah 53:3). He thought in terms of giving; we usually think in terms of getting.

3. Jesus lived His entire life contrary to the great American dream. Though He was rich, Paul writes, for our sakes He became poor, that we through His poverty might be rich. He never owned property and never expressed a desire to do so. He said that a man's life does not consist of the abundance of his possessions.

4. The greatest transaction we will ever make is to begin a relationship with Jesus Christ. We trade our weakness for His strength, our sin for His righteousness, our mortality for His immortality, our sickness for His health, our anxiety for His peace, our hatred for His love, and our stupidity for His wisdom.

And that's no Bull.

❧ January 4 ☙

Our little Michael got hold of his sister's supplies for making jewelry. Next thing we knew, he had a pearl stuck in each ear.

There was no dislodging them, so we were off to the doctor.

With some probing and prodding and digging with a little suction device, the doctor removed the pearl from one ear. The other would not budge.

The doctor recommended oil, sleeping with that ear down, and care not to do anything that would send it deeper into the ear canal or lodge it tighter. If it didn't dislodge on its own, more serious medical procedures would probably be required, maybe even surgery.

Jill and Mike prayed and asked the rest of the family to do the same. The next morning Michael could hear better. Mom checked. No pearl in the ear. A quick check of the bed found it.

Michael had become convinced of the power of prayer overnight. Now he's become our unofficial family chaplain. Once when Jill was reminding the kids not to ask Granny for presents (we accept presents thankfully, but we never ask), Michael said, "Mom, the Bible says we're *supposed* to ask!"

Even if it results in a temporary misunderstanding of some biblical concepts, we recommend exercising spirituality in young children. God, Christ, the Bible, and prayer should be as normal a part of their everyday lives as eating, sleeping, and playing are.

❧ January 5 ❧

Jill has an aviary with dozens of birds and enjoys feeding and taking care of them. She also enjoys watching fish cavort in the small waterfall and pond outside the window where she stands as she does the dishes.

One day she was watching the fish glide among the lilies when she was distracted by a commotion at the nearby bird feeder. Several orioles had been enjoying the birdie breakfast Jill had put out there when several others from the oriole family showed up and wanted some too.

The original feasters flapped their wings and loudly scolded the newcomers, driving them off, only to see them come diving back, determined to take their place at the feeding trough.

Jill was struck by the fact that these birds were arguing over and being possessive of something that was not even theirs. It had been given to them by someone who merely liked them and wanted them to enjoy it. Now they were angry because someone else seemed to be horning in on "their" bounty.

Isn't that just like us? We have been freely given all things by our Heavenly Father to enjoy. They are of temporal value. He has given them to us out of love and concern, yet we fight and argue over them.

Doesn't it seem that we should focus on the eternal gifts He has given us and be as generous with those and our material blessings with the same measure of generosity He shows us?

❧ January 6 ☙

How things change in less than a decade!

The other day, we ran across Pat's list of "Our Blessings" from 1983. Back then we lived in New Jersey, Pat was general manager of the world champion Philadelphia 76ers, our marriage had been miraculously rekindled, and we had little idea that someday we would live in Florida with our dozen kids.

Here is the way Pat's blessing list looked then:

1. My wife, Jill, her patience, kindness, and class.
2. Three healthy, gifted children.
3. Two great in-laws.
4. A lovely house that's becoming a home.
5. Our growing ministry.
6. More friends than we'll ever realize.
7. Our health.
8. A good job that is exciting.
9. A desire for more children.
10. Our cottage at Eagles Mere.
11. A pastor who is a special teacher.
12. Barbara Albrecht, our secretary.
13. Lee O'Neil, our nanny and helper.
14. Our sense of humor.

We're a long way from New Jersey now, in more ways than one, but many of the things we counted as blessings then still bless us today. An annual list is a good idea.

❧ January 7 ❧

One of the sweetest things we have experienced has been our kids caring for, watching out for, and sympathizing with one another. This was evidenced in October 1988, when Jill took Bob and Karyn to try out for the annual Christmas show at Epcot Center.

In 1986, seven-year-old Karyn had survived the long, very competitive tryouts to land a spot singing with Carol Lawrence. That was a thrill and very rewarding, though it was grueling for the family because of trips to practices and shows. We had tried to talk Bob in to trying out for the boy's part, but he wasn't interested until he went and saw Karyn perform.

"I can do that," he said. The next year, they both made it. Again it was a strain, but it was also such a rewarding experience for the kids that we wanted them to do it for as long as they could.

In 1988, we took them to the tryouts, which lasted all day. Karyn hadn't eaten and lost her energy. Though the director of the show knew her work, it was the judges she had to impress.

When the kids finally emerged from backstage after the long day, both were sobbing. Jill's heart sank, assuming neither had been chosen. As it turned out, Bobby had made it and Karyn hadn't. She was heartbroken, and Bobby was crying for her. The next year they both made it again, but we'll never forget the year Bobby shared his little sister's sorrow.

⇜§ January 8 §⇝

When we moved from New Jersey to Florida in 1986, we left it to the movers to pack everything and get it down here. Because of our schedules, neither of us could stay and supervise. A temporary casualty were the boards Jill had used for years to chart the growth of the children.

She had begun marking annual heights on each board when Jimmy was little, and she was heartsick when she realized the boards had not reached the moving van. They must have looked like wood trim or something we wouldn't have wanted. Thus began a yearlong attempt to locate them and have them sent. Jill would not give up.

Finally, the boards were located, and our former secretary had them delivered to a church where Pat was to speak. He picked them up and personally flew them to Orlando more than a year after the move. It had been some time before the move when Jill had last measured the kids, so add a year to that, and you can see how old the last markings were.

What a thrill it was to measure the kids against those old marks and see the huge leaps in their growth! It got us thinking about God's yardstick and how He likes to see those leaps, that evidence of significant growth in our spiritual lives. What a disappointment it must be to Him to check our growth against a heavenly standard and find that despite our years as Christians, we have grown so little and so slowly.

❧ January 9 ☙

Pat's lengthy experience in athletics has shown us how rare a privilege it is to be associated with a team that is the best during a certain year. When Pat was in college, he played on a baseball team that had a chance to win the college world series but lost in a heartbreaker just before the finals.

In Chicago, he saw the Bulls lose early in the play-offs after building big leads against highly rated teams.

In Philadelphia, especially after acquiring Julius Erving, the 76ers were expected to win the world championship every year for several years. The gold ring eluded them year after year, until they finally won it in 1983.

Jill finished as first runner-up to Miss Illinois in 1972, though many thought she was a shoo-in and would even be a favorite for Miss America.

The point is that you rarely see teams like the New York Yankees, who dominated baseball for decades, or the Boston Celtics, who dominated basketball. It just doesn't happen anymore. At the end of stellar careers, many great players are finding that they never competed for a championship, or if they did, they lost.

When our kids excel and get into championship games, we walk a fine line between emphasizing winning over everything else and reminding them to savor these rare, unique experiences. They come along so seldom.

❦January 10❦

Pat's good friend Jim White had wanted to be a college athletic director all his life. We were thrilled for him when we learned he had left a marketing job at Iowa to become athletic director at North Texas State University.

Shortly thereafter, however, Pat read that Jim had resigned to become assistant athletic director and promoter at North Carolina State. Pat called to see how his friend was doing.

"I just couldn't do it," Jim told Pat. "It was what I always thought I wanted to do, but once I got it, I found I was overwhelmed, in over my head, not cut out for it. Now I'm satisfied that I know what God wants me to do, and I'm doing it."

Pat was impressed that here was a guy who was willing to admit he had found his calling, and it was not what he always thought it would be. Too few guys in this image-oriented age will admit it when they have tried to become something God never intended for them.

When Jim was at Iowa he used to send friends bits and pieces of interesting things he had seen and read. Pat encouraged him to organize that little discipline, maybe get some funding, and turn it out as a newsletter.

Mainly for Men is now a regular publication of Jim White, a production that highlights gems from various books and articles to encourage Christians in the sports world. No matter where Jim White is or what he is doing, he'll have that solid ministry.

✒ January 11 ✑

We are firm believers in the "red thread" theory of child rearing. The concept has been credited to everyone from Branch Rickey to Dr. James Dobson, but regardless of who originated it, it goes like this: The red thread in a young person is an outstanding quality, skill, talent, or bent that can be developed if given the right opportunities.

In Dr. Dobson it was tennis. In Pat it was football and baseball. In Jill it was music, then teaching.

What is it in your child? That red thread can be the element that gives your son or daughter an advantage, a leg up on the competition, or—more importantly—something to make him or her feel unique and special.

There is such a tendency today for peers to ridicule one another. Some children don't have the same advantages as others. The ones on the outside of the cliques often form cliques of their own and become rebellious, join gangs, and waste their lives.

Christian kids in a secular setting often suffer the most. They are sometimes made to feel second-class. But if they have a red thread that can be developed, they have an advantage. Maybe it's something esoteric like horsemanship or science. Maybe it is sports.

The "red thread" theory is also crucial to middle children

who might otherwise lose out on attention focused on oldest and youngest children. What is your child's red thread?

✎§ January 12 ∂✎

A U.S. government Department of Health and Human Services survey reports that less than 40 percent of American mothers and fathers exercise with their children during a typical week. Katherine Armstrong, coordinator of the Children in the Schools Program of the Office of Disease Prevention and Health Promotion, says that the kids who were the leanest and most physically fit had parents who were very active physically and watched less TV.

We can and will devote more than one of these daily thoughts to television, but fitness is a big issue in our home too. We require our kids to jog a mile every morning. Yes, they complain and moan occasionally, but after a while, jogging becomes a habit.

One key is that we set the pace. We don't expect them to do what we would be unwilling to do.

We also expose our kids to all kinds of sports opportunities. Then we look for that red thread we talked about yesterday. Kids are not stupid. They will tell you when you have put them in the wrong place. Karyn never took to soccer. She loves gymnastics and dance. Bob hated gymnastics but loves baseball. Most important, we don't let them tell us what they like and don't like until they have given it a fair chance. No turning down a sport or an activity just because it doesn't sound like fun.

We want our kids to develop lifelong fitness habits with activities they enjoy.

❦ January 13 ❦

Don't ever get too busy or too harried to appreciate the fun and especially the humor in raising kids.

Jill heard two stories she thought you would enjoy:

Guests were over for dinner and a father asked his five-year-old to pray.

"I don't know what to say," the little guy said.

Dad replied, "Just say what you've heard Mom say."

So the boy prayed, "O Lord, why did we invite people over on such a hot night?"

Another little boy interrupted his mother while she was teaching a women's Bible study.

"There's a lion in the backyard," he said.

"Oh, there is not. Now don't tell tall tales."

He returned in a few minutes. "Mom, it's the truth. Come look."

She went with him and discovered the biggest, yellowest, furriest cat she had ever seen. "That's a cat, not a lion. Now you go to your room and think about lying and pray about what you've done."

In a little while, he was back. She asked, "Did you think about it?"

"Yes."

"Did you pray about it?"

"Yes. God said He thought it was a lion too."

❧ January 14 ❧

Like any parents, we would like to think our kids are perfect. We constantly nurture and teach and try to model. They know what's right and what's wrong. We want them to be loving, obedient, trustworthy, and efficient.

It breaks our hearts when we discover that one of them has lied, another has stolen something, or another has simply disregarded all he or she knows about taking care of things, getting jobs done, and taking responsibility.

Jill tends to take it personally when one of the kids is openly disobedient. When one of the kids lied to her, Jill was in tears. A friend counseled her, "This is a test for you. You can either pass or fail. You don't have to like the test, but you do have to pass it."

Recently a friend of Jim was caught speeding for the second time. His family was desperate to not have it on his permanent record. They pleaded for some alternative, and the local police came up with something interesting. They said they would throw out the charge, treat it as if it had never happened, if the boy performed eight hours of community service—in this case, washing four fire trucks and washing, waxing, and detailing four squad cars.

What a great idea! In certain cases, when we feel it is appropriate, we have started substituting community service—for the family at home—for punishment.

❧ January 15 ❧

Pat met a thirteen-year-old boy at a banquet and was so impressed with him that he invited him over for Christmas with our family. The young man, Greg McGriff, had shared his faith and seemed so mature and articulate that Pat felt it would be good for our kids to be exposed to him.

Always one to ask for life principles from strangers and well-known people, Pat asked him, "What are your goals for the coming year?"

Greg said, "First, I want to live my life to please God. Second, I want to learn as much as I can. And third, I want to do the best I can in sports."

What a lesson from a just-turned-teen! As if he'd been expecting to be asked, he had three goals and they had been categorized, perhaps unknowingly, as spiritual, mental, and physical.

Too few people of any age have an idea of what they want and expect to do in the next year. Rather than planning their work and working their plan, they just drift through life, waiting to see what happens. Sometimes they get breaks, sometimes they don't. Sometimes they meet people who can help them achieve, but most often they don't.

Pat has always enjoyed this quote: "If your goal is nowhere, any road will lead you there." We are constantly looking for that red thread in our kids that will take them where they want to go.

❧ January 16 ❧

A woman friend was at our house recently and she looked upset. We asked her, "How's life?"

"I've left him," she said, saying it all in those three words.

"Do you want to talk?" we asked.

"No, not really."

We didn't press, and as is so often the case, after she said she didn't want to, she began talking.

"He is not the same man I married," she began. "Back then he was fun. He talked and listened. We went places and did things together. Not now. Now all he does is sleep and work. We never go out. We have no friends. I'm not going to live that way."

Of course we don't condone spouses leaving one another because one has become boring or obsessed with a career. But it has been our experience that the above is the number-one lament of most troubled wives. It was true in our own marriage nearly ten years ago. Fortunately for us, Jill burst forth with some tough truth in time to see God intervene, and we are thankful our problems weren't complicated by one or the other of us seeking fulfillment in someone else's arms. Once that happens, the odds skyrocket against salvaging a marriage.

❧ January 17 ❧

Two of our kids reached the end of their ropes when Grandma and Grandpa visited. They got to go to Jim's basketball game, but they were wild and noisy in the car and ran onto the court during the game.

It was simply one of those days when the kids were bound and determined to do what they wanted, regardless of what they knew and what they had been told. It was as if they were begging for discipline. As James Dobson says, "When your child is looking for a fight, don't disappoint him. Just make sure you win."

Jill won. She disciplined the kids and sent them to bed

early, making them miss a party. Of course they protested loudly.

The next morning, however, they were docile and sweet— not cured forever, but perhaps secure in our love and correction. We are firm believers in the fact that kids may not know it consciously, but they want correction and discipline. They know they are not old enough or wise enough to govern themselves all the time.

Children need and want attention, and sometimes bad behavior is a clue that they have not gotten enough positive attention. But we think security covers the heart and mind of a child who knows his parents are there to show love by helping him grow up to be a responsible, obedient, caring person.

Our kids will soon know that we have been trying to be good parents. We won't always be right, but we'll always be there.

❧ January 18 ❧

When you have bright and talented kids—and don't we all?— you can begin to worry about your own motives. Are we pushing the kids too hard? Are we making them do something they don't want to do? Do we want them to excel for our own gratification rather than for their own development?

Jill has taken the kids to enough auditions and tryouts and performances to know how ugly it can be when a true stage parent tries to take over. The child is coached and manipulated; the directors and judges are argued with and cajoled.

That's the last thing Jill wants to be: a stage mother. Getting kids to and from rehearsals and shows is grueling and complicated. There are other children to think of, the home, the schedule. The glamour of having a child onstage can quickly fade after sitting through it all until you know every song and step by heart.

Jill is careful to monitor our kids, to be sure they are still enjoying what they're doing. And she is careful to encourage, help, and build up rather than criticize or push.

That's why it was so gratifying on Christmas Day a few years ago at Epcot when one of the older girls in the show stopped Jill to compliment Bob and Karyn, and then Jill herself.

"I'm glad you're not a pushy stage mother," she said. "You have the right attitude. You're not trying to live your life through your kids."

✺§January 19ଶ✺

When Jim was thirteen, Pat noticed one day that he looked dejected.

"How's school?" Pat asked.

Jim shrugged and said it was okay.

"Who's your favorite teacher?"

Jim told him and said why. But the conversation wasn't the tennis match Pat likes to encourage the kids to have. I put it in your court, you put it in mine. Don't just answer but also keep it going.

"How's basketball?"

Jim looked away. Bingo.

"Coach took me off the A team and put me on the B team."

Pat knows rejection. He has missed opportunities, been

overlooked for awards, wanted jobs he couldn't have. He has learned to deal with it and turn it into a positive.

"Jim, act like a champion. Battle back. Work hard. Don't sulk. Keep cheering for the other guys. You'll be a coach someday. What will you learn from this?"

"I'll learn to talk to my players in advance and not surprise them. I could have taken it better if he had just told me and not done it in the middle of practice."

That's a lesson for pro coaches too. And parents. And spouses. How often do we drop bombs with no warning? Let's resolve to keep one another informed.

❧ January 20 ❧

We were invited to be interviewed on a TV show by a hostess to whom we had given a copy of *Rekindled* a year earlier. Before we went on the air, we asked, "Did you get a chance to read it?"

"Did I ever!" she said. "It was our story all over. Husband too busy. Neglected me. Quit courting me. I felt like a second-class citizen. It was as if you had been reading my mail, it was that close to our situation.

"I had my husband read it. He felt the same way I did, and for a month he turned over a new leaf. I mean, he was really different. We had a super marriage. We did things together. He was kind and thoughtful and courteous and considerate. It lasted a whole month!

"Then he started getting sloppy again and it all went downhill. Soon it was back to the old patterns and habits, and he was the same husband he'd been for years. But that month proved to me he could do it. I'm convinced any man can do it if he really wants to.''

We asked if he was willing to try again.

"I wouldn't know," she said. "We're divorced."

We still get letters on *Rekindled*, though it came out years ago. Some are encouraging and heartwarming, but sad to say, most are the saddest things we read. Too often, by the time they see the book, a third party has entered the picture and the marriage is doomed. Preventive medicine must be administered early.

❧ January 21 ❧

When Jill turned forty on this date some years ago (well, not *that* many years ago!), friend and humorist Ken Hussar—with whom Pat wrote a joke book called *Nothing but Winners*—wrote this poem in her honor. You may sing it to the tune of "Heigh-Ho, Heigh-Ho," but we can't guarantee your family won't have you carted off somewhere:

> Four-oh, Four-oh, Jill-o just hit Four-oh,
> The hill she's climbed, she's hit her prime,
> Four-oh, Four-oh, Four-oh, Four-oh.
> Four-oh, she's always on the go.
> She packs her clan all in the van
> To go, to go, to go, to go.
> Four-oh, Jill's hit that big plateau,
> Twelve kids 'twill take to light her cake,
> Four-oh, Four-oh, Four-oh, Four-oh.
> Four-oh, when wrinkles start to show,
> No magic act can bring youth back,

Four-oh, Four-oh, Four-oh, Four-oh.
Four-oh, in sunny Or-lan-do
It's such a thrill to be over the hill,
Four-oh, Four-oh, Four-oh, Four-oh.
Four-oh, those candles really glow.
Jill's scaled the height, her future's bright,
Four-oh, Four-oh.

❧ January 22 ☙

Stephen and Thomas (T. J.) joined our family from Korea in May 1987. In December of that year, when they had been with us just those few months, Pat was reading them a bedtime story. It was called "How to Be Happy."

The boys had quickly caught on to English and were darling in how they expressed themselves.

At the end of the story, Pat asked, "So, how do we be happy?"

Thomas said, "I know! Pray!"

Pat replied, "Nice going," but now Stephen was sulking. He wanted to tell.

"Okay, Stephen, you tell me three ways to be happy, and Thomas, you can't help."

Stephen paused and repeated, "Pray."

"Nice going. Now number two."

Stephen said, "Obey the Lord."

"Great. Now number three."

Stephen said, "Obey your mother and father."

By now Thomas was busting a gut.

"I know one, I know one!"

"Okay, Thomas."

"Go to church!"

It seemed simple, two little guys fighting for Dad's attention by wanting to answer the question. Pat was thrilled. We were getting through.

❦ January 23 ❧

Pat is excited about the possibility of major league baseball coming to Orlando and his being involved in management. In fact, in a surprise move, Pat and his associates have already announced that if they were awarded a franchise, Bob Boone, the great catcher, would be the manager.

Denny Doyle, who played for the Red Sox in the 1975 series against Cincinnati, would be director of baseball operations.

Brian Doyle, Denny's brother, would be director of player development. He was the hero of the New York Yankees 1978 World Series victory over the Los Angeles Dodgers.

Denny and Brian and Brian's twin, Blake, run the Doyle Baseball School in Orlando, one of the best programs going.

Pat has been particularly interested in interacting with Brian because he is a twin and we have twin boys. We are not totally sure our Korean daughters are not twins also, though we have different birth years for them. They are close, and many of the same warnings and tips about twins apply to them.

Brian is big on twins establishing their own identities. "It's good to have the tie to the other twin," he says, "and that will never be broken. But each needs independence."

He doesn't recommend dressing twins alike all the time and says that though there is clearly an unexplainable bond between twins, they are separate individuals and should be encouraged to make their own lives.

❧January 24☙

Del Harris and his wife had three sons before Carey came along—she is now in college—and Del discovered what his friends had tried to tell him for years: there is something wonderfully special about a man's relationship with his daughter.

"I've said it before," says the former NBA coach in Houston and Milwaukee, "and I believe that she's one of the nicest people I know in the world. She's just a special person."

Carey was six when Del became an NBA assistant coach in Houston, and initially she showed little interest in the sport. She slept through some games and hid her eyes at the end of other close ones. Eventually, however, she wanted her dad to teach her to play. It was no easy job because at first she was afraid of the ball. *I'm a coach*, Del thought, *not a magician*.

But she was determined and she caught on. In fact, she went to Marquette on a basketball scholarship. Their relationship is so special that she wrote a poem any father would love:

When you're gone, I want you to know, you're on my mind wherever I go. It makes me sad to think you're gone, although I know it's not for long. My tears I'll cry when my mind's on you and all the things that we've been through. You're the father no one can replace, I'll wipe that tear from off my face. I'll smile inside and wait for you. I know inside you love me too. Whatever I do, wherever I go, you're on my mind . . . just want you to know.

❧ January 25 ❧

The number-one draft pick of the New York Knicks in 1987 was a Saint John's University star named Mark Jackson. The Knicks' confidence in him was rewarded when he had a remarkable first year and was named NBA Rookie of the Year.

His career had its ups and downs after that, but he's a sharp, high-class kid, who has recently come to Christ.

"My parents mean everything to me," Jackson says. "I couldn't repay them for what they've done for me in a million years. They were there whenever I needed them. People say my hero is [former NBA star] Walt Frazier. He is—after my father and mother."

Jackson's parents both worked when he was growing up, his father for the transit authority and his mother for a bank. "I remember so many cold winter mornings when my parents sacrificed their days off to take me to basketball games. I'm convinced that if I had had other parents, I wouldn't be a success.

"When my parents are at a game, I gain strength from them. I know I'm not only doing it for myself. I'm doing it for them."

That kind of an upbringing helped make Mark an instant success in the NBA. His coach wanted to bring him along slowly, but within the first week of the regular season, he became the floor leader for the Knicks. That kind of leadership is counseled and modeled into a kid. You can tell when a kid has been raised right.

❦§ January 26 ❧❧

Because we have so many Asian children, we are most curious about Asia and its people. It has always fascinated us that Asian children seem to do so well academically, dominating scholastic competitions and scholarships for the last several years.

When Pat ran into then U.S. Secretary of Education William Bennett at a banquet in Dallas a few years ago, he asked him about the success of Asian children in school.

Bennett told him that a study by the University of Michigan Sociology Department had determined that any superiority shown by Asian students was *not* genetic. Rather:

1. Educational excellence and achievement were high priorities in Asian families.
2. There was strong family cohesion.
3. The students worked hard.

We don't know about you, but that tells us something. It seems any student, regardless of national origin, can succeed scholastically. Academic achievement is a high priority in our home because we want our kids to honor the Lord in whatever they do. We work hard on family cohesion, which is not easy with so many children but crucial to any success we hope each child has. And the hard-work aspect goes without saying.

No, not all of our kids work as hard as the others. But we expect them to and urge them to. Even if they never thank us, they will be better people because of it.

❦ January 27 ❧

At the same Dallas luncheon we mentioned yesterday, Pat heard then Education Secretary Bennett say he thought all jobs should have a tremble factor. He said that in ancient Rome, supervisors had to stand under aqueducts after the scaffolding had first been removed.

That would result in trembling, all right. It would also result in careful supervision, good relationships with workers, and vigilance on the job.

We expect our kids to do what they are told, when they are told, and how they are told. Sure, there are people who criticize us for that. They say we are slave drivers, taskmasters, stern, mean, and too strict. Sometimes these critics are our own children!

But we have seen too many kids who are allowed to eat what they want, watch what they want on television, do what they want when they want, and take little or no responsibility. They wind up hanging around the malls or running wherever they please.

Maybe some of those kids will see the light someday and get their acts together on their own. For now, we wonder how their parents think they will ever amount to anything. In this day of super competition, it's the kids with old-fashioned, others-oriented, godly values who will survive and succeed.

In a day when merely doing your job will make you stand out on the job, excelling takes the limits off your horizons.

❧ January 28 ❧

Too often we don't know if we are getting through to our kids. Do you ever feel that way?

It seems that every day we try to reiterate to each of our children, "You are responsible for yourself. No one is going to do your work for you. You are responsible to brush your teeth without being told. You are responsible to pick up in your room, put your dirty clothes in the laundry and your clean clothes in your dresser. You are responsible for getting your lunch ready, jogging your mile, getting your morning and evening jobs done, and doing your homework. You are responsible for yourself."

Sometimes they remember this for an hour. Then we go back over it again for the eight-zillionth time. "Your mother is not the house servant." Sometimes it seems as if we are the only family in the world with this problem. We have this conviction that everywhere else, in every home in America, kids are doing what they are told without being badgered. Pat has made this theme of personal responsibility a major point in family devotions.

When Stephen at age six had been with us just a few months, he made hand puppets out of two kids' menus at a restaurant and had them talk to each other. We nearly fell on the floor laughing when he—in his inimitable Korean accent— had one puppet sternly announce to the other, "You are responsible for yourself!"

Success!

❦ January 29 ❧

We have been gone from Chicago for more than fifteen years, but because we met there and have many wonderful memories, we try to keep up with news from the Windy City. Jill's parents lived in the suburbs until 1989, and of course Pat gets to Chicago when he can to see the Magic play the Bulls, for whom he served as general manager for three years.

We were gone from Chicago several years before Harold Washington became the mayor, but we were as stunned as the locals were when he died suddenly in 1987 from a heart attack. In reading the various accounts of the tragedy, we were struck by the late mayor's seeming personal disregard for his own health.

We have been health-and-fitness enthusiasts for many years, so it was disturbing to read that his former personal physician characterized the busy, stressed-out mayor as having treated himself "like a fool."

Apparently, every warning sign had arisen in previous physical checkups: high blood pressure, high cholesterol, on-and-off smoking, not taking prescribed medication. Yet the mayor refused to keep appointments for follow-up examinations. Before he ever got back to the doctor, he was dead.

What a sad lesson to all who believe that our bodies are temples of the Holy Spirit.

❦ January 30 ❧

Too often our lessons are negative ones. We learn what to do or what not to do based on someone else's—or our own—failures. It would be much better and much easier to hear and believe those who have gone before us and not have to experience such wounds ourselves.

We recently shared the hurt of a woman friend whose two daughters had run away from home. She was heartbroken and wondering where she went wrong. Three things crossed her mind that she said she would do differently if she had to do them again:

1. She would not be a working mother if she could avoid it. "Everything spins off this," she said. "Sitters raised my kids, and I left them at day camps in the summer. I was never here to do things with them."

2. She would not have moved to an area where there was no extended family for positive influence on her kids. There were no relatives to spell her so she wouldn't have to leave her kids with baby-sitters who couldn't care as much as loved ones.

3. She would not have made her girls grow up so fast. "I didn't leave them time to just be little girls, and now they're trying to show me how grown-up they are. They're on their own at much too early an age."

We were heartbroken with and for this pitiable mother and can only hope that we and any others who know this story can learn something from her pain.

❧ January 31 ☙

Because of the many great athletes and executives Pat works with and the many impressive women Jill ministers with, we often have people in our home who can make a significant impact on our kids.

Tanya Crevier is a diminutive athlete, a professional ball

handler who can keep more basketballs spinning at one time than any other person in the world. She travels worldwide giving demonstrations and has performed in NBA cities all over the country. She is active with the Fellowship of Christian Athletes and Bill Glass's prison ministries, but more important to us, she's a friend of the family.

Pat has had Tanya perform at halftime and specialty shows, and she always demonstrates superb conditioning and consummate skill. This strong, dynamic woman from South Dakota told our kids, "Keep on keeping on. Persevere. Don't ever give up. Always do your best for the Lord."

Of course, when the woman giving the advice is Tanya Crevier, the kids are impressed.

Two days after she gave that advice, Jill got a call from T. J.'s teacher. She said the class had been working on something T. J. found especially difficult. Finally, after persevering, he succeeded.

She said he told her, "Miss Wheeler, I got it! I got it! Just like Tanya say, I stick with it and I got it!"

❧ February 1 ❧

Sometimes we are overwhelmed with the responsibility of raising one child, let alone a dozen. Each needs individual attention and care and training. It's hard to remember when we had only Jim, or only Jim and Bob, or even only Jim and Bob and Karyn. We added Andrea and Sarah before Michael was born, and even those days with six kids in the house have become part of a distant memory.

Each child is involved in activities and chores. One of our biggest struggles, of course, is getting individual time with them. We feel a tremendous burden to not simply provide for them but to also nurture and train them.

Pat met with a man from the Ringling Bros. and Barnum & Bailey Circus who told him that the now-retired animal trainer Gunther Gebel-Williams once worked 180 hours with a Bengal tiger, just teaching him to sit up. Eighty percent of his time was spent working to merely break in new animals.

Now, of course, we don't equate our children with animals, even trained ones (oh, there are days . . .). But we can relate to the heavy responsibility Williams must have felt, logging so much time just establishing the basics.

Even on those days when it seems some of the kids will never settle into an acceptable routine, we believe the Lord is faithful and will keep His promise that if we train them up in the way they should go, when they are old, they will not depart from it.

❧ February 2 ❧

Christians in the public eye are often on the receiving end of strange input. Make no mistake: we try to evaluate each bit of criticism and correction with humility and open minds (the emphasis is on the word *try*).

How would you respond to this letter to Pat?

> Sir:
> A strange letter? Perhaps . . . but for many months I personally have been offended and bothered by your totally too-casual, tieless appearance on TV and at public gatherings.
> For a man to wear a tie is a mark of class, personal

care, and respect. It is the mode of today. For you not to wear a tie shows disrespect and a personal vanity.

Furthermore, as a fellow Christian, I resent it.

You are no longer a jock, Pat . . . . You're an executive. Act like it.

The same day that letter came, Pat called to encourage Pastor Charles Swindoll, who had come under criticism for building a vacation home. He said, "It's hurt a lot, but we've had it easy up till now. We'll be better for this and better equipped to serve."

We believe in true accountability to people who love us and care about our ministry. But to expect others to follow your every whim of fashion and practice is to stifle, not build up.

❧ February 3 ☙

Speaking of criticism—now there's a cheery way to start the day—you can imagine the reaction we got when word got around that we were going to add to our family again. After we had our four homegrowns and our two Korean beauties, we added two more from Korea, twins Stephen and Thomas.

So now we had eight, but we had set no limit. We've been blessed, and Jill's love of children has no bounds. When we were informed of four Filipino boys who needed a home, we thought and prayed about it and got to work on seeing what we could do. Adopting children is a rewarding, magical thing, but the red tape and waiting is complicated and grueling.

As the days and weeks passed, word eventually got out that if everything went as planned—and it hardly ever does—we would be adding four more children to our household in 1988.

What did people say? Even our Christian friends . . .

"You're crazy."

"Why would you do that? Just for attention?"

"When are you going to stop? At twenty?"

Fortunately, there were a few people who did not question our motives. We're past the point where attention would compensate for the work involved. Our friend Eddie Donovan, former NBA coach and executive, said, "That's putting your money where your mouth is."

And Pat's best friend, Norm Sonju, said, "God has given you a special grace."

Jill has said many times, "We're not trying to be heroes. We've just been called by God to raise children."

❧ February 4 ☙

Want an idea for a great birthday gift?

Pat was giving Jill a foot rub one night when she told him the story of something a man at the local Christian school had done for his two secretaries.

At the end of the school year he arranged for them to be picked up by a limousine and taken to a salon where they were pampered by a manicurist and pedicurist, a masseuse, a hairdresser, and a beautician.

Pat arranged for various gifts to be delivered to Jill each day during the week before her fortieth birthday, and then, on the birthday itself, she was awarded a Day of Beauty.

When she called Pat from the beauty salon that afternoon, she had already been pampered for hours and was in tears. "Now I'm ruining my beautiful new makeup," she said.

The irony of it was that she had been so relaxed by the

process, she was exhausted and collapsed in bed early that evening. A word to the wise: If you provide this treat for your wife, don't plan a romantic dinner date too. She might not make it.

It is important to find the special something that will really surprise and delight your spouse. A friend of ours surprised her husband by taking him to a concert by one of his favorite artists from the sixties, one she didn't like and whom he was surprised she was even aware of. That made it all the more thoughtful and distinctive.

✑ February 5 ✑

Mike Ryan, a minister from Redwood City, California, and chaplain to the San Francisco Police Department, told Pat that 60 percent of cops' marriages break up. Why?

1. Officers are very private about their work. They don't talk to their wives about what really goes on on the street. If they did, the wives would not let them go to work. (Cops enjoy the rush of their jobs, like going into battle.)

2. They tend to work a lot of overtime, whatever it takes to get the job done, including odd hours.

That leaves little time for husbands and wives to be together. The solution, according to Mike Ryan:

1. Leave the work at the office and get into family life in a determined way.

2. Carve out time alone with the wife.

A police officer was recently shot and killed in Chicago. His wife told reporters that she had been living in fear of that all their married life, and also since childhood, because her father was also a policeman.

"It got to the point where I hated to hear the phone ring when he was on duty, especially late at night. It had to be bad news. Finally it was. I can only say that he died doing what he loved to do best."

Other than the threat to their lives, men and women in almost any profession face the same struggles with priorities.

❧ February 6 ❧

A Coach's Prayer
Adapted by Skip Hall from a poem by General Douglas MacArthur

Build me a player, O Lord, who will be strong enough to know when he is weak and brave enough to face himself when he is afraid. One who will be proud and unbending in honest defeat, and humble and gentle in victory.

Build me a player whose wishes will not take the place of deeds. A player who will know You—and know that to know himself is the foundation stone of true knowledge.

Lead him, I pray, not in the path of ease and comfort but under the stress and spur of difficulties and challenge. Here let him learn to stand up in the storm; here let him learn compassion for those who fall.

Build me a player whose heart will be clear, whose goal will be high, a player who will master himself before he seeks to master other men. One who will reach into the future and yet never forget the past.

And after all these things are his, add, I pray, enough of a sense of humor so that he may always be serious and yet never take himself too seriously.

Give him humility so that he may always remember the simplicity of true greatness, the open mind of true wisdom, and the meekness of true strength. Then I, his coach, will dare to whisper, "I have not coached in vain."

❧ February 7 ❧

Pat is really into physical fitness for the kids. When Stephen and Thomas first arrived, they were weak and without energy. Lots of good food and exercise, touching, loving, and encouragement made their faces and eyes beam and their hair shine. Most of all, they began to run and jump and play.

Initially they had been unable to do one sit-up. Not one! After six months of working at it every day, they each did 121!

When Bob was ten, he could do only forty sit-ups at a time. Pat told him, "Bob, you have to make a commitment to do these every day."

Bob said, "It's hard to make a commitment."

But he made it, and it was Bob who held Stephen's and Thomas's feet when they did their sit-ups. Now Bob can do as many as anyone in the family. As Denny Doyle of the Doyle Baseball School says, you always have to make a concerted effort to build the upper body. The lower half gets more attention because of the running and walking we do in normal living. The upper body needs special attention and encouragement.

That's why even little ball players can excel in hitting power and throwing strength. And when a big man commits himself to daily workouts, he can do anything.

The great running back Hershel Walker committed himself to hundreds of sit-ups and push-ups a day when he was a junior in high school. He still does them. Day after day after day. It's paid off.

❦ February 8 ❧

A postscript to yesterday: We took the family to our condo at the beach in August 1988, about a year after the time when Thomas couldn't do one push-up. He and Bob did a thousand each on the beach. That's the result of determination, commitment, and being satisfied with steady growth.

While we were at the beach, Pat struck up a conversation with the owner of a nearby condo. He had lent his place to one of his employees for two weeks. The employee brought his eleven-year-old son. The boy bounded from the car, eager and excited to get some time alone with his dad.

It wasn't long before the condo owner began getting calls from the boy, asking if he would take him out in the boat or play with him. Apparently the father was not really vacationing but was consumed with his work.

Imagine how that boy felt, having to ask his dad's boss to do something with him. There he was, vacationing with his dad, undoubtedly a highlight in his life. Yet the message was clear: Work was more important.

Too many fathers think that by getting things for their kids or taking them somewhere, they have fulfilled their parental duty. The fact is that kids don't want stuff and things to do. They want their dads, and that means time. Not just quality time. Quantities of time. That's the only thing that communicates true love.

❦ February 9 ❧

Many of our kids have become Christians at young ages, so we don't agree with those who say that children don't understand enough of the Gospel to make a true commitment. Though

Pat received Christ as an adult and brings that valuable perspective to the family, Jill became a Christian as a child, and many of our friends did as well.

Jesus Himself told the disciples to let the children come to Him and not to forbid them.

When Pat spoke to sixth- and seventh-graders at the Christian school a few years ago, he sensed that God was doing something in the hearts of the kids. No one complained when the session went past an hour and eventually became two hours long.

Pat asked the kids to make renewed prayers of commitment of their lives to Christ. Afterward, a friend of Bob, a twelve-year-old, approached Pat and told him in tears that he had prayed that prayer.

"I went forward to accept Christ when I was six," he said, "but I realized I never really became a Christian."

People who receive the Lord at any age need to acknowledge that they are sinners and nothing they can do will earn their salvation. It's a gift. Holy living after that is in gratitude for the gift, not to earn it. Children may need a rededication when they are a little older, but we are convinced children can be saved when they understand enough to pray.

❧ February 10 ❧

Pat sat at an Orlando baseball game with Rex Bowen, who was then eighty-one years old and scouted for the Cincinnati Reds. He had worked for years in Brooklyn with the Dodgers and in Pittsburgh with the Pirates for the legendary Branch Rickey.

It is always fascinating to talk to a veteran, and given Pat's interest in history and especially baseball, it wasn't long before he asked Mr. Bowen to list the three most important things he learned about scouting from Mr. Rickey.

"We were to look for throwing ability, running speed, and body balance," Rex said.

The old man and Pat turned to the field and compared notes on the various minor leaguers. This one Rickey would be impressed with, that one he would not.

"What, in your opinion," Pat asked Bowen, "made Branch Rickey such a special man?"

Mr. Bowen put Rickey's Christian faith at the top of the list. "It was real," he said. "It was not just lip service. Then, I'd have to say he was a truly humble man. And he wouldn't have had to be. He accomplished more than most men in his profession ever did.

"He also listened to others intently. He really heard you and valued what you had to say. He got a lot of input before he made Jackie Robinson the first black big leaguer. And then, of course, he was a spellbinding orator. He was quite a man."

❧ February 11 ❧

Kids hang on the words of their parents, whether or not they admit it. A starter at a swim meet told us that he stood near the starting platforms with his gun raised and asked Thomas, "Are you going to win?"

Thomas said, "Yes."

The starter said, "How do you know?"

Thomas said, "Because my father told me I can."

Pat doesn't recall Thomas acting or appearing as if he believed him when he tried to encourage him by telling him he could win. He feared Thomas thought Pat was just being a typical dad. But that story from the starter tells us that Thomas believed his dad. He has become a very competitive, better-than-average swimmer, and though he didn't win that race, he did better than his previous times indicated he should.

When Jim was a junior in high school, a friend asked him what college he was thinking about. We realized we were really behind in planning for that. It's hard to believe that your firstborn, who seems to have been with you such a short time, is actually having to think about college.

"I'm thinking about Wake Forest," Jim said, "but I'm not sure yet."

Pat was stunned. That's his alma mater, but he and Jim had never talked about it. It was flattering and also humbling to know that what parents do or say makes such an impact.

❦ February 12 ❦

A friend of ours told Jill this story. Her daughter invited a friend over to spend the night. The friend said, "Sure, your father's or your mother's?"

"My father's or my mother's what?"

"House. Which one do you live with?"

To the friend, it was the most natural thing in the world to live with either parent, but certainly not both. This was a junior-higher who eventually told our friend's daughter that she was the only person she knew whose parents were still together. When she was told they had been happily married more than twenty years, she could hardly comprehend it.

What a sad time we live in. Have you ever wondered what

all this adultery and separation and divorce and remarriage is doing to kids, to family reunions, to wedding pictures? What a mess!

We know of a family that was made up of a husband and wife and three kids. Then they divorced and the husband got custody of the kids. He remarried and divorced, leaving the kids with his latest former wife. She married a man who had custody of the children of his former wife.

We realize that's a little convoluted and hard to follow, but the bottom line is this: Those three kids from the original marriage were now joined with kids from another marriage. Not one of the three kids was related to anyone else in the family. They were not blood relatives of either parent. Welcome to the nineties.

❧ February 13 ❧

The doctrine of guardian angels is a wonderful, puzzling thing that people most often use to comfort children who are afraid of the dark, have bad dreams, or fear calamity. After three near misses one week in 1987, Pat is glad to know he has one on his full-time invisible staff.

He was at the National Basketball Association meetings in Whittier, California, a week before the big earthquake hit, the epicenter of which was just down the street from his hotel.

A few days later, Pat passed a spot a half mile from our house just moments after a man exploded a hand grenade that maimed three police officers.

The next night, coming home late from an engagement, he arrived at an intersection just seconds after a gas tanker struck a car, killing the driver and setting the car afire.

Do you sometimes ask yourself why you were delayed getting away from the house for an important appointment, and then come upon an accident that could have easily included you, had you been on time?

We don't claim to be theologians who can explain why so often people are spared danger in close calls while others— even many Christians—are killed every day. But we do believe that we are in the hands of God, and until He decides it is our time to be taken, we will indeed be protected by guardian angels every moment of the day.

❧ February 14 ❧

In *Say It . . . Right* (G. P. Putnam's Sons, 1991), Lillian Glass suggests ten tips to keep your marriage relationship strong:

1. Make time to talk, even if it is fifteen minutes a day. Marabel Morgan once tried to get Pat to commit to giving Jill just ten minutes of uninterrupted attention each day, and he wouldn't do it until it meant the difference in our marriage.
2. Pay close attention to what your spouse says and remember it. Don't tune out or turn off when your loved one needs to talk. And don't interrupt. Keep listening.
3. Stop beating around the bush and get to the point. Be very specific about what you want.
4. Share your worst and best thoughts. The more often you share, the closer you become. Sound familiar?

5. Apologize. Love *is* having to say you're sorry. Love is letting your spouse know you have made a mistake and how bad you feel about it.
6. Be aware not only of what you say but how you say it. Sometimes we command and demand without knowing it.
7. If you want a loving, supportive relationship, don't accuse or criticize or nag.
8. Be generous and specific with your compliments.
9. Use an upward bounce in your voice when you greet your spouse. Don't sound as if you take him or her for granted.
10. Use body language. Touch and bond!

❧ February 15 ❧

Doug Collins, former coach of the Chicago Bulls, tells the story of pro golfer D. A. Weibring, who won the Western Open. His five-year-old son, Matt, joined him in the winner's circle.

Later in Quincy, Illinois, Matt was in a kiddies tournament and his father caddied for him. When Matt won with the final putt he yelled, "Daddy, we won!"

His dad said, "No, son. You won!"

The boy was as thrilled to be in the winner's circle of a major tournament with his dad as he was to have his dad caddy for him. And then, in victory, after he had taken all the shots himself, he considered it a team effort.

That father, selflessly giving of himself and his time for his son, is logging magnificent memories in Matt's mind.

We want to be there to help, to coach, to encourage, to

train, to counsel, and also to support and cheer. Pat was always embarrassed by how his own father seemed so vocal at his games. He once presented Pat's college teammates with Popsicles until Pat had to endure "Popsicle" as a nickname for a while. Later, he drove for hours to see Pat play at Wake Forest.

But now that his father is gone, Pat realizes the sacrifices he made to be at Pat's games and how much he loved and supported him. Much as Pat tries not to embarrass our kids by being the same type of father, it was bred into him. Someday they will understand and probably be the same with their kids.

✑§ February 16 ?✑

As is often the case, the details of this story are less important than the principle. Jill got a call from a church where she had accepted an invitation to sing. The call was to inform her that the church did not allow background tapes.

We happen to believe that background tapes are one of the best things that have happened to vocalists in years. Singers don't have to rely on a pianist, sometimes a stranger or someone provided by the host church. And they don't have to sing a cappella. Some people make their own background tapes, using their own voice for harmonies. But the tapes provided by Christian music companies are also wonderful. For just a few dollars, on one little tape is full orchestration of instruments in a beautiful arrangement that only enhances the solo.

Jill was shaken by the message and didn't know what to do. She could sing without the tapes as she did years ago, but the very idea of a church forbidding them upset her.

Pat could see he needed to step in. Jill felt strongly that the decision was wrong, but she wasn't prepared to fight it. Pat was. He became the male version of the mama bear and called the organizers. Not satisfied with their rationale, he politely but firmly told them, "No tapes, no Jill."

More important than the details was the fact that Pat fought Jill's battle for her and made her feel like a queen.

❧ February 17 ❧

Even marriage counselors writing from a strictly secular viewpoint often hit on biblical principles to keep marriages together. In his *Love Tactics: How to Win the One You Want* (Avery Publishing Group, 1988), Las Vegas marital consultant Thomas McKnight lists what he calls five rules for a long and happy marriage. These are directed at wives and are designed "to keep your man from cheating":

Listen to what he has to say. The most common excuse for extramarital flings is, "My wife doesn't understand me." What he really means is, "My wife has given up trying to understand me."

Never condemn his family or his friends. Let him spend some time with his buddies, even if you don't approve of them. [We would have a problem with this one, of course.]

Don't criticize or nag him. Nothing drives a man from his home turf faster than nagging.

Point out his virtues. He'll appreciate your support and feel better about himself if you do. Give him the positive feedback he needs at home and he won't go elsewhere to find it.

Don't treat him as if he's boring you. Try to enjoy some of his hobbies.

Of course these principles go both ways. Just about any

wife would love it—after she picked herself up off the floor—
if her husband offered to go shopping with her . . . and not
just to sit on a bench in the mall while she browses.

❧ February 18 ❧

Need a chuckle today? Our little people always make us laugh.
One of our daughters saw a very good minister friend, Paul
Miller, in the driveway talking to Pat. She said, "Hey, look,
there's Saint Paul!"

Stephen and Thomas were told that in their baseball tournament they would have a real umpire. Later Stephen asked
Pat about the "ringmaster" who would be at the game.

Michael enjoyed all the preliminaries of the morning worship service at our church, First Baptist / Orlando, but when
that was over and it was time for Jim Henry's always fine
sermon, Michael wanted to tell Jill something. She bent down
to hear him whisper, "Always at this time, I want to go home!"

Later Michael tried to tell Jill how to make fudge. Among
his suggestions: "You gotta let it melt. And Mommy, you
better watch out, you know why? If it overfloats the fish pan,
you gotta take it off. You gotta keep stirrin' this. Then you
gotta let it get kinda hard—kind of, but it's not gonna be hard,
but kinda hard.

"I don't know if that's the right one for chocolate marsh-
mallow, but if it is I'll be glad."

Such comments are always cute, but they are also easy to
forget. We saved these because we knew we'd be doing this
book, but we hate to think what would happen to these memories if we didn't have a reason to scribble them down and

save them. Start a file. These will be as precious as pictures someday.

❧February 19 ❧

Pat was busy before a SunRays baseball game, making sure the field, the concessions, the rest rooms, the team, and everything was ready for the crowd. He looked forward to the family arriving. Jill had decided to bring all twelve kids.

When she arrived, however, she had only ten with her. "Where are the other two?" Pat wanted to know.

"They were throwing sand," she explained. "They think when I say something, I don't mean it. I got a sitter and put them to bed."

Pat was amused at his wife and impressed with the way she stuck to her guns, though it undoubtedly pained her and was unpopular with not only the two culprits but the other kids too. It reminded him of the twelve players on an NBA team and how they all have to be going in the same direction and have the same heartbeat for a season to be successful.

If two basketball players wanted to do their own thing, there would be a mess. And just as within the family where the age of the two culprits doesn't matter, on an NBA team the bad apples could be your ninth and tenth men, but still they could mess up everything for the whole team.

The kids really like to get out and see the team—and their dad—in action. And the two in question were reminded to be really good on those days when Mom has decided to take them to a game. Consistent, firm, fair discipline works every time.

❧ February 20 ☙

Because of our personal involvement with a certain ministry, we got a copy of the letter one of their staffers sent his colleagues when he was released due to immorality. Of course we can't tell the name of the ministry or the person, but you can picture his pain and remorse from these few excerpts. Adultery and unfaithfulness create such chaos.

> I write with a broken heart. We have decided to relocate, and I am not sure our paths will cross ever again here on earth.
>
> I want you to know how terribly sorry I am for the sin I allowed in and the destruction it brought. I ask forgiveness for my hypocrisy. I'm sure it is hard not to have bitterness and resentment toward me. I have the same for myself. Everything I love I have hurt deeply because of my sin: my Lord, my wife, my family, this ministry, my church.
>
> I am amazed to this day at what sin does to a person. I allowed one wrong thought to go unconfessed and unforsaken. I deluded myself. I would look into the Word of God and forget what manner of man I was.
>
> I know the painful reality that I am evil, desperately wicked, apart from the presence of the Holy Spirit. I am so devastated by my sin and its consequences that I often ask the Lord to take me home. My existence is constant pain.
>
> My ministry, my friendships, my home, my church— they are all gone because of my sin. I need your prayers. . . .

❧ February 21 ❧

By the time you read this, our oldest, Jim, will be in college or close to it. That's hard to believe. He has always been a sweet-natured, affectionate kid, a joy to have around. What a help he's been as we have continued to add youngsters to our home. It could have been a disaster if he and our other home-growns had resented it.

Pat will never forget the time Jimmy apparently didn't secure his surfboard on the car properly and saw it sail off on to the highway, only to be absconded with by someone behind us. Later Jim was sobbing in his bed, and Pat went to see if he felt convicted, wanted to apologize, confess, whatever.

"Talk to me, Jim," Pat said gently.

"I don't have a surfboard anymore!" Jim wailed.

After the team Christmas party in 1989, when Jim went to Church Street Station and got to play video games all evening, he told Jill, "Now I understand how useless those games are. I just finished playing them for two hours and I don't feel any better."

One Thanksgiving as we all lounged around talking, Pat asked Jim what he had learned from us about being parents.

"In my friends' homes," he said, "their parents say something two or three times and then give up. You two keep saying things until we finally do it."

That was a nice way of saying we're nags, we guess, but at least he's going to be a responsible adult.

❧February 22☙

When Pat O'Brien of CBS was at our home to tape a halftime show for a National Basketball Association telecast, he told us two stories about NBA superstars.

The first concerned Julius Erving and did not surprise Pat, as he knows well what a wonderful Christian gentleman Doc is. O'Brien looked for Dr. J. after the tough 1984 play-off loss of the Sixers to the Nets. The Philly season was over, one year after they had been world champions, and in the locker room players were screaming and cursing in frustration. Doc was nowhere to be found.

O'Brien asked for him and someone nodded to the bathroom. He knocked and Doc let him in. "Okay to talk for a minute?" O'Brien asked.

Doc, quiet and somber, nodded. It was not an interview. Just a conversation. "It has to be tough," O'Brien offered.

Doc nodded again. "It is. We didn't defend our title." He paused. "But you know, on the other hand, this gives me an extra month with my wife and kids."

The other story concerned Michael Jordan, the megastar of the Bulls. O'Brien took his two-year-old son to meet Michael, and after all the other media people had left and there was no one there to impress, Michael pulled little Sean aside and said, "Now you can help me unpack my bag."

Sean may not remember it, but his dad will never forget it.

❧February 23☙

When Bob was twelve he went out for varsity soccer because he was in a small school. It was a rare opportunity for him, but he was intimidated by all the big high-schoolers on the field.

They were strong and fast and experienced, and of course none of them wanted to be shown up by a twelve-year-old, especially a small one.

Pat went to practice and saw Bob backing off, not playing tough defense and going after the ball aggressively the way Pat knew he could. He was playing scared.

"Bob," Pat said, "you play hard. Sure you're small, but that doesn't mean a thing in soccer. You're tough. How bad can they hurt you? Who ever heard of somebody getting really hurt just because he ran into a bigger guy? Get tough and go after 'em."

Pat could see the fire in Bob's eye. He was still scared, but he knew his dad was watching and that he believed in him. He was pumped. He became more aggressive, charged the ball, got knocked over a few times but always bounced back up and got back in the game.

Then the big moment came. Bob was dancing between two upperclassmen who were passing the ball back and forth. Bob waited for the right instant, timed it perfectly, and intercepted a pass. He streaked for the center of the field, dribbling toward the opposite goal. The humiliated opponents furiously chased him, but he outran them, headed for the six-foot, five-inch senior goalie, faked one way and shot the other. Score! What a moment!

❧ February 24 ☙

Even little girls have to face persecution for their faith occasionally. Because Karyn has always been musical and physical, we have exposed her to lots of opportunities. One she especially enjoys is dance class. She has performed in the shows at Disney World's Magic Kingdom and Epcot and wants to keep working and improving.

One day in one of her dance classes, the teacher was unhappy with the performances of the girls. She stopped rehearsal and had everyone sit down. Frustrated, she said, "Girls, who are you dancing for? You're not dancing for me or your moms or your dads. Who are you dancing for?"

Karyn raised her hand. "Yes, Karyn. Who?"

"God."

"Absolutely wrong."

Another girl interjected, "For yourself."

"Absolutely right! You're not dancing for me or your mother or father or God! You're dancing for yourselves!"

A few of the other girls snickered. "Who's God?"

We want our kids to know and believe that they are to do whatever they do to the glory of God. Whether they are serving others, studying, performing, or even just playing, their activities have a target, an Honoree.

When Karyn told us that story she was upset, but not because she had been ridiculed. She was troubled that her teacher and her friends could be so wrong.

⏥ February 25 ⏥

We were at a swim meet at nearby Rollins College one fall and Pat spoke to the father of a six-year-old female swimming star who clearly has unlimited potential. They talked for a while about the dangers of being stage parents, of pushing too hard, of expecting too much.

The father of the superstar was determined to help his daughter keep it all in perspective and to have her continue with competitive swimming only as long as she wanted to.

"God has given her a gift," he said. "Now it's up to her to decide if she really wants to use it as she gets older. She can use it to go places, or she can just enjoy it recreationally."

"How bad does she want to become a world-class champion?" Pat asked.

"Real bad right now. But we're trying to make her understand that if she's going to do it, it has to be on her own initiative. We'll help her and support her and be behind her proudly all the way, but we can't do it for her. We want her priorities to be church, school, and swimming."

The girl had watched wide-eyed the Olympic swimming competition on television and saw Janet Evans on the starting platform, in the water, and on the victory stand.

"Do you see her parents there with her?" her father asked.

"No," the girl said, seeming to get the message. "She's alone."

❧ February 26 ❧

We have a woman friend who at twenty-six had no idea what she wanted to do with her life. She couldn't decide on marriage, becoming a nurse, a secretary, a businesswoman, anything. Our discussion went back and forth and was unfocused. Her parents admitted that when she was a child they didn't try to help her get on track. It was frustrating, and she was troubled.

It was gratifying to contrast her to Bob when he was eleven and in the sixth grade. He jumped in the car after school and said he had had to write a paper about what he wanted to do with his life. Pat gulped. "What did you write?"

"Five things.

"I want to get a baseball scholarship to the University of Florida.

"I want to play three years and sign with the Cardinals.

"I want to play two years in the minors and get my degree in the off-season.

"I want to play five years in the big leagues and get my master's degree in the off-season.

"Then I want to become general manager of a baseball or basketball team."

Of course, first and foremost we want him to seek God's will for his life. And many of those aspirations may change as he gets older. But we're sure glad he's thinking about his future and making plans.

❧ February 27 ❧

It is good to use certificates, awards, notes, and I. O. U.s to encourage kids. Bob once got an I. O. U. from one of his coaches that read; "Bob, I owe you a hamburger dinner for doing eighty-one push-ups! Congratulations, Bobby, but remember, while you're eating a hamburger, I'll be eating steak! Give me one hundred good ones and you can too."

That was a real incentive for Bob. He enjoyed his burger, and it wasn't long before he cashed in on the steak dinner too. Now he can do a lot more push-ups than that.

Karyn gave Jill the award she won for making a very beautiful, creative poster. Her note read, "You earned it, Mom. If you weren't here, I wouldn't even have made a poster! I'm giving this to you forever."

If teachers or coaches or counselors don't have that kind of system, why not start something in your own family. When we vacation, we often choose a Camper of the Day. Admittedly, one child might temporarily end up in tears if he expected the prize and his sibling got it. But we make sure there are enough days in the vacation so everybody gets a chance to be special.

We even have a special place setting that goes on the table for the person being honored that day. Awards and citations coming from the kids to us, like the one Jill got from Karyn, are often the result.

❧ February 28 ☙

We sent Stephen and Thomas to the Doyle Baseball School in Orlando for a week in 1988, wondering how they would feel about being shuttled off to somewhere else after they had finally settled into their new home. Sometimes orphans or adoptees are terrified at having to leave their new homes, because the last time they were uprooted they traveled halfway around the world to a strange new environment.

The boys were a little skittish when they first got there, but of course we tipped off the Doyles and they knew what to expect. Their strategy was to provide heavy doses of encouragement all week and see how the boys progressed.

At the first family dinner after their return, the boys told Pat they liked it more at Doyle than at home.

"Why?"

"At Doyle everyone is always nice to us. The coaches always root for us and tell us how good we're doing."

It hurt a little to think our kids were treated better somewhere else than we treated them at home. Of course, they were afraid to get into mischief there and didn't have to be corrected or reprimanded. But still, it was a lesson for us that we should use more pats on the backs than swats on the fannies.

It's easy to fall into a pattern of finding fault with kids, regardless of their backgrounds. Most respond much better to encouragement than to criticism.

❦ February 29 ❧

Can we ever overemphasize the power of the spoken word? Just as Stephen and Thomas flourished under the accolades tossed their way by baseball coaches, people can be deeply wounded by a careless word.

A friend of ours still remembers more than thirty years ago when, as an awkward early teen, she tripped slightly going up some stairs. Her mother, just to be funny, said, "Nice play, ox." It wasn't funny. She was vulnerable and self-conscious for years because of that one statement.

Karen and Richard Carpenter, the famous brother-and-sister act The Carpenters, saw their first hit song, "Close to You," reach number seven on the charts. In a story about them, a trade magazine referred to Karen as "Richard's chubby sister." In fact, she was not chubby at all, though maybe a little round-faced, with full cheeks.

That one comment triggered her lengthy battle with self-image, and she was soon on a destructive path toward anorexia nervosa. She died of it at age thirty-two in 1983.

The hymnwriter calls the Gospel "words of life and beauty." The New Testament writers call the Bible "the Word." Christ was the Word. We believe in the power of the printed word. But how careful we must be with our choice of words.

Children gain much of their self-image, good or bad, true or not, from the words that come from the mouths of their parents.

❦§ March 1 ೪❧

It is interesting that in this country adopted children are more strongly protected by the law than even homegrown children. It is true. An adopted child cannot be disinherited. Of course we can't imagine ever disinheriting any of our children, but we couldn't do that to our adoptees even if we wanted to.

That should be of great comfort to those of us who have trusted Christ as personal Savior. The Scriptures make it clear that our becoming sons of God (John 1:12) is a process of adoption.

Galatians 4:4, 5 says, "But when the fullness of the time had come, God sent forth His Son, born of a woman, born under the law, to redeem those who were under the law, that we might receive the adoption as sons."

Ephesians 1:4, 5 says, "Just as He chose us in Him before the foundation of the world, that we should be holy and without blame before Him in love, having predestined us to adoption as sons by Jesus Christ to Himself, according to the good pleasure of His will."

When we were going to officially adopt our four Filipino boys and our two Korean boys, we took all the kids out of school and went to court. A first-grade friend of Michael said, "I thought you already adopted those boys."

Michael said, "No, this time we're going to adopt them so we can keep them forever."

❧ March 2 ❧

One of the boys talked back to Pat in front of people, perhaps not realizing that adults—even those with visible, successful careers and healthy self-images—are people too. Adults can be embarrassed and even humiliated, especially by their kids.

Pat kept his anger in check but talked to our son later, telling him clearly that he had been embarrassed and felt belittled. Our kids' friends look up to Pat, and after all the time he devotes to family activities, he shouldn't be treated like a sibling or a stranger.

Our boy thought about it for quite a while, then penned this note to Pat:

> Dad,
> I'm sorry for embarrassing you, and I think I deserve a punishment.
> I think I should be grounded for one or two months, and that means I don't talk on the phone, I don't go over to friends' houses, etc., *but I do play basketball!*
> I'm sorry, and this will never happen again.

Needless to say, that was more response than Pat expected or wanted. Kids always seem to be harder on themselves than parents would be. We heard of one boy who was caught stealing something. When the police asked what he thought his punishment should be, he offered to let them cut off one of his fingers.

Kids' psyches are as fragile as their parents'.

✑§ March 3 ?✑

With all the kids we have, you can imagine how many school-teachers, classrooms, and situations we have encountered. Jill was a schoolteacher, we have had our kids in Christian schools and home schooled them, and we've come to some conclusions about the great teachers we have known.

A great teacher believes there is creativity within every child.

He or she knows that a child can be handicapped for life if he does not become an excellent reader, writer, speaker, and listener.

A great teacher establishes and maintains authority and consistent discipline from day one. It is always easier to start strict and loosen up than it is to start loose and then have to get tough.

A great teacher takes a genuine personal interest in the life of each student—time-consuming but essential.

A great teacher doesn't regularly give lots of homework. He or she knows the family unit is important and needs daily time together. This teacher sees parents as allies, not enemies.

The best teachers love their subjects and convey that love to their students, making learning fun.

They believe, as Bruce Wilkinson of Walk Thru the Bible says, "If you haven't learned, I haven't taught properly."

❦§ March 4 ᘒ❧

Jill tries to be creative in the ways she expresses love to the kids. She loves them all so much that she wants to touch them and hold them and kiss them, but in the rush of carpooling everyone to all their activities every day, it becomes difficult.

Once she invented a Kiss of the Day. On the way out of the van, each child would get the special kiss. It might be an Eskimo kiss, rubbing noses, a high five, a low five, kiss the nose, or any number of other fun variations. At least she thought they were fun.

The older the kids get, of course, the less interested they are in the Kiss of the Day. Jill cried the first time three of them left the van without getting theirs.

All that did, however, was make her realize that different kids, especially at different ages, need individual expressions of love.

For one it might mean a hug, for another a special look, a smile, some encouragement. Some like to be hugged and kissed, but only in private. It all depends on the individual. Jim, for instance, has never been shy about holding mom's hand, putting his arm around her, or even kissing her in front of his high school friends.

Not all kids will be like that, so it is important to find out what communicates to them. As much as they pull away or pretend not to like it, they need some form of loving every day.

❧ March 5 ❧

It is much easier to give up on kids and let them do whatever they want when they want than it is to maintain rules and discipline.

There are days when Jill is tempted to do everything for them just to avoid arguing and hassling and nagging. That would end the turmoil, but it would also teach them a bad lesson: Put up enough of a fuss and you can get out of your responsibilities.

Jill has learned that it is better to let dirty dishes sit all day if one of the kids has forgotten to do his job. Neither she nor Pat can stand the mess, but the only way the child will learn is to still have to do the dishes when the day is over.

The dishes are harder to do, and the child learns that he does not avoid responsibility by putting it off.

The last thing we want to do is to train our kids to do nothing until they are nagged or yelled at. That becomes a bad pattern that will result in an adult who does nothing until he is required to.

We don't want to worry that our kids will be irresponsible when they get out on their own. What a nightmare to imagine that a college roommate will wish he or she didn't have to room with a Williams kid!

We are trying to train up adults who can take care of themselves and their things when they are temporarily or permanently away from home.

❧ March 6 ❧

Because of Pat's background in sports promotion and entertainment, he can be fun and funny and sometimes embarrassing in public. We like to maintain a certain sense of decorum, and we never know when the man who once wrestled a bear at a halftime show in Chicago will do something to make us avert our eyes.

Once we had the whole family at a Chinese restaurant. The kids were behaving and any fears management had about such a huge crew had been laid to rest. In the crowded, dimly lit, beautifully decorated place, we quietly enjoyed our meal.

Then it was time for dessert, and at a table near ours an elderly woman was presented with a small cake. Her family sang, "Happy Birthday to Nellie," whereupon Michael told Pat he wanted some cake.

"You want some of Nellie's cake?" Pat asked, the wheels turning. The rest of us cringed. "She looks like she could spare a slice for you."

While Jill died a thousand Chinese deaths, Pat approached Nellie's table, wished her a happy birthday, and asked if he might have a little cake for his son.

When he returned with it, Michael beamed while the rest of the family tried to hide their embarrassment. One of the boys muttered, "I guess we should be glad he didn't sing to her."

Well, we hope we never get too old or too stiff to enjoy a little of Pat's serendipity.

❧ March 7 ❧

Pat was asked to speak and share his faith at a gathering in Boston that would be held in a secular setting. That way unbelievers could be invited and would not feel intimidated by a church setting.

The only problem was that the restaurant had a bar, and by the time everyone was rounded up to enjoy the program, half the crowd had been drinking.

Pat can identify with a primarily secular crowd because he did not become a Christian until he was in his mid-twenties. He is usually effective in these settings because he knows the questions and skepticism the crowd has for anyone who claims to be a Christian.

He was not prepared, however, for a heckler, and a drunk one at that. Right in the middle of Pat's testimony, a man stood and began challenging him, but he was so loud and incoherent that Pat could make out only a few of his words.

"What're you talkin' 'bout? You don' know nothin'!"

Pat, a humorist, was tempted to say, "It's all right folks, I remember when I had my first drink." Either that or ask the man if his train of thought had a caboose.

He had a sense the evening was ruined, but he felt led to just ignore the man and keep talking. He knew the Lord could work through anything, so he prayed he wouldn't get rattled and just kept going. Nineteen people came to Christ that night.

❧ March 8 ❧

You can usually get a good dose of truth out of a child.

One summer when Pat was speaking at Word of Life, an

elementary school principal approached him. He said he had a lot of trouble in his school with divorce, separation, and broken homes.

He said a first-grader came to the school open house with an adult couple, and she introduced the man as her daddy.

"And this must be your mommy," the principal said.

"No, this is my daddy's girlfriend, and I don't like her!"

Kids are straightforward and often have their own agendas. Carol Burnett tells the story of having caught her daughter in a lie. She disciplined her and sent her to bed.

Later she wanted to make sure the girl knew she loved her and cared about her and that was why she had corrected her. So she sat on the edge of the bed and leaned over her daughter, speaking quietly to her.

Carol went on and on about why she had to do what she had done and how important it was to tell the truth so people will trust you and you can be known as a person of your word. "Mommy wants you to grow up to be a good, honest person that people respect. Do you understand?"

"Uh-huh. Mommy?"

"Yes?"

"How many teeth do you *have?*"

❧ March 9 ❧

We believe in looking right, not to excess but to put our best feet forward. We don't want to become clotheshorses or slaves to fashion, but there is something about a person who knows how to dress. He also knows how to present himself, appears to take pride in his appearance without being hung up on it, and knows how to well represent his family, himself, and his employer.

We want our kids to be up-to-date and look nice without leaning toward the extremes. Whether wide or skinny ties are in or out this year or whether pastels or loud patterns are current, the classic, neat, fresh look is always in style.

Some successful men wear conservative suits or the classic navy blazer and gray slacks, and no matter what, they never go out of style.

Recently Jill was at a Magic game against the Lakers, and she was decked out elegantly. A teenage boy who sat behind Jill whispered to his mother, "That woman is someone important."

"What makes you think so?" the mother asked. "Because she's all dressed up?"

"Because she has a tan."

Well, Jill is dark to begin with, and she tries to spend enough time outdoors to keep a tan. It struck her funny, though, that she looked like someone important or a person of leisure—someone with enough time to lie around in the sun. It isn't true, of course, but it made her day.

❧ March 10 ❧

Call us insensitive, but one thing we get very tired of hearing are people's excuses for the sorry lives they lead. Don't get us wrong. We know there are cases of childhood abuse that require deep, intensive therapy to overcome.

But when we hear that someone breaks up a marriage, commits adultery, or can't keep a job because he or she was raised by parents who were too strict, well, that seems to be stretching credulity.

Many people of our generation were raised by parents of high standards. Maybe some of them didn't touch enough or express love enough, and maybe their love and acceptance of us seemed to be based solely on performance.

That can be a burden, but shouldn't it make us better parents? Shouldn't we remember those things we thought our parents could have done better, and do them for our kids?

Your upbringing does not have to determine your adult life. Your *response* to your upbringing is what counts.

That is true in so many areas of life. It isn't the problems we encounter that shape us. It is our response to them.

Pat remembers being at the 1988 Olympic trials in Colorado Springs and seeing the first fifty college basketball stars who had been cut from the original tryout list. It was probably the first failure they had ever experienced. How they handle that will determine their futures.

❧ March 11 ❧

We were talking with a young woman who had fallen in love with a local man. She had stars in her eyes when she spoke of him.

"Is matrimony in the cards?" Pat asked.

It was as if he had punched her.

"No, no, no, no!" she said. "I don't need all that hassle. My parents were divorced, remarried, all that. It's too complicated. I don't want that in my life."

She wants love. She wants the man. She wants everything but marriage.

It's sad to think that people believe they have to be locked into the patterns of their parents. Again, it is the response to your upbringing that makes the difference, not the upbringing itself.

That girl could have said, "Even if I am the first woman in my family in generations to have a successful, lifetime marriage, I will be that person."

Men who grew up in alcoholic homes where the pattern of abuse and unemployment covers the family tree can say, "It stops with me. I will not drink. I will not abuse. I will not leave. I will be responsible. The new legacy will be of men who are responsible, who honor God, and who are not destructive."

It's time for people to take responsibility for their own actions and not blame everything on heredity.

❧ March 12 ❧

Too often, dads have to learn the hard way how to raise or not raise their kids.

A friend of Pat says that he was unknowingly smothering his teenage sons. He wanted to know every detail and secret of their lives, wanted to be with them, go places with them, talk with them at all hours, even make all their decisions for them. He was pushy without knowing it.

Then the call came in the middle of the night. One of the boys had been injured in an accident. The father rushed to the hospital and began a long vigil, waiting for his son to come out of surgery, then out of a coma.

Sitting there praying and agonizing over the fate of his son, he realized there was nothing he could do. He couldn't talk to him, he couldn't operate on him, he couldn't even wake him. That was when it came to him that he had been a smothering father. He even remembered that his kids had tried to tell him that, but he was so devoted, so loving, that he just knew they understood his motives. Now, with no options and no way to have any control, he simply cherished his boy.

The son survived and is healthy again, and without his dad even talking about it, the boy has seen the difference.

"You used to know my every move and try to make every decision for me," he told his dad a year after the accident. "You used to be the biggest pain in the neck, but I like you now."

❧ March 13 ☙

In her traveling to minister and be ministered to, Jill has hit upon some keys to personal Bible study.

She believes we should study the Bible literally except when it is clear the passage is allegorical or symbolic. Too many people attempt abnormal interpretations, and you can wind up sharing theories until no one has a clue to the passage. It's the blind leading the blind.

Study the historical context. What did it mean to the people it was written to and for? What were their lives like? What made it unique to that time, and how should we apply the Scripture to today?

Study the Bible grammatically. Many expository pastors teach and preach the Scripture word by word. Study every word and phrase and see what emerges.

Remember the synthesis principle. If you have read the

Bible through in a year, you get an idea of how it all comes together like a great symphony.

Find practical principles. What does it mean to you today? Apply the Word by meditating on it. Don't be in a hurry to devour it. Think of a cow chewing her cud.

So, read, study, interpret, meditate, and then teach. Teaching the Bible is the best way to learn it because as a teacher you have to be clear on its concepts before you can relate them to someone else.

⌘§ March 14 ⁊⌘

We are often asked why we adopt. We have several reasons. Now if you asked why we adopt so many, we would have to say that if these reasons are good for one, they are good for many. As long as we have the resources, the time, and the energy, it's hard to turn away from needy children. There are days, of course, when we ask *ourselves* why so many? But we can't imagine being without any one of our precious children. Why adopt?

Because it is scriptural. We *are* our brothers' keepers. All of these kids are important to God. None are accidents. This is one way of being a missionary. These kids will come to know the Lord.

Because it is a deterrent to abortion. We would like to think that any pregnant mother would put her baby up for adoption rather than abort if she knew her child would get loving care.

Because it sets a good example. People who can should help as many children as possible.

Because every child deserves a home of his own. Harry

Holt, founder of the Holt Adoption Agency, said that no child can flourish without love and security.

Because you need the blessing and the fun. How do you know your quiver is full? (Psalm 127:3–5).

Pat can remember not so many years ago telling Jill he wasn't sure he could love a child that was not his own. Now he says, "We have four homegrowns and eight adopted, but I don't remember which is which!"

❧ March 15 ❧

When Jim was thirteen years old, he signed up for the twelve- to thirteen-year-old soccer team. His former coach was now handling the thirteen- to fifteen-year-olds, a team of bigger, stronger kids. Jim was small for his age but quite an accomplished player.

The coach approached Pat and said he would prefer that Jim play on the older, bigger team. Pat met with Jim to explain the options.

"I don't want to tell you what to do, Jim. The choice is yours. On the younger team you'll be a leader, one of the fastest and strongest kids. You'll be crucial to the team's success, and you'll be effective.

"On the older team, you'll face tougher challenges, be one of the smaller guys, and maybe not contribute as much. You'll learn a lot and have to work harder, but it will be a whole new growing experience for you."

"How do I decide?"

"I think you should pray and seek God's will on this."

Fifteen minutes after he went to bed that night, Jim came

to our room and told Pat, "I want to play on the older team. I think it's what God wants me to do."

We're not the ones to say that God speaks audibly to us or to our children. Neither would we say He couldn't if He wanted to. We do believe, however, that God will impress upon His children what they should do, if they humbly seek Him.

❧ March 16 ❧

Bill Bright, founder and president of Campus Crusade for Christ, International, was coming to town, and Pat was nervous. Pat had been put in charge of fund-raising for the move of Crusade from Arrowhead Springs, California, to Orlando, and so far, the effort had been a frustrating failure.

The committee was earnest and active, but little money had been raised. Dr. Bright was coming for an update, and there was precious little to tell him.

Pat had been involved in similar ministry-related volunteer positions, such as promoting Billy Graham and Christian films in the Philadelphia area. But this job was bigger and more complex. He was working on it, but with the state of the economy, times were tough.

When Bright arrived, Pat spoke for the committee and was forthright, though he felt sheepish and embarrassed. "Dr. Bright," he began, "the news is not exciting. In fact, it is bad. You need thirty million to make this move, and we have made little progress."

Dr. Bright's response turned the meeting and the attitudes around. "In forty years of fund-raising for Crusade, I have never raised more than we needed. If the thirty million dollars had been here when I arrived, there might have been a sense of complacency and self-satisfaction and human achievement. God wouldn't want that, and neither would I. Let's keep at it. With His help, the job will get done."

❦ March 17 ❧

Jill demands perfection, though she will accept more.

That is Pat's assessment of his hardworking wife, who, though she is involved in more activities and excels at more things than most people could imagine, still struggles with a sense of failure.

Sometimes she feels a failure as a mother, though many would feel that simply getting all our kids off to school, home, fed, and to bed would be a major accomplishment. She wants results, action, fruit from her labor. She wants perfect kids.

When all you hear all day is that someone's piece of pie is bigger than mine, or he got a drumstick and I didn't, or I don't want to go to bed now, it is refreshing and encouraging to get positive feedback on your kids from outsiders.

Norm Sonju took the time to write us about Jimmy's awards at Camp of the Woods (sportsmanship). He wrote, "What a special young guy. I am so proud of him and the wonderful job he did . . . I know both you and Jill are proud of him, and I want to let you know what a delight it was to have him here."

Not long after that, we got a call from Denny Doyle to tell us how well both Jim and Bob had done at baseball school that summer. As a junior in high school, Jim was named the most improved soccer player.

That kind of input makes it all worth it.

❦§ March 18 ?❧

You will find us quoting pastor and author David Jeremiah here frequently because we think so much of what he has to say. He told Pat how proud he was of his own son, who is growing up and making his own decisions now.

When his son was sixteen, David let him sign up for a three-day basketball shooting school that included a Sunday-morning session. Dave said nothing to his son about wishing he would make time for church in that schedule. He just waited to see what would come of it.

Dave was thrilled when his son got up on his own and went to the early church service before the shooting school.

Later he was invited to a party where the parents weren't going to be home. He called Dave for advice and Dave assured him he would trust his son's decision. His son decided to come home.

That reminded us of a story about Bob. He was at a party and had been promised a ride home. During the party, however, the adults began drinking beer. Bob was afraid to ride in the car with them, so he called Jill and asked for a ride home.

The men were probably not drunk and perhaps not even significantly impaired, but we were thrilled with Bob's decision. It is always better to take the safe route, and though we rarely talk about it, clearly Bob has been listening and watching when drunk-driver warnings are broadcast on TV.

❦ March 19 ❧

If you have ever been criticized for doing what you knew was right, you will identify with this little truism: You can expect people to misunderstand your motives when you are obeying God.

We have found that our reaction to what happens to us along the way depends on our confidence in our destination. For instance, since we know we are forgiven and on our way to heaven, it makes it easier for us to forgive. We might forgive an insult, a slight, even slander from someone others would condemn. Why? Because we know it's what God would want. We can't do it in ourselves. We are no better or bigger than anyone else, but when God wants to live through you, you find resources that are divine.

We must forgive because we have been forgiven.

We should forgive just as we have been forgiven.

We must forgive in order that we might be forgiven.

We should forgive before we need to be forgiven.

David Jeremiah says that in the matter of forgiveness, it is *always* your turn. In other words, if you feel you have done your part and all you can do, yet the other person is still angry with you, it is still your turn to forgive. We used to think you had to forgive only people who knew they needed it, wanted it, and asked for it.

No, true forgiveness is forgiving the unforgivable and even those who are oblivious to their fault.

❧ March 20 ❧

Pat has an incredible fascination with Native Americans, partly because of his love of history and also because he has a sense that there might be a wave of great athletes from the reservations that is just waiting to break onto the professional sports scene.

When a missionary returned from Arizona, where he had been ministering to the Navajo, Pat asked him about sports programs.

"They don't play," the missionary reported. "The adults don't want them to compete. They don't want one to get ahead of another."

That reminded us of the stories of an African tribe who invented a game for children in which the object is to tie. The game is not over until a certain number of points have been scored and both teams have the same amount.

In theory, that might sound interesting. There are some kids, very young ones, who need to know how to play and interact and even compete a little without the hassle of feeling bad because they were whipped. But on the other hand, if how you play the game is all that matters, why do we keep score?

There is an organized sports program for kids near us that has a basketball league in which they don't keep score. But you know what? You can't fool the kids. At the end of the game one team is happy and one team isn't, because they all keep score in their heads, and they know who won.

❧ March 21 ☙

A postscript to yesterday. Pat wishes there were a Little League baseball program or Pop Warner football or YMCA basketball on those Indian reservations. Kids deserve the chance to enjoy sports, to learn and compete, to have a chance to go on and make something of themselves.

People always think they can fool children. In a Christian school we heard about, they never used the terms *failed* or *flunked* when referring to kids who have to repeat a grade. They will talk about being held back or repeating, but not the other two F words.

It doesn't make any difference. A six-year-old was carefully informed that he would be held back a year so he would be more comfortable in first grade when he was really ready for it. All the delicate, precise language was used and the authorities felt good about the conversation. He seemed to take it well.

When he was leaving, however, the next child waiting asked him what happened.

"Not much," he announced. "I just flunked kindergarten!"

Let's quit pretending, and let's encourage kids to compete, if only with themselves. We want our doctor and our lawyer to be winners, don't you? Too often we Christians are just out there muddling around, searching in vain for God's will rather than developing attitudes of winners and champions, rolling up our sleeves and getting the job done.

❧ March 22 ☙

When our brood grew to a dozen, we knew our house had to grow too. The problem was, we were in a ranch that was already so wide on the property that we could only go up. So we went up. We moved into a much smaller place, where the kids had to double up and we were all cramped for several months while an upstairs was added to our home.

Bob complained that his and Jimmy's room was hard to take care of. They had a lot of stuff and the place was just too small.

Jill suggested that maybe living in a small house for a while was meant to teach us something.

"Yeah," Bobby said, "to help Jim and me get along better."

There's something about close quarters that makes that necessary.

People often ask if our kids fight a lot. The answer is no, and not just because they are so wonderful. They don't fight because we don't let them. Sure, they get tangled up once in a while, but even when they begin to argue, we nip it in the bud. They are stopped immediately and punished so they think twice before getting into that again.

We have found if we let it go, it will keep building until there is a real fight, and we just won't have it. They get to sit alone and think about it for a couple of hours, and that usually resolves the problem.

❧ March 23 ❧

Our friend R. C. Sproul has a wonderful passage in his book *The Intimate Marriage* (Tyndale House, 1986). It is found on pages 42 and 43 of the chapter, "The Role of the Man and Woman in Marriage," and it perfectly captures a typical storm. He writes:

> [The man] enters the courting relationship with the zeal and dedication of an olympic-bound athlete. He

gives his girl undivided attention, makes her the center of his devotion. When the marriage is achieved, our athlete turns his attention to other goals. He figures he has the romantic aspect of his life under control and now goes on to scale new heights. He devotes less and less time to his wife, treating her as less and less important. In the meantime the woman, being accustomed to the courting process, enters the marriage relationship expecting that to continue. As the marriage progresses, she finds herself devoting more attention to her husband than she did before the marriage, while he is devoting less attention to her. Now she is washing his clothes, cooking his meals, making his bed, cleaning his house—maybe even packing his suitcase. At the same time, he is becoming less affectionate (though perhaps more erotic), taking her out less, and generally paying less attention to her.

Sound familiar? It sure does to us. That syndrome came dangerously close to toppling our marriage years ago. Pat thought he had a perfect situation until Jill finally got his attention. Such marriage problems require immediate, drastic action.

❧ March 24 ❧

A few years ago, Pat spoke on the phone to his old friend Stu Inman and mentioned that he had taken our boys to the All-Star baseball game in Oakland. That made Stu think of his dad doing the same thing with him years ago. (Stu has operated teams in the National Basketball Association for the last two decades, mostly in Portland, Milwaukee, and Miami. He has served as director of player personnel, head scout, and has been in charge of college scouting.)

Now in his sixties, Stu reminisced about growing up and being close to his dad. "He took me everywhere to see ball games. I saw Jackie Robinson play football at UCLA and baseball with the Oakland Oaks before he made the majors."

The names of former greats rolled off Stu's tongue as if he had just seen them play. Many of them are dead now, but Stu—like any true sports buff—remembers all the details.

More important than the memories of all the old players and the game situations was the bond Stu remembers between his dad and him. He wouldn't trade it for anything.

There is something unique about fathers and sons. Our hope is that our kids will cherish the memories of all the opportunities they enjoy to see big games and meet great athletes. But if they are like Stu Inman and Pat, what they will really recall and treasure is the memory of a dad who cared about them enough to show his love in terms of time and priorities.

❦ March 25 ❧

Winning Mother of the Year from Mom International was a real boost for Jill, and her further involvement now as chairperson of the board for The Adoption Centre in Maitland, Florida, allows her to really exercise her gifts on behalf of many otherwise aborted, abandoned, or orphaned children.

She attended a convention for adoption agency workers in Washington, D.C., and came away stunned. She had been struggling with how hard it was to try to take care of and individually love and nurture twelve kids, but the convention changed her attitude.

She felt like small potatoes when she met mothers of nineteen and twenty-four and thirty kids. There were several single mothers with fifteen to twenty handicapped kids! Jill returned with a whole new outlook.

It isn't the number of kids you take in that counts, of course. What matters is what you are able to provide for them. During those times when Jill wishes she could have a relationship with our twelve like the one Maria had with her charges in *The Sound of Music*, she has to remind herself that this is real life.

There will be imperfections, squabbles, tears, and frustration. But it will all be worth it. When Jill can pull back a little and think about the family she has brought together, the homegrowns and the adoptees, she wouldn't trade any one of them for anything. She sensed even as a child that mothering was her calling, and this is what life is all about.

❧§ March 26 ?❧

We have always been impressed with the spirit and humility of Billy Graham. Sometimes you have to compare him with some of the shrill, egotistical, money-grubbing TV types to realize what a modest person he is. He never features himself, never grovels for money, never shows off.

He was asked what he wanted to be remembered for, and his answer was surprising yet telling. This from a man who has preached to and reached more people than anyone else in history: "When my life's over, I want to be remembered as a man who was fun to live with."

He will be remembered as a great man of God, a man of the Word, a preacher and evangelist extraordinaire, but those around him say he will indeed also be remembered as a man fun to live with. He has a good sense of humor. He is others-oriented. He is not contentious. What a legacy!

Too often we Christians act as if there is a rule that says we can't enjoy life. We feel we have to go around looking like cheerleaders for a funeral.

Our assistant coach, George Scholz, is a big advocate of fun. He writes, "Choose to have fun. Fun creates enjoyment. Enjoyment invites participation. Participation focuses attention. Attention expands awareness. Awareness promotes insight. Insight generates knowledge. Knowledge facilitates action. Action yields results."

❧ March 27 ❧

Our friend David Jeremiah tells the story of his renting a car to drive to Camp of the Woods, where he was to speak and minister for a week.

He stopped for gas and asked for diesel because a sticker on the gas cap said, "Diesel Fuel Only."

Not long after, the car sputtered and stopped. Towed to a service station, Dave was told, "You're using the wrong kind of fuel."

"But it says, Diesel Fuel Only."

"So it does," the mechanic said. "But I've been under the hood. That engine has spark plugs. It runs on unleaded gasoline, and it won't run on diesel. That's why you're here."

Dave says the cost of the towing and the work was worth

the illustration. The moral? It doesn't matter what you say on the outside. It's what's happening inside that counts.

Pat ministers every year at camps too, and he often likes to ask questions of the staffers. He asked waitress Wendy Powell at the Word of Life Inn to list the three most important things her parents did for her.

She said, "First, they led me to Jesus Christ.

"Second, they showed me love and loyalty.

"And third, they trusted me, which made me want to be worthy of their trust."

That was good counsel for us.

❦§ March 28 ❧❧

You never know who your path will cross when you simply follow the Lord and try to do His will. In 1973, Pat moved from being general manager of the Chicago Bulls to the same job in Atlanta with the Hawks. He didn't know he would be there only a year before going to the 76ers, but the range of people he met in that short time—especially those who turned out to be leaders—made the time in Atlanta more than worthwhile.

He looked for someone to give an invocation at the start of the basketball season and was directed to the governor of the state, a professing Christian. Pat asked. The man said yes. Fellow by the name of Jimmy Carter.

He was invited to lunch with the owner of a local UHF station that carried the Hawks games. Guy named Ted Turner.

Visited the tiny studio of a Christian TV station owned by an independent minister. Pat Robertson.

Jill urged Pat to spend a morning listening to a man

who had developed a unique approach to Scripture study called Walk Thru the Bible. A man named Bruce Wilkinson.

We were invited to visit First Baptist in Atlanta while looking for a church. Someone said the controversial new assistant there had taken over after the church split over his hiring. We thought he was pretty good and stayed there during our time in Atlanta. The preacher's name was Charles Stanley. The rest of the country now agrees he's pretty good.

❦§ March 29 ?❧

Other people who were unknown and have become known since crossing our paths include Barry Manilow, Cecil Day, Kay Arthur, and even Hal Lindsey.

Pat was arranging for a Halloween party at the New York Knicks game against the 76ers in the Philadelphia Spectrum in 1974 during his first season as general manager. Someone called and asked if he could play a tape over the sound system as the crowd filed in. Sure, why not?

The guy showed up, a skinny little person with a prominent nose and wire-rimmed glasses. "Where can I take my tape?" he wanted to know.

Pat was busy. He pointed to the engineering booth and the guy hurried off. Soon everyone was listening to Barry Manilow's first hit, "Mandy," and Pat had met, while hardly noticing, a future superstar.

Pat was asked to speak at a Christian company and share his testimony. The invitation came from the owner, the late Cecil Day. The company? Days Inn.

Jill went to a weekly Bible study in Atlanta during 1973,

taught by a woman who traveled from Chattanooga each week to teach it. Jill thought she was great. Kay Arthur.

And soon after Pat became a Christian in the sixties, he used to drive for miles to attend Bible studies taught by a guy who hadn't even written one book yet, let alone a half-dozen best-sellers: Hal Lindsey.

◄§ March 30 ৡ►

Pat had been asked to speak at the First Baptist Church in Elkhart, Indiana, where David Graham was pastor. Graham agreed to make Pat's flight arrangements.

While on the phone to the reservations office in Nashville, this Indiana pastor happened to speak with a reservationist who discovered he was a pastor.

"Oh, I miss my pastor," she said. "He used to be here in Nashville, but he's been gone almost ten years now. We still miss him."

The pastor? Jim Henry, who moved to First Baptist in Orlando and is now our pastor. It's a small world.

That story, besides being an amazing coincidence, also shows the depth of feeling people can have for their shepherds. There are excesses, of course, and the wise and humble pastor will always turn his people's attention back to the Lord.

But not all feelings of love and devotion for one's pastor have to lead to cult-type worship and dangers like the Jim Jones fiasco. Some pastors are worth the devotion of the flock, especially if those pastors are faithful to the Word, love their people, and have their family priorities in order.

We have had great pastors over the years, including George

Sweeting, Warren Wiersbe, Charles Stanley, Jim Henry, and many others. We know they are just men, but we love them and are grateful for the part they have played in our spiritual growth.

❧ March 31 ❧

Our Karyn has seen nine more children join our family since she was a little girl. Though she still gets lots of love and attention, no doubt there must be times when she wishes she had her mom and dad all to herself.

It was interesting for her to chat with Donna Schmidt, the wife of former Philadelphia Phillies star third baseman Mike Schmidt, when she was at Disney. Karyn, along with Donna and Mike's two children, are part of a Disney kids advisory board.

Donna told Karyn that even though there are only two Schmidt children, each cherishes moments alone with their mother. So that feeling isn't unique to big families.

That is the toughest part of our job as the parents of so many children. We know each of them wants and needs time alone with each of us, and all we can do is the best we can. It's hard to have time alone with each one every day; in fact it is nearly impossible. But we do try to focus on that and do it as much as possible.

Sometimes private moments can be shared in brief snatches, speaking individually with one of the kids, sharing a look or a touch or a whisper, even with others around. Even saying something aloud that applies to only one of the bunch can make him feel special, and it shows on his face. On special occasions we make sure we get time alone with a birthday child, and when carpooling puts us in a situation where it is just us and one other, we take advantage of the time to really connect.

❦§ April 1 ❧

One of our favorite speakers and teachers is theologian/scholar R. C. Sproul. He attends Orangewood Presbyterian Church, where our kids go to school. His ministry, Ligonier, is based in Orlando, and he is a Magic season ticket holder. Our kind of a guy.

Once we heard Sproul say that a person should try to learn one new thing every year. One year Pat learned surf fishing with a net. But when Pat decided to work on music for a while so he could sing a duet with Jill, she was stunned.

Music has never been Pat's thing. He has no rhythm. He can carry a tune, but he has never sung in front of a crowd. Regardless, he worked with Jill, and at a marriage conference where we were speaking, he did it. He actually stood in front of the crowd with Jill and sang the melody to her harmony.

The result was a standing ovation, either for his courage or for the fact that we were through, but nonetheless, he had done it. He had conquered an inhibition, invested the time, and accomplished something new.

The ovation showed the crowd's delight, but Jill was even more thrilled. For him to devote himself to doing something with her and for her made her feel special and loved. She is now working on her jump shot and hopes to be able to help out the Orlando Magic should they get into an important game and find themselves short of personnel. Just kidding.

❧April 2❧

Don and Carol Lough run the Word of Life Inn in New York. A few years ago, when their daughter Jodi was attending Liberty University and working at the inn during the summer, Pat asked her what she was looking for in a husband.

She said she wanted someone who was:

A growing Christian.
Missions minded. Either already heading or interested in going to a mission field.
Moral. Someone who had kept himself pure for his wife.
Musically inclined or at least appreciated music.
Able to challenge her intellectually. A reader.
Not into television or videos in a big way.
Interested in sports.
Attractive.
Not absorbed with getting married.
A lover of children.

Of course such definite and clear answers made Pat want to know the parents' secrets to raising such an articulate thinker. The Loughs said they tried to be consistent in their life-style, acting the same in public as at home. They encouraged their kids to talk to them a lot. They controlled the TV and spent a lot of creative time together as a family. They always disciplined immediately for bad attitudes, weren't afraid to apologize, and were undyingly loyal to each other and the kids.

❧ April 3 ❧

There was a wealth of information and teaching in yesterday's entry, wasn't there? We learned a lot from Jodi Lough and her parents.

Our job as parents is not to make our kids hopelessly dependent on us but to make them secure enough to be independent. We know many parents—and this is a temptation for us too—who nag and bug and cajole their kids to get them to do anything. Their daily existence is nothing but yelling and badgering kids to get up, brush their teeth, have breakfast, straighten their rooms, get dressed and out to the car on time, remember all their stuff coming and going, do their chores, and on and on and on.

Perhaps things get done, but where are those kids going to be when they don't have anyone standing over them all the time, telling them what step to take next? Kids need to know what their responsibilities are and when they have to be accomplished. Then they must face the consequences if they don't get the jobs done.

We want our kids to learn to get along on their own so that when we take them to summer camp or sports camp they don't stand by the car and wail but head for the new opportunity, hardly looking back.

They know we are there for them. They know we'll miss them. They know we love them. And most of all, they know how to get along away from home and out from under our constant supervision.

❧ April 4 ❧

Pat's friend Bill Curry, former head football coach of the Kentucky Wildcats and now the Alabama Crimson Tide, tells a wonderful story of a special person in his childhood.

Mrs. Miriam Berry was his choir director at College Park Presbyterian, and she was a woman who could control him even when he was a rambunctious twelve-year-old. He says he was so unruly that one teacher tied him to a chair and taped his mouth shut.

But not Mrs. Berry. She had a way with the kids that made them want to do what she said and to stay long after rehearsals were over.

Once she asked him to sing a solo at a Christmas concert and made him feel comfortable with it by rehearsing every line and note and phrase with him until he knew it perfectly. The night of the concert he was ready, proudly standing before the congregation in his starched robe, hair just so.

Then stage fright struck and his mouth went dry. His knees knocked. His memory was gone. Nothing would come out of his mouth.

As the music played, another voice carried the melody and the lyrics. It was Mrs. Berry, singing for him, then singing with him until he got on track, and carrying him through to the end. Later people complimented them on the beautiful duet, not knowing that this wonderful woman had actually renewed his confidence and saved face for him.

❧ April 5 ☙

A few years ago Pat became a Civil War buff. That entire period of American history fascinates him, and he has learned a lot from the hundreds of books on the subject.

He knows women, especially housewives, work long and hard now, but consider the pioneer wife. She worked so hard and long that she usually collapsed into bed as soon as the sun went down. Historians say she worked sixteen hours a day just to survive.

Many women had to chop wood, and even if their husbands did that, it was the women's responsibility to collect and bring it in and get the cooking fire going so the family could eat. Most women milked the cows, got water from the well, and mixed cornmeal mush with milk or molasses.

After the meal and the cleanup, the wife had to tend her own garden and often work in the fields with her husband as well. In her spare time she made medicines, tended the sick, and made soap and candles and clothes. For lunch she had to cut meat and chop vegetables for a thick stew. Then it was back to her many chores.

Dr. David Hawke, an historian and author of *Everyday Life in America*, says that laundry day was the only break from the arduous routine, and that was torturous in itself. It usually took an entire day of boiling kettles of water in the kitchen and carrying them outside for the scrubbing job. On top of that, women couldn't vote, own property, or speak in public.

You've come a long way, baby.

❧ April 6 ❧

Swen Nater, a six-foot, eleven-inch UCLA basketball star center, who wound up enjoying a long career in the National Basketball Association, was deep into drugs more than a decade ago, and his life was falling apart.

The giant who led the NBA in rebounding for a couple of years and ended his career backing up Kareem Abdul-Jabbar had a problem like so many other successful and visible athletes.

That's why it was so moving and such a thrill to be at Camp of the Woods in the summer of 1987 and hear Swen, now a coach at a Christian college, sing a solo, "There Is a Savior," the beautiful song made popular by Sandi Patti.

Gordon Purdy, who had introduced him, was in tears after the solo and said, "Who ever would have thought ten years ago that this man, whom we watched playing basketball, would stand here singing about a Savior who changed his life?"

The older we get in our Christian lives, the sweeter is the picture of a Christ who not only forgives and saves and satisfies but who also turns lives around.

We don't know what it is about the spotlight or athletics or success that makes people turn to drugs. It seems those people would have less reason than anyone to do drugs. And we don't know all the reasons Swen Nater was drawn into that destructive world. But we praise God as Swen does that "for each tomorrow, and yesterday, there is a Savior who lights our way."

❧ April 7 ❧

We heard a humorous Christian speaker say that when her husband tried to do the laundry for her, he put all the colored clothes in with the whites and it all ran together. The whites now had tinges of all the other colors in the wash and came out looking gray.

Of course, if you drop anything red into a laundry of whites, everything comes out pink. It's not what you want in a wash, but as the old pastors used to say, it'll preach.

We once heard Edith Schaeffer, widow of the great Christian scholar and philosopher Dr. Francis Schaeffer, say that the lives of people in too many Christian families are separated like laundry.

Each has a different circle of friends and colleagues and acquaintances and goes his separate way. Mrs. Schaeffer advises that we keep our families together and, in essence, wash them at the same time until they come out tinted by our common faith in Christ.

When that doesn't happen, disaster looms. A friend of Pat, who came to Orlando with his family and immediately set about excelling in his career, was brought up short when he returned home from work one night and found his kids sitting on the floor with notes from his wife pinned to them. She had left.

"I had spent my adult life reaching the top of my profession," he said, "and it cost me everything I loved."

❧ April 8 ❧

The man we mentioned at the end of yesterday's entry took the entire blame for his failed first marriage. "I was consumed with my work and never let it go. I thought the ice wouldn't freeze unless I was there to watch it.

"It took finding my children sitting on the floor of a living room with no furniture left to get me started rearranging my priorities. I could make twice as much money as I do now, but I don't want to. My new wife and my kids are happy, we get three square meals a day, and I get a new suit every year. What more could I want?"

A friend told Pat that a man in her office brings his personal problems to work every day, "and it's killing us. All he talks about is what is wrong at home, and it drags everybody down. He's made a crusade out of his kids, with their pictures literally lining every wall of his office. It's sad, and the marriage is going to end."

The same day Pat heard about that, a man called who had read *Rekindled*. "My wife left me five months ago," he said, "and I'm a wreck. I built my business into a forty-million-dollar company, but I'm worthless at the office. I can do nothing productive because my mind is torn up and totally distracted by the mess I've made of my life."

We see and hear such stories almost every day and can only pray for people to see their need of Christ.

❧ April 9 ❧

Pat could hardly believe it the day in January 1987 when the news came of the death of Pete Maravich. Pete had been one of the greatest college basketball players in history, averaging more than forty-four points a game in his last three seasons at Louisiana State University under his father/coach Press Maravich.

He went on to play ten years in the NBA, first in Atlanta, where he was when Pat joined the club as general manager in 1973. One of Pat's final duties there was to trade Pete to the New Orleans Jazz (now the Utah Jazz) for a raft of future draft choices that made the Hawks competitive for years.

Pete had become a vibrant, outspoken Christian, and he was playing a pickup game of basketball with Dr. James Dobson and some of his friends before a scheduled "Focus on the Family" radio interview.

They were taking a break, and Dr. Dobson asked Pete how he felt.

"I feel great," Pete said, then fell to the floor. At first Dobson thought Pete was joking, then realized he was in trouble. He died within seconds.

Our pastor, Jim Henry, said, "Pete Maravich, the king of the courts, this past week made his appearance in the court of the King."

❧ April 10 ❧

We ran into Gaye Wheat, wife of Ed Wheat, who wrote *Love Life for Every Married Couple* (Zondervan, 1980), and she asked about all we were doing. Her husband's book was a major factor in the turnaround of our marriage, so we were pleased to tell her of our huge, happy family and many of our activities.

She said, "You be sure to enjoy every minute of it, because we never know what tomorrow holds."

The Pete Maravich story from yesterday is proof of that. It

reminded Pat of something he has heard from many pulpits on the suddenness of death: "Life is short, death is sure. Sin the curse, Christ the cure."

It is easy for Pat to think of his own father when someone brings up the suddenness of death. Just after Pat's final collegiate baseball game, he took the long ride home to Delaware with a bunch of buddies. His dad had been to the game at Wake Forest, and of course, Pat fully expected to see his father when he arrived home.

They took a leisurely trip, as graduates will do, trying to enjoy themselves while commiserating over a tough loss that had knocked them out of contention for the college world series.

When they got home, Pat's mother pulled him off to the side to tell him of his father's death. He knows the pain of things left unsaid, and he'll always remember that day.

❦ April 11 ❦

When we think of Ed and Gaye Wheat, we always think of the acronym Dr. Wheat used in his book *Love Life for Every Married Couple.* It was B-E-S-T and stood for Blessing, Edifying, Sharing, and Touching. That was his prescription for an offending spouse to try to win back an offended mate.

Blessing means praising her. Edifying means building her up. Sharing means telling her your hopes and dreams and even problems and including her in your plans. Touching is self-explanatory, except that Dr. Wheat recommended heavy doses of nonsexual touching. When a wife has been neglected, the wrong kind of touching can be misinterpreted and turn her off.

Most interesting about Dr. Wheat's prescription is that though a scared-to-death husband, who is applying this much later than he should, is looking for immediate results, Dr. Wheat says results may never come. Yet the B-E-S-T principles still apply if only because they are the right things to do. You are hoping to win back your spouse, yes. But you apply these whether or not she ever responds.

Hanging on to the spouse of your youth after having neglected her or having deeply offended her in some way is like trying to hang on to a wet bar of soap. Squeeze too tightly and she shoots from your hand. Hold her too loosely and she slides away. A gentle but firm grasp is called for.

❧ April 12 ☙

The B-E-S-T principles have become a foundation for our marriage and even for our children, and they remind us of how important word choices are. In the Blessing and Edifying and Sharing categories especially, well-chosen words make such a difference.

Jill still remembers sharing at the All-Star baseball chapel meeting in Kansas City in 1973, when then Cincinnati Reds manager Sparky Anderson raved about her and said she was gorgeous. It was just a sentence, a nice compliment from someone who appreciated her. It will soon be twenty years since that comment, and she still roots for Sparky's teams.

At a summer swim meet, Thomas was swimming his leg of the one-hundred-meter individual medley relay. It is a grueling event, even for a little guy who has worked hard preparing for it. We were impressed to see Sarah at one end of the pool, on her knees, screaming encouragement to him as he made his turns.

Later we overheard Thomas tell her, through a huge grin, "I was tired when I heard you going wild for me, and then I wasn't tired anymore. I just went *whoosh!*"

A married couple we know has a signal between them. They can tell when they start disagreeing about everything, so they just give each other the eye and everything stops. "It's like we hit a breaking point," they say, "and we regroup, clear the air, and reconcile immediately." Good advice about words.

⮜§ April 13 ҙ⮞

Parents love to hear just the right words from their kids too. Doesn't it warm your heart when one of your children compliments you without being urged to by your spouse? How sweet to hear a child say, "Great dinner, Mom. That was good."

Or to have a child say you look great, or that he is proud of you, or that he loves you. Spontaneous, unforced, unbribed, un-begged-for hugs are wonderful too.

Mark Twain said he could live two months on one good compliment.

When David, one of our Filipinos, was eleven, he wrote this beautiful Christmas note to us:

> Mom and Dad, thank you for adopting me. You both are very special to me. I thank God also for bringing me here so that I could learn how to play baseball, basketball, soccer, and how to swim.

.I thank you also for letting me do all those things.
What do I like about my dad? I like my dad because
he taught me how to play baseball and he spends time
with me.

How we long to be worthy of that sweet praise from a child.
Our kids have always been thoughtful about expressing themselves that way, and we like to think we have modeled that to
them. It is hard to keep up with appreciating the people in
your life and telling them so, but it sure is worth it. It makes
the hard work all that much more worthwhile.

❦§ April 14 ?❧

Touch is so important. Some experts believe that wives need
twenty significant touches a day just to keep their equilibrium. Men need to be touched encouragingly and affection-
ately too, whether or not they admit it. Hardly any husband
would feel uncomfortable in public with his wife's hand
through his arm or her arm around his waist while walking or
around his shoulder while sitting.

Inappropriate public displays of affection are out, of course,
but most men are proud to be seen with their wives. They
enjoy having it show that their wives enjoy being with them
too. It is nice to have it be obvious that she is still in love, still
happy to be with him, and isn't just hanging with him because
she can't get out of the marriage or didn't realize she was too
good for him. Yes, men can be a little paranoid too.

Most of all, though, the touch, whether in public or in
private, is therapeutic, soothing, confidence-building, and encouraging.

One of the saddest and most moving anecdotes we have ever heard about the life of Marilyn Monroe is from her childhood, when she was little Norma Jean Baker. She was raised in a series of foster homes where she mostly felt neglected and unwanted, often ignored. But one of her foster mothers touched her cheeks while helping her apply her makeup. "I'll never forget that touch," Marilyn said years later.

❧ April 15 ❧

We have heard Chuck Swindoll talk about turning points in people's lives, and what he outlined was certainly true in our case. When our marriage was on the ropes in 1982, the four characteristics Dr. Swindoll attributes to turning points were evident, especially in Pat's experience.

In fact, Dr. Swindoll was one of the first people we told of our salvaged marriage and our renewed love. He was the one who suggested the title for the book *Rekindled*.

He says that real turning points in a person's life will:

1. Happen in normal events. Pat first became aware of the deep problem by pressing Jill on why she had been so quiet at breakfast and at church.

2. Be sudden and unexpected. Jill's response nearly left Pat breathless. When she told him he had killed her emotionally, he was stunned to the core.

3. Impact others in our lives. Our turn of events impacted our whole family and even how we interacted with friends.

4. Prompt changes in us. Pat cried and prayed and wrote copious notes about the changes he knew needed to take place in his relationship with Jill. He became more focused on her needs and the home, and it changed even the way he

dealt with friends and acquaintances. People noticed. He was no longer on a mission to get to the next project. He cared. He listened. He had become a whole person again. It was a true turning point.

❧ April 16 ❧

Pat is nearly ten years older than Jill, and now, in his fifties, he is running at a frenetic pace few people can understand: volunteering to help raise money for ministries, speaking, providing for a huge family, serving as president of two professional sports teams. Many people ask, "Why do you do it?"

Pat has always had high energy and meets the day eager to get things done. But now, realizing that these opportunities may never come around again, he feels the need to enjoy it all.

Life is short and tenuous. It is hard not to think of the Pete Maraviches who died more than ten years younger than Pat.

David Jeremiah recalls that when he was forty-six, he received a letter of invitation to a meeting of the Future Christian Leaders. At the bottom of the page, it said in small print that he could come only if he was under forty-five. He called his wife and said, "You're married to a has-been."

Janet Chusmir, executive editor of the *Miami Herald*, died at sixty of a brain aneurysm. She left a grown family grateful that they had been able to enjoy her for that long.

As an executive, she had encouraged her female colleagues that they should not forsake domestic pleasures while climbing the corporate ladder. She said they needed to remember their nurturing skills. "I always remind myself that I can't hug a newspaper," she said.

❧ April 17 ❧

Having worked for so long in the NBA, Pat has interacted with hundreds of young black men. These men, many from humble backgrounds, face difficulties that millions of dollars in salaries often can't overcome.

A June 4, 1990, editorial in *U.S. News & World Report* says that "for black children, the likelihood of living with both natural parents until the age of 17 dropped from 52 percent in the '50s to 6 percent in the '80s. Not having a man in the house has disastrous economic consequences and young males grow up without the role model and disciplining presence of a working father."

One of the fortunate ones in the NBA is Wayman Tisdale, the ninth leading scorer in NCAA history while at Oklahoma and the second pick in the 1985 NBA draft behind New York Knicks center Patrick Ewing. Tisdale played his first four NBA seasons in Indianapolis before being traded to the Sacramento Kings.

Wayman was raised the son of a preacher in Tulsa, and he agrees he was one of the lucky black kids who grew up with both parents in the home. "To have both my parents together and to have both my mother and my father influencing my life—they're still a big influence on my life now—I feel like I'm one of that six percent still."

Wayman says his father was the "backbone of our whole family. I want to be like my father. . . ."

❧ April 18 ❧

We were saddened last year to hear of the death of the great pro and college football coach George Allen. Allen made up one of Pat's favorite lists of the characteristics of a Champion and of an Also-ran. It went like this:

A Champion is ambitious, coachable, aggressive, a leader, a take-charge guy, hardworking, physically tough, and mentally tough. He hates to lose, can't stand failure, takes advice, is eager to learn, asserts himself, sets an example, and is respected by teammates. He takes over in a crisis, never misses a practice, stays in shape, and never gives up.

An Also-Ran has no drive, is a know-it-all, a mouse, a follower, a watcher, a corner-cutter, a hypochondriac, a complainer, and a quitter. He doesn't care whether he wins or loses, never listens, gripes, works by himself, always kicks himself, never tries to lead, worries about what people think, always has excuses to be late or cut practices, often has an injury that keeps him from working out consistently, gives up easily, is frequently distracted, and can't stick till the end.

When you watched a George Allen team in action, you knew the type of a ball player he wanted around him. Long after he had retired from an illustrious pro coaching career, he accepted the position of head coach at Long Beach State, a program that had been in disarray. He led the team to a near .500 season and called it his proudest year. A classy guy.

❧ April 19 ❧

Pat loves to ask people abrupt questions to get their attention. When he spoke at a lawyers' luncheon, he was seated at the head table near an attractive young female attorney.

He asked, "Do you have a good marriage?"
She appeared shocked, then said, "Yes, I do."
"Why?"
"Well, God is at the center of it." Then she named three other principles:

1. We spend lots of time together.
2. We have many of the same interests. Of the fifteen things I like to do most, my husband does twelve of them with me.
3. We have fun when we're together.

For once, someone was ready with an answer that got Pat's attention more than his question got theirs. As impressive as her list was the fact that she was ready with it at a moment's notice. That proved she and her husband don't just work at a good marriage but they also analyze it and talk about it and keep it growing.

It is never the right time to coast in a marriage. Just like in your professional life or your spiritual life or even your educational life, if you are not growing, you are stagnating, and that means dying. There is no neutral. Push for higher ground or you'll slide back further than you were before.

❧ April 20 ☙

To balance the letters of criticism and correction we receive, God also provides people who write wonderfully encouraging notes. It's nice to get a boost occasionally from someone. A man wrote to Pat a few years ago after hearing him speak at a men's breakfast:

> I was very impressed with your witness and encouraged by the fact that there are Christians like yourself who are not afraid to let their colleagues, clients, and competitors know they are Christians.
>
> The first time I heard of you was when I was attending a Sixers game and my father told me who you were and that you were a Christian. I was amazed that a general manager of a National Basketball Association team could remain a Christian. After all, being a Christian is not just something one does on Sunday to pass the time before the basketball game. It is a full-time commitment—seven days a week.
>
> Too many times people seem to be afraid to let those they work with know they are Christians. After hearing your witness, it is encouraging to know that it can go both ways.

Letting people know early on that you are a Christian makes it easier to stand for the Lord in the workplace.

❧ April 21 ❧

Los Angeles Dodger pitching great Orel Hershiser benefits from sound advice he received from his lawyer, Robert Fraley.

Fraley told Orel to ask himself four basic questions every month:

1. Is your wife happy, and does she still care about you?
2. Are your children happy and healthy, and do they know you?

3. Are you financially secure?
4. Do you still have your friends?

If you can answer yes to those questions, your career is just fine. They appear simple, but a closer look shows that for their simplicity, they are crucial. We know many successful businessmen, executives, and athletes whose marriages have become casualties. We have been saddened to hear sorry tales of people who have scaled the heights of fame and fortune, only to lose their children.

We have seen very successful, wealthy people make unwise investments and purchases and suddenly find themselves bankrupt.

Saddest of all, we have seen people get too big for their friends. When their lives start to fall apart, they have nothing and no one to fall back on.

These aren't bad questions for anyone to ask himself regularly, even if he can't say yes to number three.

❧ April 22 ❧

It is becoming less and less popular to believe in a personal, literal devil and hell. But we are from the old school. We believe the Bible, and we believe writers like Moody Memorial Church Senior Pastor Erwin Lutzer.

In his *Living With Your Passion* (Victor Books, 1983), Dr. Lutzer outlines three common methods Satan uses to bring us down when we are tempted sexually:

1. He works undercover. His first "cover" is the flesh (immorality, impurity, envy, drunkenness, etc.). When we struggle with sensuality, we usually attribute it to our flesh, but demons are also used to intensify our desires. The devil wants

us to think we were "born that way." He wants us to develop a sense of helplessness and rationalization.

2. He causes spiritual blindness during temptations. He blinds us to the consequences. When temptation comes, we don't visualize the broken homes and the chaos of weeping children.

3. He uses the slow approach. He often uses this style with committed Christians. He is gratified when we "only sin in our minds" because he wants us to believe we can handle our own sins when we really get serious about them.

Remember Samson? He said no to Delilah three times before he gave in. As long as you are in the vicinity of sin, he will eventually get you.

It behooves us to guard the gates.

✘§ April 23 ?✘

How often does it seem that conversations with your kids aren't conversations at all? We have a fear that too often all we are doing is giving commands. Do this. Don't do this. Don't do that.

It's not easy, but it is crucial to make time to slow down, stop, look a child in the eye, and have a real conversation. It doesn't have to be the obligatory, "How's school?" or "How was your day?" unless you know that will spur your child to react. Usually, kids just say school was okay and their day was fine.

Rather, try bringing up a subject in which you know the child is truly interested. "Think the Dolphins will win this weekend?" Your child might do a double take, wondering if you really care what he thinks about pro football.

You might ask, "Are you still interested in cheerleading next year? What kind of competition is there? Who is considered the best choice?"

If you know your children's friends—which is easily accomplished by having them over frequently—you can ask, "Does Stacy still have her braces? Are they still giving her problems?"

Those are yes or no questions, but if your child wants to talk, he or she will usually be reminded of something of interest about the person. Lob a conversational serve into his court and see where he hits it.

❧ April 24 ❧

Dr. Jerry White, director of the Navigators, wrote a book called *The Power of Commitment* (NavPress, 1985), which makes some excellent points about commitment in marriage. He says, "The ultimate glue in a marriage is not love, sex, an emotional feeling, children, or law. It is commitment. The conscious decision to stay together and make it work."

He lists four commitments for a lasting marriage:

1. An initial commitment or a renewing of that absolute commitment to stay in the marriage no matter what.

2. A commitment to remain faithful in mind and body. Sexual unfaithfulness never happens on a whim. All the excuses of a miserable physical relationship or lack of communication cannot justify marital infidelity.

3. A commitment to love your spouse. People *fall* in love, but they decide to *stay* in love. We must commit to self-sacrificial love whether or not it is reciprocated.

4. A commitment to work on your marriage. No marriage can stand neglect and still survive. Any automobile mechanic

will tell you that maintenance, not repair, is the key to lengthening the life of a car. We dare not neglect the maintenance of our marriages.

❧ April 25 ❧

One of the most painful things about reading the letters generated by our book *Rekindled* is noticing in them the desperation of the spouse who has seen the error of his or her way.

The marriage is nearly shipwrecked, the offending party finally sees his fault, but now it is too late. The letters have a same-ish quality about them. The writer is pleading with us to help, which we are glad to try to do.

A typical letter:

> I am writing with tears, having just again finished your book. My story mirrors yours. Several months ago my wife said she no longer loved me. I immediately told her I would make any changes she felt necessary. We have seen a minister and a Christian counselor, but she's simply given up. She moved out to be on her own and think things over.
>
> My purpose in writing is to thank you for writing the book and to ask whether it might be possible for Jill to talk to my wife, just to assure her that placing our marriage in the Lord's hands will help heal our relationship.
>
> I know my request is a bold one, and I know with your schedule and commitments this might not be possible. I am drawn to make this request, however, because I am seeking any godly means possible to win back my wife.

We made the call, but only God knows what will happen.

❧ April 26 ❧

There are some *don'ts* that are as appropriate to parenting as some *do's*.

We don't want to do for our children things they can do for themselves. Have you had a child come into your room in a rush of a Sunday morning, frustrated because he began buttoning his shirt at the wrong hole and now has fastened the shirt lopsided?

The temptation is to quickly unbutton and rebutton it for him, just to save time and keep moving. It takes only a few seconds to say, "Oh, see, you just got off the track there. Unbutton it and start over, making sure you start either with the top button in the top hole, or the bottom button in the bottom hole." Then, while he's doing that, you are still free to keep getting yourself ready.

Another *don't* we attempt to live out is that we don't want to remind our children of their past faults. That's an easy, bad habit to fall into. We want to model our sin-forgiving God, who has the ability to forget confessed sins. He says, "Their sins and their lawless deeds I will remember no more" (Hebrews 8:12).

More *don'ts?* We don't want to compare our kids to one another, discipline them in public, say things to them in anger, miss a chance to offer a compliment, or let a day go by without expressing spoken and physical love.

How much better to express love and encouragement than to say something in anger you will never be able to take back.

❧ April 27 ❧

A common complaint about marriage is that husbands and wives view sex differently. Men see sex as something separate from everything else. It can be a comfort at the end of a busy, bad day. It can be recreational and needs no reason.

Women, however, tend to see the elements of life interconnected. They can't simply warm to sex when they are frustrated or upset about something else. If a husband has not been affectionate or even communicative during the day, it can seem insulting and presumptuous for him to expect his wife to be instantly amorous when they go to bed.

It is crucial for husbands to act loving and attentive, even when sex is not the next item on the schedule. They might be surprised how much expressions of love and compassion and help improve the sex life of the marriage and the marriage itself.

We would be wrong to generalize, but it does seem that too many men can take or leave the small, intimate details of sex. Rather than realizing how much his wife enjoys being made to feel special, being talked to, cared about, and cherished, a husband thinks that an enjoyable session of sexual activity will mean as much to her as it does to him.

If he spent the time to find out what she likes and appreciates and what makes her feel more passionate, a small investment in such daytime psychological and emotional foreplay would result in surprisingly pleasurable results.

❧ April 28 ☙

When we find ourselves overreacting to small problems, we have to remind ourselves that bigger crises may present themselves later in our lives. We have all seen mothers scream at their children for small infractions: a torn dress, a forgotten hat, a chore left undone. It becomes a major issue, a shouting scene with a slammed door, tears, a federal case.

How will that same parent respond if her child is injured or killed, or if her husband loses his job or his health or his mind? If we scream at our kids for childish faults and mishaps, what emotion have we saved for things that require appropriate indignation?

Will there be any anger and verve left for a serious infraction? Do we think that by overreacting to minor problems, we are ensuring our kids won't dabble in drugs, get pregnant, crash a car?

Former football star and now prison evangelist Bill Glass says that in Jeremiah 12:5, God asks his people, in effect, "If you have trouble crossing the Jordan, how do you hope to cross it at flood stage?" God is trying to teach us through the small problems how to handle the big ones that inevitably come.

❧ April 29 ☙

We received a nice letter recently from the mother of a serviceman we invited for Thanksgiving. She writes:

> I wanted to send you this thank you from the bottom of my heart.

You had our son over to your place on Thanksgiving for a home-cooked meal. He really enjoyed himself. This was the first holiday season he's been away from home, and he was feeling kind of lonely.

It is a wonderful thing to have a boy to your home who is serving his country.

I am trying to get a program like that started here. We've got a couple of bases within an hour of us. Keep your fingers crossed that I'm successful. Since someone is doing this for my son, I'd like to do it for someone else's child.

We are happy to be able to do that, and it really was not in any way an inconvenience. There's always room for one more at the Thanksgiving table, isn't there? Our guest was shy but seemed to enjoy getting to know a little about our family.

We spoke of our work and activities and asked him about his. We didn't make him feel obligated to stay long, but we urged him to do what he wanted while he was with us. The letter from his mother indicates that this small, simple gesture meant a great deal to her son.

We recommend it.

❧ April 30 ❧

Marie Firsching, a guest in our home, had some interesting insights on holiness, so we asked her to put them in writing. She titles this short treatise "The Paradox of Holiness," and we thank her for letting us use it here:

Our Lord says that we should be perfecting holiness in the fear of the Lord (2 Corinthians 7:1).

But He also says that all of our righteousnesses are as filthy rags (Isaiah 64:6).

No matter what we do, we cannot discipline ourselves into holiness. We are only holy and forgiven because we are covered by the blood of Jesus Christ.

However, the apostle Paul says that to strive for the mastery, we must be temperate in all things (1 Corinthians 9:25). Don't be disciplined to a principle; be devoted to your Savior and to His will for your life.

We need to walk through the doors of both discipline and commitment before we can become devoted. Jesus said we love Him if we keep His commandments (John 14:21).

Jesus was the most paradoxical Man on earth, but He was never inconsistent in His relationship with His Father. It is easier to be a fanatic for a principle than to be devoted and faithful to our Lord.

Perseverance is the key that turns discipline into devotion.

❧ May 1 ☙

Mid-life crisis: fact or fiction?

There have been a lot of books written on the subject of mid-life crisis, and those—mostly men—who have suffered from it will swear it is real. We are not in a position to say otherwise, but it is interesting that more and more experts are saying it may not all be as scientific as they once thought.

Pat has wondered if he was in mid-life crisis when he felt an urge to apply for every interesting job that came open in his field. On the other hand, he's been doing that all his life. After twelve years in Philadelphia, people thought he was crazy to take a risky job with a group of owners who had no team, no arena, no franchise, just a willing city, a wing, and a prayer. It has worked out beautifully.

The idea of a mid-life crisis being defined as buying a hot car and leaving one's wife, however, is becoming passé. We are now hearing experts say that basic personality traits remain constant through adulthood, and that people who complain of mid-life crises probably complained of other emotional trauma earlier in their lives.

So are mid-life crisis victims really victims, or are they just complainers? Pat heard a psychology professor say that intro-spection and career changes have nothing to do with age. The prof said mid-life crisis might be an excuse for aberrant be-havior or relationship and career failure. Interesting.

❧ May 2 ☙

In all our dealings with professional athletes over the years, we reluctantly have to say that their thoughtfulness quotient leaves much to be desired. Their level of appreciation is fre-quently zero, no matter what favor you do for them or what you bestow upon them.

We don't know the reason. Perhaps they have been pam-pered so much for so long that they have simply lost the ability to handle small social details like thank yous.

A pleasant exception is one of the biggest modern-day stars in baseball, Dave Winfield, former Yankee and now California Angel. He was in Orlando for a convention, so Pat left tickets to a Magic game at the box office for him and his wife. A week later, a letter arrived. It would have been wonderful anyway, but given our experience as outlined above, it nearly knocked us off our feet. It read in part:

> Dear Pat, I am sorry I was only able to wave at you at the game, but I want to thank you for leaving tickets for my wife and me. We were quite impressed with the young talent on your team as well as with the enthusiasm of the crowd. The arena itself was quite a surprise. It is beautiful and really a good place to watch a basketball game. . . .

Dave's is an example of protocol we can all follow with a little effort. It was not cursory but friendly and detailed. That it is so rare is unfortunate.

❧ May 3 ❧

The coaches usually handle the postgame radio call-in show, but after a recent game they had to catch a plane for a road trip, so Pat took the calls.

These calls frequently debate highlights of the game, coaching decisions, and the play of favorite players.

One of the calls came from a teenager on a car phone who identified his hometown and with a smart-alecky tone asked if a certain player on our team was related to Bozo the Clown. Then he hung up.

Pat ignored the comment. There is little you can say on the air in response to a no-class comment like that without falling to that level.

The next day Pat's phone rang at the office. It was the kid's father, a doctor in a nearby town. "I heard that comment last night," he said. "It was my son. I want to apologize for his behavior and tell you that I have dealt with him and he is writing a letter of apology to the player.

"We're all here trying to make a living and earn our keep, and comments like that of my son are not tolerable."

We have a feeling that boy learned a valuable lesson from that bit of teenage indiscretion. It appears he has a father who doesn't think it's cute to be rebellious and a smart aleck. Someday that kid might look back on the experience as one of the best things that ever happened to him.

❧ May 4 ☙

Bo Jackson, the former Kansas City Royal and Los Angeles Raider, says that the only person he knows who is stronger and more stubborn than him is his mother. When he was growing up, she cleaned people's houses during the day and a motel at night. She also raised ten children by herself.

"And people say playing two sports is hard," Bo says.

His mother was the only parent he ever knew, and now she is the most important person in his life. He says he would drop anything, anytime, anywhere to go to her if she needed him. "She's all that matters," he says.

He remembers that they were always short of food when he was growing up, and because he was big and strong, he became a bully to get other kids' lunches. What he couldn't steal, he says, was "a father's hug or a father's whipping when I needed one."

People see the stellar athlete hitting a prodigious home run in an all-star baseball game or making the big gain in the NFL play-offs, and they see him endorsing the products for several sponsors. They may think he has achieved so much because he was blessed with a great body and natural ability.

It is important to remember that Bo also has a self-sacrificial work ethic which keeps him in shape to take advantage of his abilities. But most of all, it is clear he was raised with discipline by a woman of character who molded him into the professional he is today.

❧ May 5 ☙

We hear all kinds of unbelievable reasons people cheat on their spouses. Some say that everyone cheats occasionally, so why shouldn't they? The fact is, the worst percentages we have heard from secular surveys say that about half of men and 30 to 40 percent of women cheat. That, we hope, would not be true in the church, but even if everybody you knew, inside and outside the church, was cheating, it would still be wrong.

Some people justify their cheating because the third party is more sexually attractive than the spouse. First of all, so what? Second, it usually isn't true. It is amazing to see some of the duds for whom people throw away their spouses and families. Usually the reason for the affair has little to do with the attractiveness of the other party; the excuse is often that the other person "understood me better, made me feel more like a man [woman]." Too often these cheaters are simply trying to regain their youth.

Unfortunately, the offended party often knows about an affair but pretends to look the other way, hoping it will go away and take care of itself. We don't recommend that. By confronting the adulterer, you eliminate the appearance of condoning his or her actions, and you take a stand that says you refuse to be treated so shabbily.

Divorce is not the only option after an affair, but the odds of reconciliation are minuscule indeed.

❧§ May 6 ?❧

One of the most important aspects of Dr. Ed Wheat's B-E-S-T principles for marriage is T for touch. A pamphlet entitled *25 Ways to Increase the Romantic Warmth of Your Marriage*, distributed by Scriptural Counsel of Springdale, Arkansas, is excerpted from his book *Love Life for Every Married Couple*.

In it, Dr. Wheat explains his reasons for the list of nonsexual touching exercises as follows:

> Our need for a caring touch is normal and healthy and we will never outgrow it.
>
> But if touching is so valuable and pleasurable, why is it necessary to advise couples to do more of it? The answer lies in our culture. While our western civilization is highly sexual, it frowns on or ignores touching apart from sex. This is particularly true for men, for whom there are only three acceptable kinds of touching in today's world: the superficial handshake, aggressive contact sports, and the sexual encounter.
>
> Men have been conditioned to turn to sex whenever they feel any need for loving closeness. No wonder experts believe that our extreme preoccupation with sex in this society is actually an expression of our deep, unsatisfied need for the warmth, reassurance, and intimacy of nonsexual touching.

. . . You may take it as a sobering warning that most of the time marital infidelity is not so much a search for sex as it is for emotional intimacy.

❧ May 7 ❧

Bobby Malkmus, a scout for San Diego, is a former big-league ball player. He managed the Spartanburg (South Carolina) Phillies for Pat when he was general manager there in the 1960s. Malkmus is a Christian who played a major role in Pat's conversion.

Recently he sent a document he had drawn up called God's Contract. You may find some of its clauses interesting:

> The parties of this Uniform Member Contract are God, His Son Jesus Christ, the Holy Spirit and Member [you]. . . .
>
> God will receive members permanently (John 10:27–29) upon their professions of faith in His Son (John 1:12).
>
> Members become heirs and joint-heirs with Christ (Romans 8:17) and are paid all the promises of the Bible (Proverbs 28:20).
>
> Allowances: "My God shall supply all your need" (Philippians 4:19).
>
> Duties: Share with others the Gospel of Good News (Mark 16:15).
>
> Termination: None. Member lives forever in heavenly places (John 3:16).
>
> Special covenant: Forgiveness of sins (1 John 1:9), becoming a new person (2 Corinthians 5:17), a mansion in heaven (John 14:2, 3), His grace meets member's every need, no more wants (2 Corinthians 12:9).

Worth signing.

❧ May 8 ❧

It is difficult to overemphasize fun and enjoyment in the Christian life. So few people seek and take advantage of the abundant life Christ wants us to have.

George Matthew Adams has been quoted as having said, "The one who does not get fun and enjoyment out of every day in which he lives needs to reorganize his life. And the sooner the better, for pure enjoyment through life has more to do with one's happiness and efficiency than almost any other single element."

The Orlando Magic administration and coaches like to emphasize to the team that playing hard, conditioning, playing together, total team defense, fundamentals, and execution leads to overachievement, which leads to wins.

Winning is fun, and fun leads to enthusiasm for doing things the right way. And the cycle goes on.

Teams win because they work hard and have fun together, and stadiums are filled when teams win. You can have every promotion, every halftime gimmick ever invented, but what brings the people back is consistent victory and quality basketball.

What we as Christians need to realize is that the more fun we have with our faith, the more victorious we will be in our personal growth and our interaction with other believers and with the world.

Fun and enjoyment in life can be valuable gauges for our spiritual temperature.

❧ May 9 ☙

The legendary sports commentator Red Barber still has a weekly radio show in Tallahassee. He tells a revealing story about Branch Rickey.

The Rickeys had a son and five daughters, and as the daughters approached marrying age, one of them asked their father at dinner what one qualification he thought a young man should possess if he wanted to marry one of his daughters.

Rickey took the question very seriously. He considered many character traits and abilities and eliminated them one by one. Wealth? A man could be rich today and broke tomorrow. Health? Important but not predictable. Good looks? No. Social standing? No. Sex appeal? No. A marriage based on sex alone isn't going to be a marriage very long.

Mr. Rickey surveyed a long list, considered first this attribute, then that one. As quickly as he thought of one, he ruled it out. He said later, "I finally came to the most important single qualification a man should have to marry one of my daughters. It is infinite kindness. [That] will sustain a marriage through all its problems, its uncertainties, its illnesses, its disappointments, its storms, its tensions, its fears, its separations, its sorrows. Out of infinite kindness grows real love and understanding and tolerance and warmth. Nothing can take the place of such an enduring asset."

❧ May 10 ☙

Red Barber also enjoys telling the story of a conversation he once had with the great Yankee and later Red Sox manager Joe McCarthy. At a Red Sox spring training, Barber asked

McCarthy to define managing. Barber says he was ready with his pencil and notebook, eager to take notes.

"Managing," McCarthy said, "can be summed up in two words: *memory* and *patience*."

Hearing Barber tell of McCarthy's explanation—that he had to remember each player, each play, each attribute, each strength, each weakness, and then have patience to teach and keep reminding, we were reminded immediately of parenting.

As Al Lopez, another manager, once told Barber, "Managing is reminding. We teach only once or twice. We never stop reminding."

Isn't that a picture of parenting? When our kids seem to have never listened and learned, we need to remember that the teaching has been done. The learning has been done. What is needed is the reminding of those people who are simply too young to retain too much too long.

Repetition, patience, reminding, and continuing to invest in the minds of our children is the price of raising responsible adults. When we are frustrated and at wits' end, we try to remember that our job is not unlike the big-league manager who teaches once or twice and spends the rest of his time reminding. Our goal is higher and more noble than a pennant.

❧ May 11 ☙

We love salvation stories, as most Christians do. There is always something special about the way God calls people to Himself.

Our good friend, former big-league baseball player Clint Hurdle, has shared his story:

I came into the baseball chapel just out of the shower after pregame practice. I put my uniform on, half listening to the speaker. It was Mike Blaylock, and he delivered the Gospel message of Jesus Christ. I had heard it before, but he was crystal clear.

At the end, he asked people to follow him in prayer if they wanted to receive Christ. I put my head down and thought that then would be the time. I'd given everything else a chance. But I finally decided there were a couple of things I hadn't tried.

It was eight years before I finally prayed that prayer in 1983 at the age of twenty-six. For eight years I ran around as a lost soul. The picture of me on the cover of *Sports Illustrated* was of a man who was headed for hell. There are millions of people like me, thinking they've got it all together. They have the world by the tail, but they're losing their souls.

A lot of people had a lot to do with my coming to Christ. God's network is immeasurable. It was through Baseball Chapel that I had an awakening, a reawakening, a rude awakening, and finally a real awakening. I still have a long way to go, but that was when the transaction took place.

❧ May 12 ❧

It is just as bad to accept unwarranted criticism as it is to ignore valid, constructive criticism. Successful people are rarely discouraged from doing what they want and believe they can do by the opinions of others.

The Polish piano virtuoso Ignace Paderewski was told by his first music teacher that his hands were too small for the keyboard.

May 12

The Italian tenor Enrico Caruso was told by a mentor that his voice sounded like wind whistling through a window.

When Guglielmo Marconi asserted that the discoveries of German scientist Heinrich Hertz could be applied to worldwide wireless communication, he was told his ideas were contrary to the laws of physics.

When Benjamin Disraeli first tried to speak in Parliament, the members hissed him to silence and laughed at him when he said, "Though I sit down now, the time will come when you will hear me."

When a person knows what he wants to do and has no doubt he can accomplish his goals, criticism won't deter or discourage him. In fact, it will often prove an impetus, a challenge, a mountain to be climbed. The inappropriately criticized person will simply work harder and longer until his efforts are rewarded.

Let nothing stand in the way of your mission.

❧ May 13 ☙

Pat received another of those encouraging letters late last year. It came from Jerry Howarth, the Toronto Blue Jays play-by-play radio broadcaster. He wrote:

> Hi Pat, you might not remember me but I was in Tarpon Springs a couple of years ago when you gave a testimony.
>
> Included in your message was a challenge to read the Book of James for thirty consecutive days. I finally got around to doing that about six months ago. It was a wonderful experience and a practical guide to Christian living.

Barry Banther led me to a personal relationship with Christ in March of 1987 after many good years in the church. He and Janice have been friends of ours ever since. He's a unique individual.

Thanks again for motivating me. Now good luck and God bless you as you motivate the Orlando Magic and raise that large and blessed family. I'll be praying for you.

When we hear from people like that, expressing themselves so generously, it makes us want to remember those people who have impacted our spiritual lives. Letters of thanks and encouragement don't have to be complicated or gushy.

Jerry Howarth merely reminded Pat of a speaking engagement and told us what the result was in his life. It took him time and effort, but the dividends in our lives are incalculable.

Everybody needs inspiration and motivation once in a while.

❧ May 14 ☙

The idea that spouses have a right to pursue their own interests and fulfillment, even if it means the abandonment of their children, is becoming more accepted. People who leave innocent spouses often run to counselors who assuage their guilt by encouraging them in their pursuits of personal happiness. "It's time to do something for you, something you want to do," they tell them, and the result is chaos for the family left behind.

At an L. A. Clippers game last year, Pat ran into Douglas Mann, who has a sports ministry among Southern California athletes. Douglas has a real burden for the National Hockey League, which seems to have the fewest Christian believers of any sport. He is aware of only ten or so out-and-out Christians in the entire league.

Doug says that when he is with any of those few, their number-one prayer request is always the same: Pray for escape from temptation on the road.

Athletes are targets for frustrated and needy women. The jocks seem to be most attractive because they are macho, wealthy, well-known, available, and—in a strange way—nonthreatening. Athletes are in town for only a few days at a time, and groupies believe they can "enjoy" them without commitment.

Sadly, it is the people left at home who suffer the most. Christian athletes try to band together and avoid temptation on the road, and they need our prayers.

◆§ May 15 ?◆

Isn't it interesting that in a day when a Christian risks his social standing by being drunk or running around with someone else's wife, he can still be proud as a peacock. Pride seems to be acceptable these days, for some reason. Even some church leaders strut around as if they are God's gifts to the masses.

Scripture is clear on this point, however: "Let nothing be done through selfish ambition or conceit, but in lowliness of mind let each esteem others better than himself" (Philippians 2:3).

That was penned by the same man who came to this conclusion about himself in his letter to Timothy: "This is a faithful saying and worthy of all acceptance, that Christ Jesus came into the world to save sinners, of whom I am chief" (1 Timothy 1:15).

True humility brings benefits. The truly humble person can hardly be insulted. If he is already aware of his standing before God, he knows he was worth the ultimate price of sacrifice, yet he also knows that spiritually his sin has made him worthless.

The truly humble person will live to be generous and expect little from anyone else. We are not talking here about people who are down on themselves and always shuffling around with their eyes to the ground. Rather we are recommending living our lives in such a way that we know clearly who we are and who we are not. That is true humility.

❧ May 16 ❧

There is a cautionary statement that must be made in light of yesterday's entry. Being consumed with our own unworthiness can also be a form of pride. No one can be as bad as I am. I am the reason for the death of Christ. Poor me. I'm helpless and worthless. No. It is important to emphasize the fact that God loves us in spite of ourselves. It certainly isn't because of our goodness.

The goodness of people is the aberrant foundation stone of humanism. Strangely, it takes less faith to believe in the depravity of man than to believe in the basic goodness of man. How much history do you have to read or news do you have to watch to realize that man is basically evil?

Even if we compare ourselves to ruthless dictators and say we are not that bad, most people know their own hearts. They know how they feel and act in private, what they really want for themselves if they were only bold enough to say so.

The problem is, people don't want to believe this. They are hung up on improving their self-esteem, not lowering it. The more a person believes he has the answers to life's problems and is convinced that eventually he will begin to feel good about himself, the less likely a candidate he is for receiving the Gospel.

The martyr Jim Elliot said, "He is no fool who gives up what he cannot keep to gain what he cannot lose."

May 17

People who do what they love for a living seem to be high achievers compared with those who simply find a job in order to finance their household. Notice we didn't say that high achievers simply happen to love what they do. Rather, they discover through trial and error, all during their maturing and educational process, what they love the most. Then they make a career of it.

These are the people you hear say that they would work at the same kind of job for nothing. Because they love it so much, they do it well and are often rewarded handsomely. This is such a crucial truth—that you should work at what you love to do anyway—that if your area of enjoyment doesn't pay well, we would recommend adjusting your needs and wants, moving to an area where the cost of living is lower, and keeping at it.

There is always fear before a person lands a position in the area he loves. Guilt is also a factor. You wonder, how could someone pay me to do this when I enjoy it so much? If you find yourself in that position, you'll soon be working at 100 percent of your capacity.

If, on the other hand, you are doing something you don't really love, simply plugging along every day trying to make ends meet, you are probably not working to your potential. It is not easy to free yourself and take a chance at doing what you really love, but it will be worth it in the long run.

❧ May 18 ❧

For some reason, the world admires and respects specialists as opposed to generalists. Even doctors are better compensated if they are specialists.

Once you find the area you love, narrow your focus so your expertise is recognized, and be sure it is the part of the discipline you like most anyway. Admittedly, we rub shoulders with people who are at the top of their professions in the sports world, so they are mostly specialists by default. Even sports executives have specialized and are making deals, evaluating talent, scouting, and staying close to the sports they love.

If you are working in a factory but really love to work on cars, start looking for that mechanic's job. Start on your own time, building a client base. If you are a homemaker but you love to speak, start making yourself available and become known as an expert in an area you enjoy.

We have all taken jobs to pay the bills, but the day will come when that isn't enough motivation to get out of bed every morning. That's when you need to have found your area, taken your risk, quit your job, and started doing what you really love.

A popular book by Marsha Sinetar titled *Do What You Love,*

the Money Will Follow (Dell, 1989) stresses this idea. Be sure it is legal, doable, makes you feel good about yourself, and keeps you busy. Then you can't lose.

❧ May 19 ❧

We once heard an illustration that brought home the necessity of redeeming the time we are allotted. A speaker compared the 1,440 minutes in every 24-hour period with a bank deposit of $1,440. He said to imagine that is deposited for you every day and that you can have as much of it as you want to do with as you see fit—with one condition. Whatever you don't use would be removed from your account. Obviously, we would take out every last penny every day and use it. The analogy to time is obvious.

A significant portion of our 1,440 minutes every 24 hours is well invested in sleep. But what about the remainder? Do we fritter away time and wonder where it went? Do we see time fly by while we sit idly in front of the TV?

Everyone needs time to do relaxing things, battery-recharging activities, thinking, reading, chatting. But we have to remember that if we are not doing something productive, something with others in mind, something for the Kingdom, we are letting our time bank dwindle.

There is no saving up minutes to be used tomorrow. Find a way to spend them, to invest them today. Don't feel guilty when you are not running here and there. There is nothing wrong with doing something now that will make you a better person tomorrow. But look at people who seem to slide through life with nothing to do. They are underdrawn at the bank of time, and they will never see those minutes again.

❧ May 20 ☙

Leo Buscaglia is a fun speaker we enjoy. We especially liked what he had to say about Julia Child, the TV cook with the appropriate name. Though a past-middle-age woman, she is youthful in her enjoyment of life.

Buscaglia says he likes her attitude. He watches her because she does such wonderful things. "She beats this and whisks that and drops things on the floor. She wipes her face with a napkin. Then she throws her soufflé in the oven and talks to you for a while, all these wonderful, human things."

Buscaglia says what he loves best about Julia Child is that when she finally says the soufflé is ready and pulls it out of the oven, if it has caved in, she merely says, "Well, you can't win 'em all. Bon appétit."

Buscaglia says, "I love it! That's the way we have to live our lives. You can't win 'em all. Bon appétit. I know people who are still flagellating themselves over mistakes they made twenty years ago. They say, 'I should have done this' and 'I should have done that.'

"Well, it's tough that you didn't. But who knows what surprises are in store for tomorrow? Learn to say Bon appétit. Sit down and pig out on today!"

Sounds biblical, doesn't it? "Therefore do not worry about tomorrow, for tomorrow will worry about its own things. Sufficient for the day is its own trouble" (Matthew 6:34).

❧ May 21 ☙

One of Pat's heroes in the history of sports was the legendary Green Bay Packers coach Vince Lombardi. He was once quoted as having said, "Winning isn't everything; it's the only thing." Critics use that line to say the coach was concerned more about winning than sportsmanship, but anyone who knew or even closely observed the man knew he was a man of true character.

Few people know that Lombardi himself was a college football player at Fordham, an arch rival of the Pitt Panthers. Lombardi was one of the Fordham linemen, who were known as the seven blocks of granite.

Fordham and Pitt met three times during Lombardi's last three years in college. Each game ended in a scoreless tie, and the brutal contests are still rehashed to this day by people who witnessed them or played in them.

Today people would be bored by a scoreless tie, but such games were a thing of beauty in the old days, when the blocking and tackling fundamentals were the bedrock of the game. Low-scoring contests then were as exciting and dramatic as no-hit baseball games today.

That few people see the beauty in a no-hitter is a sign of the times. It takes a true sports fan to appreciate execution and dedication to every fundamental move. Fans of Lombardi and lovers of true sport can appreciate a great play by the home or visiting team and true athletics the way they were meant to be played.

❦§ May 22 ?❧

Too few people know the difference between intimacy and sex in marriage. When sex wanes, intimacy wanes, and the marriage is the worse for the latter even more than the former.

Wives may be too tired or upset about something to be interested in sex, but they would not be opposed to intimacy:

being held, being caressed, being kissed, being talked to. But far too many husbands are so quickly turned on sexually by intimacy that they want more.

If couples can be honest with each other, the wife might find that occasionally her husband is perfectly willing to be merely intimate without expecting sex. He needs to know this in advance, of course, and realize that he is showing his love by not wishing to satisfy only physical needs.

The wife must occasionally be willing to allow intimacy to lead to sex, even if she hadn't planned for it. In other words, don't fight it. But the signals should come from the wife, because if the husband thinks sex is next on the schedule and finds out it isn't, both parties will wish they hadn't been physical at all.

Indeed, many wives say they reject even nonsexual physical intimacy because they know their husbands are frustrated at stopping there. We recommend heart-to-heart talks in advance. Both partners will be pleasantly surprised at how much fun intimacy can be and how it will enhance the sexual relationship as well.

❧ May 23 ❧

One of the traps of our modern society is that we have become fun junkies. There is always a new thing, more excitement, an event, a concert, a party, a promotion, a purchase that gives us something to look forward to.

Unfortunately, such material and emotional highs are addictive, and it takes something bigger and better to make us feel as good the next time. If you have bought the car of your dreams and now two years later it's time to buy again, will the same car thrill you? If you took that trip of a lifetime this year, do you feel the need to top it next year?

People who live for these highs are often miserable, either because they can't afford to feed the cravings for everything to be bigger and better or because they find that no matter how they please themselves, the pleasure is fleeting.

How much better to learn to enjoy the real, lasting, important, even eternal things of life. Can you appreciate the gap-toothed smile of a six-year-old as much as you can enjoy front-row seats at a great event? Can you enjoy a relaxing evening with your spouse, watching an old movie on television and eating popcorn before the fire, as much as you can a trip to Hawaii?

If we can learn to enjoy people, God, serving others, and the simple things of life, we will be easier to please. We will be happy without pursuing the next high.

ᥥ᥉ May 24 ᥬ᥎

We are pastor people. We like and appreciate pastors and have benefited from sitting under some wonderful ones. Fortunately, none of them has been too heavy. (Sorry, we couldn't resist that.)

No matter who your pastor is, however, or how on top of his ministry he seems, he could probably use some encouragement occasionally. Pastors are people too.

Sometimes it is easy to think that generic compliments are the only way to encourage a pastor. How much better to be specific. Rather than simply telling him he preached well or wrote a good sermon, how about telling him that you took his advice and it worked.

Depending on the age and family situation of your pastor, you might offer to take in his kids for an evening so he and his wife can go out by themselves. You might want to provide a hot, home-cooked meal some evening, even when no one is sick or out of town. Just be sure they know it's coming!

If you have spare time, see if the pastor can use you for anything. Maybe he would like company when he goes calling at the hospital or visits shut-ins. If you are handy, offer to help him with a home fix-it project he hasn't been able to finish.

Sometimes it is these offers of small favors that really make a difference in a pastor's busy life. Try it.

❧ May 25 ❧

We all disagree with somebody sometime. The quote, "If two people always agree, one of them is unnecessary," has been attributed to everybody from Ruth Bell Graham to Mahatma Gandhi. There is some truth to it. The key to disagreeing is to keep from arguing. Here are a few possible ways:

Don't hide from disagreement. You could be wrong, and isn't it better to be corrected early, before you make a huge mistake? Embrace the problem. See what you can learn from it without being personally offended.

Ignore that first instinct, which will usually be to defend yourself from someone who clearly knows nothing about what he is talking about. That's defensiveness, and it leads to arguments, not solutions.

Don't fly off the handle. Once you have lost your temper, you are no longer discussing, you are arguing.

Hear the person out, then see where you agree. If he is right, even on a minor point, admit it and apologize. If your critic has been hostile, this will take some of the wind out of his sails.

Be thankful for the input. That may be the hardest thing to do, but grit your teeth and say it anyway. Don't lie. You have to mean it, but it still might have to be forced from your lips. In time you *will* be grateful. Just be sure to give yourself time to think before you act.

◆§ May 26 ?◆

The fast pace of modern life has generated high-powered workers who believe that their down time has to be quick and competitive too. Rather than really relaxing, lying on the beach, or taking a leisurely hike to unwind from the rigors of their normal existence, people schedule vacations that include competitive sports and survival ordeals.

The joke is told of a man who told his business associate, "Joe, you have to take time to slow down and smell the roses."

"You're right," Joe said. "I will."

The next morning, the man met Joe at the front door of the office building on their way in. "I smelled forty-seven flowers this morning," Joe said. "How many did you smell?"

There must be an addiction to the adrenaline of executive life that makes many vacationing execs stay in touch with their offices by phone. Some men have simply changed the location of their offices for a week or two, running things from lounge chairs on the beach rather than from behind their desks.

Pat likes to keep up on happenings in the sports world when he is away, but he is learning that it's just as important to really tear yourself away from business activities and let the world spin without you for a while.

Then you can return to your lifework refreshed and ready to hit it again.

❧ May 27 ❧

As our kids become teenagers—our oldest two already are at this writing, and in a few years we will have at least eight teens at once!—we realize that we have to base our yes and no decisions on principle. It is no longer enough to say, "Because I said so." Emerging adults have the right to know why. They don't have to understand totally and they don't have to agree. They still have to obey, but as Josh McDowell says, "Rules without relationship leads to rebellion."

So, where do parents look to formulate their principles and policies? We can't simply base our rules on our own upbringing. In Jill's day we didn't even know about touch-tone phones, and in Pat's day they didn't know about phones at all (smile). It is a new day and there are new temptations and problems, so it's better to have underlying principles than specific rules for every situation.

First we need to know whether Scripture speaks directly to an activity: "All Scripture is given by inspiration of God, and is profitable for doctrine, for reproof, for correction, for instruction in righteousness" (2 Timothy 3:16).

Then we are not afraid to seek counsel from people who are accountable for us spiritually: pastors, teachers, counselors who have been through these waters before.

We try to ask whether an activity will help or hurt our child spiritually. Their spiritual lives are our responsibility.

❦§ May 28 ❧

Ever wonder why men say they'll never understand women? Probably because they won't, for they don't take the time to learn women's language.

Don't we both speak English? Sure, but women and men mean different things when they speak.

For instance, when a wife wants to go out with her friends and wants her husband to stay home and take care of the kids, she usually asks permission. "Is that all right with you, honey?"

When a man wants to go out with his friends, obviously expecting his wife to stay home and take care of the kids, he usually simply informs her.

Any request by a wife is seen as nagging, because a man can't stand being told what to do. So he puts off fulfilling the request to show his independence, which makes the wife repeat it, making her appear even more of a nag.

Women seek emotional intimacy and want to have rapport. Men seek independence and would rather simply report. Each needs to borrow a little from the other's traits. A woman needs to develop confidence in her husband's love and approval by not coming hat in hand to ask permission for everything. And a man needs to borrow from the feminine side and be considerate and compassionate, developing rapport with his wife and considering her viewpoint on his activities. He could also take out the garbage the first time he's asked.

৩৪ May 29 ৵৵

While that borrowing of traits we suggested in yesterday's entry is taking place, it is important to realize that some of those personality makeups are natural and have always worked that way. And they aren't all bad.

There are those who would say that a strong, competent man and a sensitive, caring woman are negative stereotypes of co-dependents. We disagree. While there is room for movement on both sides, the traditional traits of the husband and wife are often valued by each other.

Militant feminists may think these things have gone out of style, but they have forgotten to check with the masses of happily married couples. These personality traits still have a lot to offer and in many ways fit well with the biblical standard of man as the self-sacrificing, loving, spiritual head of the family.

Any wife would be happy to submit herself (notice the difference between that wording and the often misinterpreted idea of a husband subjecting his wife) to a man who truly loved her as Christ loved His church.

There was and is much to be learned from the women's movement. Too many men treat their wives as servants and almost as nonentities. But to pretend that men are supposed to have changed and become supersoft and open about their feelings is wrong.

৩৪ May 30 ৵৵

As our children grow toward dating age, we need to be able to help them determine the difference between true love and infatuation. It is simple, really, but when a person is infatuated, he is incapable of reason anyway. The time to talk to kids about such matters is long before they "fall" in love.

Of course, true love is not something you can fall into. It is not a state of being. It is an act of the will. You love someone by loving him or her in word and deed. Infatuation is a state of being in which you have no control over your feelings. You are helplessly, haplessly, hopelessly enamored with someone and no one can talk you out of it.

Kids think no one has ever had a relationship like theirs before. They could go off to a desert island somewhere and gaze into each other's eyes for years and simply enjoy being in each other's presence. That is not love.

For one thing, that kind of feeling is generally focused on someone the kid hardly knows. He's in love with a smile, a hairdo, a personality. He desires a relationship for the rush it can give him rather than for what he can mean to her.

Infatuation, puppy love, crushes can be fun and exciting, but they always end. People who get married while in the middle of that often worry that they have made the biggest mistake of their lives. And they usually have. Love isn't something you are *in*. It's something you *do*.

❧ May 31 ❧

The debate over alcohol rages on. Is it a disease, a weakness, a habit, or just plain irresponsibility? We are sympathetic to people who are alcoholics and are trying to recover. They didn't realize their proclivity to the disease, and now they suffer the consequences.

But it is interesting how society responds to alcoholism. Witness this piece, written anonymously:

Is Alcoholism a Disease?

If alcoholism is a disease, then it is the only disease that is bottled and sold, and it is the only disease contracted by the will of man.

It is the only disease that requires a license to propagate it, and that requires outlets to spread it.

If alcoholism is a disease, then it is the only disease that produces revenue for the government, that provokes crime, that is habit-forming, that brings death on the highway, is spread by advertising, and is the only disease without a germ, virus, or cause. It just might be that it's not a disease at all.

We would be the last people to call ourselves experts on alcoholism, and it may be insensitive to pretend that there is no disease related to alcohol abuse. But the above raises some valid points worth sharing and thinking about.

❧ June 1 ❧

Here are some things we have learned to avoid as parents:

Putting Off Discipline. When kids need to be corrected, and frequently they do, it is good to pray and think and even study the Scripture for applicable passages. But don't put off correction any longer than necessary, for instance, not longer than an hour. We know parents who are aware of a child's truly serious misbehavior, yet they haven't even talked to the child yet because they are trying to react perfectly. When they get around to it, it may be too late.

Showing Disunity. You won't always agree with your spouse on discipline. When one begins a lecture or announces a punishment, the other should not say, "Now don't be so harsh," or "No, it needs to be more severe." If you really believe your spouse is doing the wrong thing, ask to speak to him privately. When the sentence is handed down, it should be from a position of agreement.

Partiality. This is a particular danger in homes where there is a mix of homegrown kids and adoptees. Some parents in this situation favor the adoptees, believing they need more attention. Others favor their "own" children, forever making it obvious which child is which.

Be careful even about which kids you always find yourselves gravitating to for conversation. The best, most secure setting is where the kids truly know you love them all the same.

❧June 2 ☙

We have heard it said that a man's best friend is most often his wife, while his wife's best friend is usually another woman. Women's relationships tend to be more intimate than men's, but women are also more critical of their friends and expect more of them than men do.

One prescription for a long married life is a best friendship between man and wife. Too many couples love each other but don't like each other. If you and your spouse are not true friends, it is likely one of you is unhappy.

True friends who are happily married tell each other they love each other nearly every day. They kiss every day. They agree on the directions their lives are taking. They talk, spend time together, enjoy each other, share secrets.

Happy couples believe their partners have become more

interesting, not more irritating. And they take on problems together, clearing the air, setting things right quickly rather than letting every difference escalate into an argument.

It is not necessary to be totally honest with your partner all the time. Small irritations and peeves can go unreported if you realize that your partner could have just as many he is overlooking about you. Save the firepower for the major things. Everyone who lives together and gets along learns to live with idiosyncrasies. Remember, overlook them; don't harbor them for subsequent ammunition.

⋖§ June 3 §⋗

Ever since we discovered it on the east side of Orlando, we have shopped for groceries almost exclusively at Gooding's Supermarket. We have been impressed with the outspoken Christian ownership and the refusal to sell lottery tickets despite the competition from every other grocer and convenience store. The market also employs several handicapped and retired people.

One day Jill was in Gooding's and realized that the retiree bagging her groceries was Doc, a man who had done the same for her at another grocery before she discovered this one. He said she was right. He had moved to make his wife's commute easier, and now he too had discovered Gooding's.

Jill remarked about how impressed we had always been with the store. Doc was happy with it too, but for a different and surprising reason. "You know the best part about working here?" he asked as he put the bags in the van.

"Tell me," Jill said.

"They employ so many young people! My boss is just a

kid, and is he ever fun to work for! These kids have drive and ambition and ideas. Most of all, they've got enthusiasm. I love it."

It was refreshing to hear an elderly person say something positive about youth and change. It seems we often find older people cranky about change and innovation. Here's a man with the opposite view!

❧ June 4 ❧

Good relationships, especially marriage relationships, don't just happen. They are created by decisions made by each spouse. That's why husbands and wives need to remember that they are in positions to keep love alive. Each is in control of the future of the relationship.

Here are a few rules to help keep love alive:

Remember that love accepts, it doesn't change. If it is your plan to change your mate with a major reclamation project, you are headed for trouble. Sure, people like to change in small ways to please their partners, but if you give the impression you are going to start an overhaul from the ground up, you will seriously offend your partner. Accept quirks.

It's not so much what you say as what you do. It is important to tell your spouse you love him or her frequently, but it is even more important to prove it. Thoughtful gestures are remembered far longer than empty phrases. If you are saying one thing and doing another, you are living a lie.

Love believes all things and forgives all things. True lovers don't punish each other for foolish, hurtful things. We all make mistakes. Be quick to forgive.

Don't expect your spouse to meet all your needs. He or she

will be a major part of your life, but you need friends, a personal relationship with God, a strong church life, and your own pursuits. It will make you a more exciting partner too.

❧ June 5 ❧

J. Allan Petersen, who wrote *Hi-Fidelity Marriage* (Tyndale House, 1986), has this to say about faithfulness to one's spouse: "A call for fidelity today is like a solitary voice crying in the sexual wilderness. What was once labeled *adultery* and carried a stigma of guilt and embarrassment now is an *affair*—a nice-sounding, almost inviting word wrapped in mystery, fascination, and excitement—a relationship, not sin."

In his book he lists eight facts about affairs:

1. No one is immune.
2. Anyone, regardless how many victories he has won, can fall disastrously.
3. The act of infidelity is the result of uncontrolled desires, thoughts, and fantasies.
4. Your body is either your servant or it becomes your master.
5. A Christian who falls will excuse, rationalize, and conceal, the same as anyone else. It is as if his entire value system has been rearranged.
6. Sin can be enjoyable, but it can never be successfully covered.
7. One night of private passion can spark years of family pain.
8. In spite of all of the above, failure neither has to be fatal or final.

❧June 6☙

Writer Martin Buxbaum tells a story that reminds us of one of Paul Harvey's famous "The Rest of the Story" offerings:

A poor Scottish farmer was out walking one day when he heard a cry for help from a nearby bog. He ran over to find a boy sunk almost to the waist in the black muck. Extending his walking stick, the farmer pulled the boy out.

The next day a horse and carriage came to the Scotsman's small home and a gentleman stepped out. He offered a reward to the Scotsman, who refused it. The farmer's son came to the door, and seeing him, the nobleman made the farmer an offer. He said, "Let me take your son and give him a good education. If he is anything like you, he'll grow into a man you can be proud of."

The Scot liked the idea and shook hands on the deal.

In time, the farmer's son graduated from St. Mary's Hospital Medical School in London. He later became Sir Alexander Fleming, the noted discoverer of penicillin.

Years later, the nobleman's son was stricken with pneumonia but was saved through the use of penicillin. Thus the great favor had been returned. The nobleman was Lord Randolph Churchill. His son's name was Winston.

You never know whom you're going to run into, whom you might assist, or what the outcome might be. Of course we aren't to do favors in hopes of reciprocation. But once in a great while, a simple act of kindness results in something quite wonderful.

❦§June 7❧❧

At a Pro Athletes Outreach meeting in Tampa, Christian Financial Concepts founder Larry Burkett shared a wealth of information and insight with the gathered Christian athletes. His insight is good for anyone, famous and wealthy or not.

Burkett concentrated on the fact that the athletes should control their spending. He said that on the average, pro football players leave the game about 20 percent further in debt than their average annual income. That comes from aggressive spending, poor business decisions, and trusting the wrong people.

Bottom line? Spend less than you make.

He also encouraged the assembled athletes to develop marketable skills. For every superstar who lasts ten years in his profession, there are dozens who are washed up or washed out within two or three years.

All players should use their status to increase their future work opportunities before their careers are over.

He also advised the athletes, as he advises everyone, to become debt-free. Proverbs 22:7 says that "the rich rules over the poor, And the borrower is servant to the lender." He recommended that the athletes buy only those big-ticket items they can afford now and pay off their homes while they are still making big salaries.

Finally, he reminded them, "You won't be playing forever. There's nothing like having a surplus fund to ease your transition from sports to a new career."

❧ June 8 ❧

A few years ago, Pat was having fun with his new skill learned that year: surf fishing with a heavy net. He and a friend needed help with the poles, so Pat turned to a couple on the beach and asked the man if he cared to join them.

The man, whose name was Chance, eagerly stepped in and began to labor with the guys. They pulled in a seven-pound tarpon.

Chance seemed to enjoy it, and the guys cast and pulled again several times before Pat began to feel bad for Chance's wife, Rose, who stood watching from the beach.

"Can we have Chance for just one more pull?" Pat asked her.

Her answer was one for the books, or at least for this book.

Rose said, "Chance will decide when to stop. He makes his own decisions. That's the way he was when I met him, and I fell in love with him and married him. I'm still in love with him and I'm not going to change him now."

Perhaps occasionally Chance is insensitive and does his own thing and Rose feels left out. But Pat sensed from her loving answer that though sometimes Chance might be exasperating, Rose knew what she was getting into. It was Chance's independence that had attracted her and apparently kept her interested.

Not only was she married to man who would not be nagged or henpecked but she was also proud enough to let everyone know about it.

That's a lesson.

❦§ June 9 ?❦

We will never forget that January day in 1988 when we finally decided to go ahead and make official our interest in four Filipino boys. We already had eight children, half of them adoptees. We called the woman at the agency.

"What's up?" she said.

"We're going to do it," Pat said.

She didn't miss a beat. "I'll send a cable tonight."

We sat there thinking the heavy thought that the cable would arrive shortly at an outpost in the southern Philippine Islands, where an eighty-five-year-old woman would read it. She would then gather four boys around her and tell them in their own language that a father and a mother and brothers and sisters were waiting for them.

We didn't know how they would react, but to us the whole thing was another miracle. It was such an intense concept that all we could do was sit and stare. There were no words. God had chosen these boys for us and us for them. They were virtually on their way. And while there would be lots of delays and frustration along the way, emotionally they were ours from the moment Pat said, "We're going to do it."

We were numb and scared. The idea of a large family was no longer new to us, but twelve? From another country this time and not Korea? We knew so little about them or what we might be inheriting. All we knew was that they were now ours.

❧ June 10 ❧

Eight months later, we were still waiting and worrying. To give you an idea what that's like, let us share with you just one piece of the correspondence we received during our ordeal in trying to get our four Filipino sons, David, Peter, Brian, and Samuel. This came from a missionary with the Bethany Christian Home for Children, the Philippines, in August 1988.

> Dear Pat and Jill,
>
> I just came home from a conference in Manila. Imagine my surprise when I got there to find that the court order for the boys' abandonment decree had not been sent. I saw someone who agreed to send for the order immediately.
>
> Monday we sent all of our papers to the Holt agency so Marilyn Manuel could take them with her when she leaves for Oregon tomorrow. That should enable you to start on the visas. I hope it won't take a long time.
>
> You may have been puzzled about the boys' health when I told you I was taking them to a doctor for checkups. His diagnosis was incorrect but we followed up with medication until our former missionary doctor came to visit. He made further tests, found the error, and stopped the medication. We are so thankful for his visit.
>
> Three of the boys sang with the children's choir last Sunday. I wish you could have been there, but soon their noise will fill your house.
>
> It won't be long now.

❧§ June 11 ᘓ❧

Want to know how to really bug your kids? Maybe you already know how. Most parents do. But the Bible instructs fathers to not provoke their children to anger, so we should focus on what bugs kids so we can avoid it.

Two of the things that seem to bother kids the most are when parents hang around them at inappropriate times, and when they correct their kids in front of their friends.

Experts say that despite a lot of thinking otherwise, an equal number of kids will turn to their parents first when they are having a problem as will turn to their friends. That should be encouraging, and you can bet that those parents who are turned to are the ones who have carefully developed strong relationships with their kids.

After getting good grades and getting into college, kids care most about dressing fashionably—or at least not dressing un-fashionably. Pat will never forget the day he took one of our boys to see the emerging new basketball arena in Orlando. It was in the final stages of construction, but there was still heavy equipment and scaffolding about, so visitors had to wear hard hats—even Pat and anyone he brought around to see it.

"No way," our son said. "I'm not going in."

"Why not?"

"Not with that silly-looking hat. I don't want to look like a fool." Pat didn't bug him. They went back later, bareheaded.

❧ June 12 ❧

The story is told that Woodrow Wilson, president of the United States, lay ill on March 19, 1920, in a bed that had been used by Abraham Lincoln.

Wilson, who had marched through post World War I Europe as a hero to the cheering throngs on his way to Versailles, now found that the cheering had stopped. The Presbyterian layman, former president of Princeton University, and governor of New Jersey had just received word of a major setback. The Senate of the United States had rejected his recommendation that the U. S. join the League of Nations.

That night, the president couldn't sleep. His friend and physician, Carey Grayson, stayed at his bedside. At about three in the morning, President Wilson summoned the doctor. "Please get the Bible there and read from Second Corinthians chapter four, verses eight and nine."

Dr. Grayson read these words to the sleepless president: "We are hard pressed on every side, yet not crushed; we are perplexed, but not in despair; persecuted, but not forsaken; struck down, but not destroyed" (2 Corinthians 4:8, 9).

What a balm Scripture can be to a tortured soul! If Woodrow Wilson could think of the Bible at one of the lowest points in his life, how easy it should be for us to turn to the same source when our trials come and the world seems to be closing in around us.

❧ June 13 ❧

Kids of all different ages have unique relationships with their parents. We mentioned Don and Carol Lough earlier—the couple who run the Word of Life Inn in New York. They tell the story of their twenty-three-year-old son walking in on them while they were on their knees in prayer.

At first he was startled. Later he embraced his mother and sobbed on her shoulder, he had been so moved.

When our Jim was fourteen and we dropped him off at camp, his counselor told him, "Be grateful your father is here. Ninety percent of the kids who come here show up with only their mothers."

And then there's little Michael. At age six he wanted to try out the new computer but complained that he didn't know how to spell yet. Jill told him, "Just sound things out." Here is the precious result:

> dere mom i'd lack to staey home weney i'm sick and woch tv and driegck soop and driegck te i lack to do all cienz of stuf laieck play a rawnd i love you vare vare vare vare vare much bi bi i love you vare vare vare much bi bi momy my lover bunch scool is prite fun but i laieck to stay home bi bi my lover bunch.

And the translation:

> Dear Mom,
> I'd like to stay home when I'm sick and watch TV and drink soup and drink tea. I like to do all kinds of stuff like play around. I love you very much. Bye-bye, Mommy, my lover bunch. School is pretty fun, but I like to stay home. . . .

❧June 14❧

Apparently Benjamin Franklin's negotiating style was relentless. He persevered with patience until he won without making his opponent lose face. If it is true that a man convinced against his will is of the same opinion still, try these tips from one of the early masters. He said that if you don't win the bargain today, go after it again tomorrow and the next day.

Here are some of Franklin's negotiating strategies:

1. Be clear in your own mind as to exactly what it is you are after.
2. Do your homework so you are fully prepared to discuss every aspect and respond to every question and comment.
3. Be persistent. Don't expect to win the first time. Your job is to simply start the other person thinking.
4. Make friends with the person you are bargaining with. Make your argument in terms of his or her needs, advantages, and benefits.
5. Keep your sense of humor.

Keeping that sense of humor is difficult in Pat's line of work. He has a sense of humor all right, and people enjoy hearing him use it at speaking engagements. But it has not always been easy to keep his equilibrium when flesh-peddling agents are representing spoiled kids who think they are entitled to millions of dollars before they have shown they can even compete in the NBA. But Ben Franklin's tips have been of real value.

❧ June 15 ☙

A friend of ours, Betsey Grippi, was called to meet with her nine-year-old son's second-grade teacher. She nearly panicked, wondering what could be wrong.

Little Jeff is a Korean adoptee, and Betsey felt he had been adjusting well. But now this. Her heart pounded as she parked and made the lonely walk through the parking lot, up the walk, and into the school. The teacher betrayed nothing as she greeted her and showed her to a seat.

"What I wanted to talk to you about is this," the teacher began slowly. "Jeff is doing so well that I wanted to meet the woman who is raising him."

Parents' psyches are so fragile. We live and die for each of our children, doing the best we know how and then worrying that we aren't doing enough.

When Jim was upset at not getting enough playing time on the school basketball team, we didn't know what to do. He was miserable. A friend encouraged Pat to call the coach. No pressure, just to talk. "He's not sacred. If it was a teacher, you'd call." Pat called and told the coach how upset Jim was.

"I don't want to tell you how to do your job, but if you can work him in a little more, we'd appreciate it."

The next day Jim started, scored the team's first four points, finished with eight, and the team won by thirty.

We have to communicate with those impacting our kids.

❧ June 16 ❧

What's a parent to do about allowances?

We like Larry Burkett and Gary Ezzo's ideas on the subject. Both of these outstanding Christian financial experts recommend not giving kids money just for the sake of their having cash. Neither should an allowance be related to good behavior, like a bribe.

An allowance should not appear to be pay for normal chores

and family duties, such as cleaning up his room or feeding the dog. Rather, an allowance should be a planned, organized system of teaching money management. A child is entrusted with a certain amount and is expected to give some, save some, and wisely spend some.

Kids can first start managing money when they get a few dollars from relatives at birthdays or Christmas. Then, by the time they are old enough to be entrusted with an allowance, they already know that they are to give and save and spend wisely. When a child first starts managing money, he should be taught the fun and fulfillment of buying something for someone else. If all kids do is wait to see how much they have left for themselves after giving and saving, they are developing selfish, materialistic habits.

As the child matures, he can be taught the difference between short-range and long-range saving, saving for a rainy day, and even staying out of debt. If you can raise a child with an aversion to credit, may your tribe increase!

❧June 17❧

One of the greatest athletes of our day is Cleveland Browns quarterback Bernie Kosar. Bernie's mother, Geri, says that she and her husband wanted their kids to engage in those activities they enjoyed to keep them "tired and out of trouble." She says they always knew where the kids were at ten at night: in bed, asleep.

Their son Brian played college baseball, and his parents gave his games just as much attention as Bernie's NFL games. When they had a game on the same day, Dad went to Bernie's and Mom to Brian's. She listened to the Browns on the radio and videotaped the baseball game for her husband.

We know another family that has a high school basketball player, a junior high baseball player, and an elementary school soccer player. Their policy is that everyone goes to everyone else's games. Since the youngest has had to fidget through the oldest's games over the years, the oldest has to make it to as many of the youngest's games as he can.

The result has been a family truly interested in one another's activities and pursuits. The older children cheer heartily for the younger, and the whole family is closer because of it.

With a dozen kids involved in all kinds of activities every day, it is a challenge to get them where they are supposed to be. Someday we'll tally how many games and performances we've seen.

❧ June 18 ❧

For decades people have made money telling others how to be more sociable. Just about any management or success-oriented motivational program has its roots in the book Dale Carnegie made famous, *How to Win Friends and Influence People* (revised edition, Simon & Schuster, 1981).

Though the advice in that book is profound, it is also so simple that it has become the bedrock of business and social success in this country. Forgive us for grossly summarizing, but much of the thesis can be boiled down to getting other people to talk about themselves. That's it. Feel awkward in a new social situation? Don't know what to say? Ask the person you run into to tell you about his family, his job, his home.

People love to talk about themselves; they are their favorite topic of conversation. Think about it. The person you enjoy being with most makes you feel special. That person enjoys hearing your latest exploits and achievements.

Part of being interested in another is hearing, noticing, catching, and using his or her name. A secret to this is to plan ahead, decide to concentrate, and then use his name two or three times as early in the conversation as possible.

"Ray? Nice to meet you, Ray. And what do you do, Ray?" It may sound ridiculous, but Ray doesn't mind. He likes his name. Get your kids to learn these simple rules, and who knows, you may raise the next Barbara Walters. At the very least, your kids won't become wallflowers.

⋹§ June 19 ?⋺

Joe Garagiola and his family have their priorities in order. Joe, former catcher for the Saint Louis Cardinals and childhood friend of Yogi Berra, has been a media star since his playing days and has had two regular stints on the popular "Today" show.

After his first four years on that program, 1969–1973, Joe wanted out because he could see himself pulling away from his family. He found work with more regular hours, giving himself time for his wife and kids.

A few years later, his son Steve followed in his footsteps and eventually became a sports anchorperson in Detroit. He was earning six figures as the sports guy at five, six, and eleven o'clock at night, but soon he was as frustrated as his father had been. He overheard his daughter tell his wife, "Sometimes I feel like I don't have a dad."

That was it. He asked to be relieved of the 11:00 P.M. duty, which is the most visible and highest paid position. People thought he was crazy or had another job in the works. Soon he was out of a job and wound up in a smaller market for less pay.

Steve and his father think it was the best decision he ever made. And when his dad was invited to be a regular on the "Today," show again, at first he turned it down. Didn't want to move away from the kids and grandkids. How about four days a week? Nope. Three days a week? That was palatable, and his wife comes along. Money and fame are far down the list to the Garagiola family.

❧ June 20 ☙

One path to peace is through the right pace. Consider the following, author unknown:

> The Lord is my pacesetter, I shall not rush; He makes me stop and rest for quiet intervals. He provides me with images of stillness that restore my serenity; He leads me in ways of efficiency through calmness of mind, and His guidance is peace.
>
> Even though I have a great many things to accomplish each day, I will not fret, for His presence is here. His timelessness, His all-importance, will keep me in balance. He prepares refreshment and renewal in the midst of my activity by anointing my mind with His oils of tranquillity.
>
> My cup of joyous energy overflows. Surely harmony and effectiveness shall be the fruits of my hours, for I shall walk in the pace of my Lord and dwell in His house forever.

Everyone has a different pace threshold, just as they do a pain threshold. Some people can go from morning to night at a frenetic pace that would leave others exhausted. The key is to find your own best rhythm. If you do better at a leisurely pace, then settle into it and you can accomplish prodigious tasks by sticking with them.

Some people are starters and not finishers, but they can inspire all kinds of projects. Find your place and your pace.

June 21

Many people have heard the name Harry Bollback and know that he is a musician and executive who has worked for years with Jack Wyrtzen, founder and director of Word of Life. Few know, however, of his dramatic call to missionary work and his exciting tenure in the jungles of Brazil.

Though his father had dedicated all three of his children to missionary service and had seen the other two go, the senior Bollback hoped Harry might become a professional musician and even play at Carnegie Hall one day. After his conversion at youth camp, Harry dedicated his music to God and played weekly for Jack Wyrtzen rallies.

After serving three years in World War II and getting married, Harry returned to the States and to his weekly playing at the rallies. One night when Wyrtzen was giving an invitation for people to commit themselves to missionary service, he noticed that the piano accompaniment had stopped. The pianist was coming forward.

Bollback took an accordian into the jungles of South America, and he and his partner made forays into the territories of some of the fiercest Indian tribes on earth. One such contact looked good at first, but soon the Indians chased Bollback and his partner down the river, firing poison arrows at them. Only the miraculous intervention of God made every arrow miss and spared Bollback for a life of service to the Kingdom.

June 22

We enjoy hearing Ray Ortlund, former pastor of the Lake Avenue Congregational Church in Pasadena, California, and now the host of the "Haven of Rest" radio broadcast. One night he spoke on the subject "When God Doesn't Answer Prayer," and Pat took some notes.

Dr. Ortlund first said that we must pray the proper way. It is one thing to ask God for the desires of our hearts, but we must also come to Him in reverence, asking only for those things we believe are consistent with His will.

We are not to hold grudges. When we hold a grudge against someone, God won't hear us. We are willfully sinning and trying to hide it from God, and that blocks our communication with Him: "Therefore if you bring your gift to the altar, and there remember that your brother has something against you, leave your gift there before the altar, and go your way. First be reconciled to your brother, and then come and offer your gift" (Matthew 5:23, 24).

We must treat our spouses right. Many people are not kind and loving to their mates. If this relationship is not right, don't expect God to answer your prayers in other areas.

God may say no. He loves us too much to grant a request that would cause us great pain in the future.

Sometimes He says yes in a surprising way, as He sent Jesus the Deliverer. Watch for His answers.

◄§ June 23 ?►

Our culture says that to be successful in life, we need beauty, brains, ability, and things. We like the more spiritual approach to true success. It says we need faith to live by, a self to live with, and a purpose to live for. The true believer will be successful when he glorifies God by living for others. We know this is antithetical to society's view.

Read this story of the famous preacher Harry Rimmer to your kids and see if they can determine where his values lay.

One day Rimmer was rushing to catch a train. In his haste, he knocked over a little boy and his fruit stand. Now he faced a decision: catch the train or stay and help the little boy get set up again.

Rimmer set down his case, knelt, and helped the boy get up. Then he helped him set up the stand and paid him for the damages. As he apologized and turned to leave, he was stopped by the boy's words: "Mister, are you Jesus?"

When was the last time you were mistaken for Jesus?

In truth, we may get opportunities in life to emulate Jesus Christ. The question is how we will respond when the time comes. We were always impressed with how Dr. Lehman Strauss took such loving care of his wife when her health failed late in life. Harry Bollback told Lehman, "If trouble hits, I hope I'll do the same."

Strauss replied, "Not *if* trouble hits. *When* trouble hits."

◄§ June 24 ?►

Hospitality is both a virtue and—we think—a spiritual gift. Certainly it is biblical, and the Golden Rule applies to it perfectly.

Not everyone has the space to designate a full-time guest room. If all your kids are still at home, you may have to designate one of their rooms as the guest quarters.

Start with a list of those details that have to be taken care of before the occupant can be officially said to have moved out. Not every evidence that this is someone else's room has to be covered or stashed somewhere, but certainly you don't want GI Joes or other action figures on the floor if Grandma will be using the room.

Then there should be a list of what needs to be done to make the room livable for the guest. Fresh linens, of course, dusting, vacuuming, air freshening. Just keep in mind how you would like it if you were the guest.

Reading material?

Extra blankets?

A clock?

A radio?

A TV?

You want your guest to have experienced your best hospitality and to be able to feel as if he or she has been in the home of people who would do what Jesus would have done.

❧ June 25 ❧

We heard Dr. D. James Kennedy interview family counselor Gary Smalley on a wife's greatest needs, and we were struck by how universal those needs are. In fact, not only do children need the same basic kinds of strokes—with obvious adaptations—but so do husbands.

Smalley said that the greatest need of a wife is security and that a man should tell his wife he'll never stop loving her. Not just, "Hey, I married ya, didn't I?" And isn't this also a need of a husband? A lot of petty jealousy would be cured if husbands were regularly reassured too.

He also said that a wife needs regular, meaningful conversation, a half hour to an hour a day. That sounds crazy to men who have never tried it and luxurious to women who have never enjoyed it. But it is time well invested.

Wives crave romance, Smalley says. Walk with her. Hold her hand. Here again, husbands are not immune to this need. Most men love to be touched in public by their wives so that everyone knows they are with their husbands and are happy about it.

Hold her regularly. The number-one physical need of a woman, says Smalley, is nonsexual touching. He recommends eight to twelve touches per day for greatly enhanced emotional health. We say make that reciprocal, and don't leave out the children.

That means a whole lot of healthy physical interaction will be going on, and that is as it should be.

❧June 26❧

The Associated Press cited a study by the National Bureau of Economic Research to confirm something Christians have suspected or believed for years. Are you ready? Couples who live together before marrying have nearly an 80 percent higher divorce rate than those who didn't, and they seem to have less regard for the institution.

What a surprise, huh? After years of respected advice columnists saying it isn't a bad idea to live together for a while before marriage to make sure of the compatibility of the partners, sin is coming home to roost. Fornication is still sin, no matter how modern society dresses it up.

Of course, the authors of the study do not want to moralize. They maintain that they are not saying cohabiting *causes* breakdowns in relationships but that people who choose to live together generally bring to the relationship less commitment to the long term. Uh-huh.

The study was based on a survey of nearly five thousand Swedish women because, the researchers say, "Swedes tend to precede American social trends by ten to fifteen years."

An estimated two million American couples live together unwed, or about 4 percent of all couples. Cohabiting has quadrupled in the last ten years and shows no sign of slowing.

Here is another area in which Christians can take a stand and be salt and light in a fallen world.

◈§June 27?◈

"And we know that all things work together for good to those who love God, to those who are the called according to His purpose" (Romans 8:28).

The above is probably one of the most abused verses in all of Scripture. Too many people let it trip lightly off their tongues when they can think of nothing else to say to someone who is bereaved or ill.

In spite of that, the verse is true because it is Scripture. While we should be careful not to be too glib with it, it is important to remember that blessing does come from difficulty.

For one thing, it can be a means of spiritual growth. We don't mind pain when we are working out, but we don't seem to appreciate it in the spiritual realm: "My brethren, count it all joy when you fall into various trials, knowing that the testing of your faith produces patience" (James 1:2, 3).

Trials can teach us how to comfort others when they suffer:

> Blessed be the God and Father of our Lord Jesus Christ, the Father of mercies and God of all comfort, who comforts us in all our tribulation, that we may be able to comfort those who are in any trouble, with the comfort with which we ourselves are comforted by God. For as the sufferings of Christ abound in us, so our consolation also abounds through Christ.
>
> 2 Corinthians 1:3–5

Continued tomorrow.

❦ June 28 ❧

When we are suffering, God has our attention. When else do we have time to "be still, and know that I am God" (Psalm 46:10). Many people make their major decisions in life when they are on their backs, as the cliché goes, with nowhere to look but up.

It is only then that we can determine what is really important in life. Is it our health, or is it our relationship with Jesus Christ? There is nothing wrong with getting well, unless wellness has taken the place of God as the object of our affections.

Suffering sometimes is part of God's sovereign plan for our lives. Satan tempts us most when we are under the weather. He wants us to believe we are unworthy of God. It is at those times we need to remember that "we do not wrestle against flesh and blood, but against principalities, against powers, against the rulers of the darkness of this age, against spiritual hosts of wickedness in the heavenly places" (Ephesians 6:12).

Pain and suffering in this life is only temporary. God may choose to heal us by medical means, or He may wait and do the job Himself when we see Him in glory.

"Whereas you do not know what will happen tomorrow. For what is your life? It is even a vapor that appears for a little time and then vanishes away" (James 4:14).

"So teach us to number our days, That we may gain a heart of wisdom" (Psalm 90:12).

❦§ June 29 ?❧

Paul Anderson, once the world's strongest man, played a large role in Pat's conversion. He came to speak at the Spartanburg, South Carolina, ballpark when Pat was general manager of the Phillies there in the mid-1960s.

At five feet, nine inches tall and 375 pounds, Anderson was an imposing figure who performed amazing feats of strength. *The Guinness Book of World Records* entrant and 1956 Olympic gold medalist also told the crowd, in a voice that needed no electronic amplification, that if the strongest man in the world needed Jesus Christ, what about them?

Anderson has run youth homes for years, but a few years ago he was stricken with kidney disease. In a letter to us, he gave an update that evidenced the spiritual tenor of the man:

> My health is improving slowly, and I ask you to con-
> tinue praying for me. I have no sad story. I am able to

work out hard, even though I am not walking yet. If I never take another step, I praise the Lord that He has allowed me to take as many as I have; I will praise Him from a wheelchair. This is not the talk of a martyr, because I am certainly doing everything I can to be mobile once more.

His praising God from a wheelchair reminded us of Joni Eareckson Tada. She admits she never would have chosen her situation, but now that she is in it, she is determined to glorify God.

❧ June 30 ☙

When Jim was thirteen, we watched him play Y League basketball. His team was good and reached the play-offs. When they took a twenty-point lead, we relaxed and started dreaming of a championship. Then things started deteriorating.

They could do nothing right, and their opponents could do nothing wrong. Just as in a pro game, there are ebbs and flows, and the trailing team usually makes at least one significant run at the leaders. This run succeeded, and with just a few seconds left on the clock, Jim's team trailed by one.

He was determined to do what he could to turn it back around, and on a pretty play he led a teammate with a perfect bounce pass. Jim's friend was fouled while shooting and was awarded two free throws. To rattle him, the opposing coach called two time-outs before he shot.

If he made one shot, they would tie and go into overtime. If he made two, they would win. He missed them both.

After the game, he sat alone and crying as we watched. Jim

was the only one to go and put his arm around his teammate and walk him toward the locker room. On the way, they passed the referees. Jim stopped them and told them they had called a good game.

That was one of those days when we couldn't have been more thrilled. It is one thing to see a child do what his parents tell him, but it's another altogether to see him—on his own—be even more charitable than they might have been.

❧ July 1 ❧

Let's start this month—and this day—with a quiz. Don't peek at the end of this entry for the answer, which has nothing to do with today's thought. It's just for fun. Your question for today: Who said this?

"Children today are tyrants. They contradict their parents, gobble their food, and tyrannize their teachers."

Cheerful people are fun people. They are great to be around. They brighten our days. The problem is, where have they all gone? It seems in our childhood we remember more cheer. Maybe our memories are screening the realities of life and making nostalgia seem sweeter than it should. Life was never really a Norman Rockwell painting, but compare your childhood with today. Weren't there more smiles back then?

Apparently we are going to have to provide the smiles ourselves today. Maybe it's all part of being Christians in this society.

Jim told Jill she was the prettiest woman at his baseball game. "Thanks, Jim," she said. "That's nice to say."

"You were smiling," he said. "The other mothers were all sitting there like this." He imitated dour women with their heads down, scowling. It takes only a smile to be pretty and cheerful.

Now, the answer to today's quiz: Socrates!

❧ July 2 ❧

Many people see athletics as a pursuit rewarding only to those who have no brain. Ever notice how jokes about football, for instance, always make the players out to be oafs who wouldn't know how to find their classrooms?

That scenario doesn't jibe with the body of wisdom that has come from great football coaches over the years. Consider these gems:

George Allen, pro and college coach, said, "The more I study people, the more I am convinced that the difference between one man and another, the successful and the unsuccessful, the great and the ordinary, is this: energy, determination, purpose, and how badly he wants to win."

Paul "Bear" Bryant, the legendary coach at the University of Alabama, listed five things members of good teams need: to know what is expected of them, an opportunity to perform, to know how they are getting along, guidance when they need it, and rewards according to their contributions. He adds, "If anything goes bad, I did it. If anything goes semigood, we did it. If anything goes really good, you did it."

Lou Holtz, coach at five colleges, including the University of Notre Dame, has a philosophy consisting of three simple rules:

1. Do what is right. You know the difference. If you have any doubt, get out your Bible.

2. Do your best.
3. Treat others as you would like to be treated.

❧ July 3 ❧

A few years ago, Pat received a letter from a man who had attended a meeting where Pat spoke. The man and his wife had been considering bringing three handicapped children into their home, after having been married seventeen years without starting a family.

He wrote:

> We both had dreams to chase and children just didn't seem to be part of the program. Then we read in the paper about three children who were considered difficult to place because of their ages and their special needs. My wife raised the prospect of our doing something about it, and I agreed.
>
> The prospect of bringing strangers into my household did raise my anxiety level. What [your speech] did for me was simple. Anybody who can have five first-graders and still laugh about it can convince me that newcomers in my household is NO PROBLEM. I left Orlando with the assurance that my wife and I are doing the right thing and that the consequences of our decision will be a better life for all involved.
>
> I hope you can appreciate the impact you have made on our lives. In a few minutes I found the rationale to take on this responsibility. My wife and I thank you very much. Of course, the adoption process has just started, and the agency may decide we do not have a "fit." But in any event, the process will not stop because we have

cold feet. I feel this is the start of another chapter in our lives, and we know it will not be our last.

❧ July 4 ☙

The family was God's idea, and it has been important to generations of God's people since the beginning of time. A legacy of faith in Christ does not come by accident. Because of failures within families in the Old Testament, Judges 2:10 tells us, "When all that generation had been gathered to their fathers, another generation arose after them who did not know the LORD nor the work which He had done for Israel."

As heads of families, we should look for ways to shore up, to improve, to keep from making the mistakes our ancestors made in their relationships with God.

Even the church functions most effectively when it functions like a family. Some churches, sadly, are like dysfunctional families. Family members and parishioners should read the Bible with family references in mind. Scripture is replete with them.

As you study your family and your church, ask yourself these questions, as suggested by Dr. Gary J. Oliver, clinical director of Southwest Counseling Associates in Littleton, Colorado, and visiting associate professor at Denver Seminary:

Does your family spend time together?
Does it demonstrate good communication patterns?
Does it deal with conflict constructively?
Do you encourage and build up one another?
Are you committed to the Lord?
Do you have a clear commitment to the family?

❧ July 5 ❧

Sometimes witnessing, sharing our faith in Christ with someone else, seems harder than it needs to be. Somewhere we have gotten the impression that witnessing means stopping people on the street or going door-to-door and spelling out the entire plan of salvation to others. Then we are expected to lead them in a prayer of acceptance and begin to disciple them.

Well, of course there are people who do that and do it effectively. You would have to admit, however, that at best that is not the typical believer's experience. Besides being more natural and attractive, an easier way to witness is to *be* a witness all the time. It is true that you rarely see someone who was "exampled" into heaven by the life-style of a believer, but there is something to the idea of planting seeds rather than doing the planting and harvesting all at once.

During one of Pat and Bob's times alone together, Bob mentioned that witnessing was hard for him, especially with teammates. Pat told Bob that at baseball tryouts, Bob's coach had asked Pat about the card he saw Pat carrying when he ran in the mornings.

"I just told him it was a Bible verse I'm memorizing," Pat told Bob, who was wide-eyed. "It was just the planting of a seed. He asked a question and I answered it. Who knows where it might lead? It may open the door to my talking to him more, or he might ask more questions. We are witnesses all the time."

❦§ July 6 ?❧

We are militant pro-lifers. We believe abortion is wrong even in the case of rape and incest (what is the point of murdering the innocent party?). And we believe former Surgeon General of the United States C. Everett Koop when he says he has never known of an abortion being required to spare the life of a mother.

We have been impressed with Kay James, former director of public affairs for the National Right to Life Committee and founder and president of Black Americans for Life, which seeks solutions for women with crisis pregnancies. She now works for President Bush under the secretary for Health and Human Services.

A reporter once asked James how she would handle it if she became pregnant as the result of a rape. She said, "I usually give a scenario of a woman who has four children and finds herself pregnant again. Her husband is an alcoholic and, because of his disease, abuses the woman and her four children. He does not provide for the family, and the woman does not know how she is going to provide for them either.

"Many people say it would be irresponsible to bring another child into that situation. That kind of summarizes why I'm involved with the pro-life movement. That woman was my mother and that fifth child was me. I was born on the kitchen table.

"And no, I cannot imagine any circumstance where I would reach inside myself and take that human life that was growing there."

❧ July 7 ❧

Mickey Mantle, the legendary Yankee, once said, "If my kids had my father for a dad instead of me, they might have become ball players, especially Mickey, Jr. But you've got to play from the time you're five, like I did with my dad."

You can sense the sadness in Mickey for those years when he was away from home six and seven months at a time, too busy being a ball player to be able to help his sons do the same. In light of that, maybe it's just as well they didn't become ball players.

Floyd Patterson, former heavyweight boxing champion of the world, owns a gym where amateurs work in hopes of becoming professionals. Several years ago, he noticed that every evening when he left the gym, a young boy who had been watching just sat outside. Finally Patterson asked him his name and whether he would like to try boxing. He gave him some equipment and let him fool around in the gym. Realizing the boy had nowhere to go, Floyd let him stay upstairs at the gym, where there was a bed and a kitchenette.

Patterson had a wife and two daughters, but he felt for the eleven-year-old and began asking him over for meals. "It's amazing he had not already gotten into trouble," Patterson says. "There wasn't even a father's name on his birth certificate. His mother was sixteen when she had him."

Floyd says, in his self-effacing manner, "The thing mushroomed to the point where we adopted him." Simple as that.

❧ July 8 ❧

A lot of strange things surrounded the death of Pete Maravich in January 1988. He had been speaking a lot about the brevity of life and how our existence on earth could end in an instant.

Then there was the interview done several years before by Andy Nuzzo of *The Beaver County Times* (Pennsylvania), in which Maravich was quoted, "I don't want to play ten years in the NBA and die of a heart attack at age forty."

Which is exactly what he did.

Late-night radio talk-show host Larry King had just undergone bypass surgery around that time, and among the greetings he received was a Bible from Pete Maravich. It arrived the day before Pete died.

Enclosed was a letter from Pete that read:

> Dear Larry,
> I'm so glad to hear everything went well with your surgery. My prayer is that you remain open and that God will touch your life as He has mine. Once I was a disbeliever. When I could not fill my life with basketball, I would simply substitute sex, liquid drugs, or material things to feed my internal shell-like appearance. I was never satisfied. I have finally realized after 40 years that Jesus Christ is in me. He will reveal His truth to you, Larry, because He lives.

Ironically, Pete's prayer at the all-star chapel the year before had included, "Make us realize the shortness of our days."

✥ July 9 ✥

Other elements of the Pete Maravich all-star chapel service prayer that we found interesting:

"Father, Your word says that 'man is like a mere breath; his days are like a passing shadow. . . .' Give us that know You the desire and power to boldly and confidently witness what Christ has done in each of our lives. . . ."

Maravich had gone from being an egocentric star to a meek and humble Christian. When his friend John Lotz lost his father, Pete wrote this letter, of course unaware that his own demise of a heart attack would occur some time later:

> My heart goes out to you and your family. I walked down this same lonely road only a short time ago. I want you to know that your dad meant a great deal to me. We had great fellowship the times that we talked.
>
> He always encouraged me and always kept his eyes on Jesus. Not only was he a loving example of our Savior, but he was also blessed with a sense of humor. Only eternity will tell of his many accomplishments and contributions.
>
> He and your mother raised beautiful and respected sons. It has been a great privilege for me to know the family. During this time may His grace and peace be yours in fullest measure.
>
> Your friend and brother, Peter

Pete left a legacy of more than Hall of Fame basketball talent.

❧ July 10 ☙

"If I were raising a child today, I would be a lot tougher about what he or she watched than ninety percent of today's parents are," says Vance Packard. "I say this because I spent five years studying the changing world of children. I think the sheer amount of time children now consume watching TV is a national scandal. They spend about as many hours a year in front of the tube as they spend in front of teachers.

"I wouldn't allow them to have a TV set in their rooms. Having a set so readily available puts too much pressure on children to watch excessively." This from the author of *The People Shapers* (1977). He knows whereof he speaks.

We have become ferocious about television viewing in our home. There have been times in our distant past when we were glued to the screen for hours in the evening, but no longer. We don't use it as a baby-sitter; in fact, the kids are not allowed to turn it on without permission, and they are not given permission unless all their homework and chores are done, and—and this is every bit as important as those prerequisites—there has to be a program on worth watching, most often sports.

We don't watch just to watch. We don't watch just because there is nothing else to do. There is *never* nothing else to do in a house with thousands of books and tapes and plenty of people to talk to.

We control the TV so it won't control us.

❧ July 11 ☙

We are told in the New Testament to hold fast to our faith. Sometimes that is easier than believing that Jesus is upholding His end of the bargain: "I am with you always, even to the end of the age" (Matthew 28:20).

We praise God that Jesus Christ has unchanging qualities: "Jesus Christ is the same yesterday, today, and forever" (Hebrews 13:8).

He also has an unchanging purpose. Our salvation was His motivation: "The Son of Man did not come to be served, but to serve, and to give His life a ransom for many" (Matthew 20:28).

His Word is also unchanging: "The grass withers, the flower fades, but the word of our God stands forever" (Isaiah 40:8).

His work never changes. Through the Holy Spirit, He is still at work in the lives of His children. He is continually convicting men of sin.

Best of all, His love never changes. The foremost evidence of God in someone's life is love. Three times in John alone, Jesus admonishes His disciples to do as He has done: "A new commandment I give to you, that you love one another; as I have loved you, that you also love one another" (13:34). "This is My commandment, that you love one another as I have loved you" (15:12). "These things I command you, that you love one another" (15:17).

❧ July 12 ☙

Danny Ferry is a six-foot, ten-inch tall basketball playing machine who made his mark at Duke University and went on to play pro ball in Italy and then in the NBA.

His story is instructive on how parents can best provide for and encourage a kid with prodigious talents and physical attributes.

Danny's father, Bob Ferry, is six feet, eight inches tall and was an NBA player before becoming a general manager. He spoon-fed Danny basketball from the time he was five until he went to Duke. Dad Ferry had nothing but heredity to do with Danny's reaching six-eight when he was fourteen years old. But he did see to it that his son went to the best basketball high school in the country (DeMatha in Hyattsville, Maryland) and that he was playing inner-city basketball in the Washington, D. C., area as young as twelve.

That experience gave him all kinds of moves, but more important, it gave him confidence. He knew that if he could compete against high-schoolers and collegians at that age, his future looked bright. By the time he was a junior at Duke, he was dominating the conference and headed for the pros.

Ferry credits his father for all the basketball input and for getting him into the right schools, but he also says he was lucky that his mother "drove me everywhere. She spent a lot of time on the road taking me places."

July 13

"It is my pleasure that my children are free, happy, and unrestrained by parental tyranny. Love is the chain whereby to bind a child to its parents."

That was the feeling of a relatively well-known father of four sons: a man named Abraham Lincoln.

Lincoln's eldest son, Robert Todd (Bobby), pursued the education his father lacked and enrolled at Phillips Exeter

Academy as a precursor to Harvard University. In early 1860, before he became president, Lincoln visited Bobby at Exeter and brought an address to the students.

At first some of the students were offended by the homely appearance of the shabbily dressed politician, but one recalled it this way: "Not ten minutes had passed before his uncouth appearance was absolutely forgotten by us boys, and, I believe, by all that large audience. . . . There was no more pity for our friend Bob; we were proud of his father. . . ."

The Lincoln family suffered severe tragedy. The second son died before reaching four years of age, and Lincoln regretted the time lost with him. He spent a lot of time with Willie and Tad, the last two Lincoln boys, and to the consternation of the staff, virtually let them have free rein in the White House. He even let them have a menagerie of animals that roamed the place. Willie died at eleven and Tad at eighteen, six years after his father had been assassinated. Lincoln's wife, Mary, never recovered from the losses.

❧ July 14 ☙

We are in that stage of parenthood when we have to be aware of and guard against negative peer pressure. That very statement implies that there is such a thing as positive peer pressure, and we believe that. That's why our kids are either home schooled or attend Christian schools. That's why they go to camp. That's one of the many reasons we go to church.

But we don't want to be guilty of isolating our kids from the world. Otherwise, how will they play any part in the fulfillment of the Great Commission?

Things we do to help our kids resist peer pressure:

Keep them talking. We want to know what is going on in their heads, what they are thinking about, planning, doing.

Build family loyalty. We spoke before about trying to get as many members of the family as possible to attend any public performances or games in which the others are involved.

Know where our teenagers are all the time. People criticize this because they say we are not allowing our kids to develop and grow up. If drugs and social diseases are signs of development and maturity, we'll pass.

Know who is influencing our kids. Have you heard a new name mentioned by your child a lot lately? It's time to get to know that someone. Have him or her over to your house and see for yourself whether this person is having a good or bad influence on your child. Your job is to guard the gate.

July 15

Is it possible we are in the last days? Many people think so because of the wars and rumors of wars, persecution, and all the rest. Yet the Scripture tells us that Jesus Himself said we should not view these things as the end (Matthew 24:6). He says, "See that you are not troubled; for all these things must come to pass, but the end is not yet."

Rather, He gives us instructions. We are to keep watch: "Behold, I am coming as a thief. Blessed is he who watches, and keeps his garments, lest he walk naked and they see his shame" (Revelation 16:15).

We are never to waver: "And now, little children, abide in Him, that when He appears, we may have confidence and not be ashamed before Him at His coming" (1 John 2:28).

We are to be patient: "You also be patient. Establish your

hearts, for the coming of the Lord is at hand. Do not grumble against one another, brethren, lest you be condemned. Behold, the Judge is standing at the door!" (James 5:8, 9).

We are to be active: "Go therefore and make disciples of all the nations, baptizing them in the name of the Father and of the Son and of the Holy Spirit" (Matthew 28:19).

And we should be ready: "Therefore you also be ready, for the Son of Man is coming at an hour you do not expect" (Luke 12:40).

Are you ready?

July 16

Do any of us ever get so old that we are allowed to take our marriages or our spouses for granted? We see marriages of twenty and more years fall apart, sometimes seemingly for reasons that could have been avoided. So, as we approach our twentieth anniversary in the fall of 1992, we are thinking about maintaining the romance in our relationship.

We have both always been concerned about our physical appearance and fitness. We eat healthy foods and work out. No one would fault us if we beefed up and got soft after all these years together, but who wants to be less attractive to his mate than he was when he married?

We still flirt. A touch, a wink, a smile, a phrase that turned us on in our youth can have the same effect now. We can forget we are past the halfway point of the Bible's allotment of three score and ten and enjoy a guilt-free romantic rush.

We maintain our independence. We each have activities that keep us busy and keep us circulating in our own orbits.

Our individual activities were part of our mutual attraction when we met, and within reason they can still be.

We still try to be courteous to each other. It's not easy for any couple who have lived together two decades to maintain good manners and not take each other for granted. But it sure makes for a more harmonious home and relationship. The please-and-thank yous that grace society also set the tone at home.

◄§ July 17 §►

Have you had the experience of seeing a dear friend grieving over the loss of a loved one and not knowing what to say? If you have not been down the same road, the best thing to say is nothing. The best thing to do is to be there, not smothering, not babying, simply being available.

People with the best intentions often encourage their suffering friends to "just call and let me know if there's anything I can do." No one ever calls. They are too hurt, too stunned, too numb. They don't want to bother anyone.

But indeed, many things need to be done, don't they? Meals cooked, errands run, calls made. These are things you can simply do, without waiting to be asked. Some will need the input of the bereaved, and we need to be sensitive if we find we have volunteered to do something he or she really doesn't want us to do.

But usually, acts of kindness are much appreciated. A hug, a squeeze, a shared tear can also be meaningful. Anything but the old bromide that we know how he or she is feeling, especially when we can't and don't. If you can relate because you lost a loved one too, then say so. But don't suggest solutions or assure the person he will get over it.

Simply saying that you recall how hard it was when you lost your loved one implies it is not as hard now. The person knows you have been there and that you do understand.

❧July 18❧

A few years ago Jill was in real estate school—trying to find something to fill those idle hours, you know—and Pat decided to stand in the gap. He was going to be sole parent to our then eight kids for a whole day. He planned, scheduled, and was ready.

As soon as Jill was out the door, he organized everyone, got all the chores done, and then entertained the kids the rest of the day.

They went here and there, did all kinds of fun things, and were exhausted by the end of the day. Pat took them to dinner and then took them home. When Jill returned, they all wanted to know about her day, and then Pat recounted theirs.

"Here's a question," Pat announced to the kids, hoping they would tell Jill what a great day they'd had. "What was the highlight of your day?"

It was almost unanimous. "When Mom came home!" they chorused.

That doesn't change the fact, however, that experts say father input is one of the most important influences on successful people. In a survey of adult achievers, homework, fancy schools, and even wealth finished further down the list than attentive dads. Mother love and attention were considered givens, but the major difference between achievers and nonachievers was how much personal attention they received from their father. Are you listening, Dad?

❧ July 19 ☙

One of the crucial voids in our marriage before it was rekindled was a sense on Jill's part that Pat didn't really know her. She wondered how in the world he would do if we were on a show like "The Newlywed Game." And this was after we had been married ten years!

Jill wanted Pat to become a student of her. What did she like and not like, enjoy and not enjoy? It seemed he was an expert on everything and everybody except his own wife. When we heard James Dobson interview Christian educator Howard Hendricks a few years ago on "Focus on the Family," we were reminded of our own situation.

Dr. Hendricks pointed out that a man wants his wife to understand him too. He wants her to understand that what he is doing at the office or at the plant is one of his sources of fulfillment. It is one of the things he lives for.

The problem, according to Dr. Hendricks, comes when a man gives himself inordinately to his job. He becomes married to the job rather than to his wife. His work now becomes an excuse to let things get out of balance.

Hendricks added that the great temptation in all men is to let legitimate concerns—their desire to be task-oriented, to achieve, to make an impact, to have meaning in their work—become such ends in themselves that in the process they mortgage a marriage and a family.

❧ July 20 ❧

Here's a nice note we received from a woman who heard Karyn sing when she was eight years old:

> Dear Pat and Jill,
>
> I so enjoyed your daughter singing tonight. We also had a son who accepted Christ as a preschooler and was baptized then. Our next son was led to Christ by his older brother, also at a young age. Our adopted daughter, who came to us as a baby, received Christ very young.
>
> Now my youngest son has asked Jesus to come into his heart and he asks me to ask Jesus to make his owies better all the time. He also leads the blessing sometimes at our dinner table, thanking God for the flowers on the table, his favorite food, or anything else he sees.
>
> He also prays for my sister, without any prompting. She was run over by a truck while bike riding and has had several operations.
>
> Please tell other parents that they shouldn't wait around to lead their children to Christ. We never know how long we'll have our children here with us. Our first-born son went home to be with the Lord when he was seven, nine days before his eighth birthday.
>
> Psalm 41 was a great help to us as we did receive a new song in our lives. We now have three children and are richly blessed in so many ways.

❧ July 21 ❧

Speaking of leading a child to Christ, our church put out a flyer with information adapted from a Church Training Department article called "Helping a Child Understand Salvation."

The pastor and his staff urge prayer before the time when a child expresses an interest in receiving Christ. Then, when the child does bring up the subject, here are four basic rules to remember:

Each question deserves an answer. Spoon-feed the answers, don't force them. Attention given to every question helps the child establish a feeling of self-worth.

Give attention to questions as soon as possible. A child needs an answer while his question is uppermost in his mind.

Find out why the child is asking the question. A child's question does not necessarily mean he is under conviction. Question him further.

Be open and available. Parents must be receptive and available to the child. Caring about everyday things shows the child your readiness to care about other things.

A child shows he is ready by serious meditation, sober thoughts, or expressions of worry over his sin. Many children show a change in behavior. Each child responds in his own unique way.

We are convinced that believing parents know best when their children are ready to receive Christ.

❧ July 22 ❧

A twenty-year veteran policeman specializing in working with troubled teens asked hundreds of them this question: "If your parents were seated with us, right here and right now, what would you like to tell them?"

He found their responses startling and brutally blunt. He selected seven of the most common and calls them the things kids are dying to tell their parents:

Keep cool. This was the number-one thing kids in trouble with the law wanted their parents to do. Don't fly off the handle. Don't go into a rage.

Show me who's boss. Kids don't want cruelty. They want their parents to be strict, consistent, and fair. They want specific boundaries and they want to know the consequences for stepping over the line. Jails are full of people who never had anyone enforce a rule until it was too late.

Be parents, not peers. Kids don't want parents to look or act like kids.

Tell me if there's a God, and does He really care?

Get tough with me. Scare me. Convince me what I'm doing is wrong and that it will get me nowhere.

Call my bluff. I don't want everything I ask for. Don't back off from your threats.

Be honest with me. It doesn't do any good to try to fool me. Be real.

❧ July 23 ❧

Pat sees books and magazines and hears of cassettes and seminars on tips for getting along with people and working better. We are always amazed at how the principles emphasized in these programs also work in the home—most of them because they are others-oriented, biblical, and thus, of course, right. The motive for exercising them may be wrong, (i. e., just to get ahead or be successful rather than to emulate Christ), but if the advice is right, the motives are our choice.

For instance, many of these programs insist that a person should not force his ideas on other people. Doesn't that sound good for siblings, spouses, and parent/child relationships?

Diplomacy is the key. When differences surface, talk them out. Sound familiar? Honesty is the best policy. Cooperation gets things done.

Stay calm. Don't lose your temper. This is similar to the advice from troubled teens to their parents from yesterday's entry. And of course, it is biblical: "A soft answer turns away wrath, But a harsh word stirs up anger" (Proverbs 15:1).

Use tact. Consider the feelings of others.

Be reliable. If you say you are going to do something, do it. Don't put it off, thinking you will get around to it later. That always shows. It's true at home too, isn't it?

Keep your sense of humor. People who find humor even in difficult situations get along much better at work and at home.

❧ July 24 ❧

One of the men we admire and enjoy reading and hearing is Dr. Jay Kesler, former president of Youth for Christ, International, and now president of Taylor University.

He says a person cannot claim to have a Christian marriage if the Christian part consists only of words shared at the marriage altar. The element that makes a marriage Christian involves the daily activity of Christ in marriage difficulties.

It includes the willingness to realize that your original commitment and covenant is worth fighting for . . . to realize that you and your mate are caught in the midst of pain and pressure from the world. Together you may actually be victims of forces larger than yourselves.

Dr. Kesler says, "We need to always remember that Christ demands obedience—a radical commitment to Him regardless of how we feel. Our obedience includes not only receiving His forgiving love but also passing it on to others."

Do you know of people who darken the door of their churches only for christenings, marriages, and burials? Someone has said they get water sprinkled on them, rice thrown at them, and dirt shoveled on them. Then they call themselves Christians. Others come to church only on Easter and Christmas, then complain that the pastor only preaches on the birth of Christ and the death of Christ. Let's make our marriages and our lives truly Christian.

❦ July 25 ❧

John A. Huffman, Jr., minister at St. Andrew's Presbyterian Church in Newport Beach, California, is such an insightful speaker that we subscribe to his printed sermons and always benefit from them. We especially appreciated his message on what God has to say about your job, based on 2 Thessalonians 3:6–16.

He made clear that God wants us to view our jobs as sacred privileges, not only as necessary evils. They are not just a drudgery to put up with in order to pay the bills. One of the reasons we get bored with our jobs is that we have not dedicated our careers to the Lord.

There is no place for a lazy Christian. The Thessalonians loafed around, waiting for the return of Christ. We are called to an energetic life of action and service.

Our jobs give us opportunities to provide for our families. The apostle Paul told Timothy that anyone who does not provide for his relatives, especially for his own family, has disowned the faith and is worse than an unbeliever. We should not only refuse to feed him but we should also stay away from him!

Jobs provide Christians with opportunities to produce quality workmanship. Simply do your job these days and you'll stick out like a sore thumb. Do quality work and you'll rise like a star.

That's a sad commentary on the state of affairs in today's marketplace.

❦ July 26 ❧

It was a thrill when Elisabeth Elliot visited our home. The great missionary and teacher and author was the widow of the martyred Jim Elliot.

Elisabeth is a woman of prayer, and she has much to teach us about it. On her radio program "Gateway to Joy," she admitted that she, like Martin Luther, finds prayer hard work. She quoted Luther:

> It is a tremendously hard thing to pray aright. Yea, it is verily the science of all sciences even to pray so that the heart may approach unto God with all gracious confidence and say, "Our Father, which art in heaven." For he who can take to himself such confidence of grace is already over the hill of difficulty and has laid the foundation stone of the temple of prayer.

Someone else has said, "Perfect prayer is not attained by the use of many words but through deep desire."

Elisabeth Elliot emphasizes that "it is the work of a Christian to pray. It is the way to make a living, in the spiritual sense." When we pray, she says, we are workers together with God.

"Why should we pray? Because we follow a Master who prayed. If Jesus, who is God, needed to pray, can we imagine that we could do without it? God's omnipotence is not impaired by His having ordained our participation in prayer. He has given us a means of helping others by prayer."

❧§ July 27 ❧❧

One of Vince Lombardi's coaching secrets was that he never let up on the practice field. Every mistake was challenged and corrected on the spot. Nothing was overlooked. After he left the Packers, no coach was as relentless on the practice field about little things that led to big things, and the Pack was never the same. They have had their ups and downs but have never been as successful as they were under a coach who majored on the minors, because he knew the minors added up to the majors.

Success is accepting the challenge of the difficult. In the inspiring words of Phillips Brooks, "Do not pray for tasks equal to your power. Pray for power equal to your tasks. Then the doing of your work shall be no miracle, but *you* shall be the miracle."

Success is relative and individual and personal. It is your answer to the problem of making your days add up to a great life. There are no secrets of success. Success is doing the things you know you should do and not doing the things you know you should not do.

Most counselors will tell you that the majority of the troubled souls who come to them know precisely what their problem is and how to solve it. What they lack is the will, the motivation. They would rather have a quick fix. Generally, the solution lies in backtracking to where they stepped away from what they knew they were supposed to do. They are experts on it. A counselor need only get them to admit it and get to work.

❦ July 28 ❧

We are ministers all. We each have our own special gifts of ministry to share with those around us.

Ministry is caring for a sick friend or serving food at the community mission even when we are too tired to prepare our own next meal.

Ministry is listening twice as often as we speak.

Ministry is loving our friends and, at the least, forgiving our enemies—letting God do the loving through us in His divine way when we are incapable.

Ministry is clearly calling out the injustices we see around us.

Ministry is seeing and listening as though through a child's eyes and ears.

Ministry is laughing at our own inconsistencies but never laughing at another's.

Ministry is pouring new role models into tired old vessels.

Ministry is catching the vision of a new day and passing it along to the ones who linger, run, stumble, or fly through our paths.

What is your definition of ministry?

If we look around us, we will find a vast mission field with untold numbers of people who could use a little ministry. If we leave the task to others, we will miss out on uncounted blessing and fulfillment, all of which could be laid at the feet of Jesus as an offering.

❧ July 29 ☙

One of the columnists we enjoyed reading when we lived in Chicago was Mike Royko, now with the *Chicago Tribune*. It isn't that we always agreed with him. Many times we didn't. But he is usually humorous and always to the point. You never wonder where he stands.

A few years ago, Royko did a column on the dropout rate in Chicago schools. Everyone was pointing the finger at everyone else, from the superintendent to the board and from the parents to the teachers.

Royko stood with the view of a man named Bernard Epton, whom few outside Chicago would know. He is one of the many otherwise nameless politicians who have tried to win the mayor's race in Chicago. During his unsuccessful campaign, he was surprisingly succinct and candid.

In a meeting of the candidates, a parent stood and asked in a belligerent tone, "If you're elected, what are you going to do about keeping our kids from dropping out of school?"

The question, Royko reports, brought a cheer from others in the crowd. A more conventional candidate would have scanned his mind for a diplomatic and politically astute response, such as the formation of a blue-ribbon task force to study the problem.

But Epton merely said, "Nothing. They are your children. It is your responsibility to keep them from dropping out of school." Unfortunately, this astute man was not elected.

❧ July 30 ☙

Scripture is clear that it is harder for a rich man to enter the Kingdom of heaven than for a camel to go through the eye of a needle. But we are aware of many wealthy people who have their priorities in order and who glorify God with their resources. True, they may have a tougher time with distraction to their spiritual lives, but people through the ages who have honored God with their money are credits to the cause of Christ.

One extremely wealthy silver investor gave over a million dollars to Campus Crusade for Christ, International, just before the silver market went bad.

His response? "I'm glad I gave that money to the Lord's work or else I might have wasted it. I know now it is well invested."

Rich DeVos, co-founder and president of Amway, has three principles of accountability:

1. The more one has, the greater his accountability: "But he who did not know, yet committed things worthy of stripes, shall be beaten with few. For everyone to whom much is given, from him much will be required; and to whom much has been committed, of him they will ask the more" (Luke 12:48).

2. If one is held accountable, he must be given the freedom to make his own choices.

3. Accountability must always include evaluation.

Too many people want independence and think money can bring it to them. But we all serve something. What do you serve, God or money?

❧ July 31 ❧

Married couples should do more than live together. They should love together. Didactic? Oversimplified? Obvious? We haven't always done that. Have you? Why do so few married couples really love each other in word and deed?

Perhaps they have forgotten that physical love in a marriage is something you have to earn and learn over time. Romance and love take time and a setting of priorities.

Perhaps they have forgotten that any part of a relationship that is neglected will weaken. Are both parties avoiding sex or romance? Is it too regulated to a specific day and time? Try variety, serendipity, surprise.

Perhaps they have forgotten what it was like before the kids came along and became the center of the home. We are fine ones to say you shouldn't build your lives around your children when our lives seem entwined with twelve. But we have learned to have a private love life all our own.

Perhaps they have forgotten that all of life involves change and that, like the Christian life, the love life is a series of new beginnings.

Rejoice in the familiar but exult in the newness of your mate. Is he or she looking differently, acting differently, working somewhere else, interested in new things? Celebrate that! Build a new relationship upon it. Soon you will once again be doing more than living together. You'll be loving together.

❧ August 1 ❧

What can be sadder than regret? If people knew how to avoid it, everyone would, wouldn't they? People live with the hunch that they are doing something they shouldn't, or not doing something they should, and they just know they are going to regret it. Sure enough, they do. The problem is, they think the fun or enjoyment or ease of their lives is more important than how they are going to feel later about what they have done.

Take the case of Leo Durocher. Now in his eighties, Leo the Lip looks back on a career as a baseball manager who places sixth on the all-time win list. Many believe he should be in the Hall of Fame. He lives alone in comfort in Palm Springs, California, but he has regrets.

"I've got a lot to make up for," he says. "I threw away some of the best years of my life, ignoring God. Terrible. I was just terrible. I just wish, while I was so busy being a ball player and a manager, that I had remembered the Lord. All the time I used His name in vain. It was vile; it was awful; it was stupid. There was no reason for it. No excuse. A trillion times I did it. Now I'm not perfect, but I'm eighty to ninety percent better than I was."

Here is a man who was one of baseball's immortal greats. He should be able to reminisce about playing with the Gas House Gang, the 1934 St. Louis Cardinals—of whom he is the only one left—and about being a contemporary of Babe Ruth. Yet he looks back with regrets about his relationship with God. A lesson for us.

❧ August 2 ❧

Our friend Waddy Spoelstra—former Detroit sportswriter and the impetus behind the Baseball Chapel program—tells an Andre Thornton story in his *Closer Walk* newsletter. Thornton was the power hitter for the Cleveland Indians who lost his wife and a child in a car crash but still maintained a strong testimony for Christ.

When he was at the peak of his career, a teammate complained that the reason the Indians were not winning was that "we have too many Christians on this team." It is a common criticism that Christians are too meek and mild to be competitive.

"I was having a good year," reflects Thornton, "but the comment was obviously directed at me."

The following year the complaining teammate was traded somewhere else, but when his and Thornton's paths crossed again, he had a surprising bit of news for Andre: "Guess what? My son goes to Fellowship of Christian Athletes meetings at school."

Like Jesus, when Andre was reviled, he didn't strike back. That takes a man. He just kept doing what he knew he was supposed to be doing: speaking out for the Lord, doing his best at his profession, and keeping himself fit to be the best he could be. He set records for the Indians that will stand for decades.

Interestingly, few people would know or remember the name of the teammate who criticized him.

❧ August 3 ❧

Sometimes when people ask us why we have this seeming compulsion to rescue every otherwise homeless kid, we think of a beautiful statement penned by John M. Perkins, the great black founder of the John M. Perkins Foundation for Reconciliation and Development:

> The morning I saw I was a sinner I wept. I wept because I saw that God still loved me.
>
> I grew up without the family's circle of love. I believe that behavior is determined by love. I think it is so important for kids to be wanted. I think part of our situation in the ghettos today has to do with so many babies being born who aren't wanted.
>
> The dignity of the ghetto is crying out. I hear it crying out. I think warped behavior is dignity crying out for affirmation, crying out to be loved. To be loved.

Our kids are of four different nationalities. We have found that the only people who have any trouble with the mix are people outside the family. We don't ignore the diversity. We celebrate it. We are all Williamses, we're brothers and sisters, we're all one family. But we are made up of beautiful individuals who have national heritages and homelands that contribute to the family mosaic.

❧ August 4 ❧

All parents want their children to succeed in school. From Jill's background as an elementary schoolteacher and our active roles in Christian schools, home schooling, and sending

211

our twelve off every day, we have developed some hints for getting the best academic performance out of children:

Create the right environment. Kids should have pleasant, well-lit, well-resourced, and individual places to study. Each needs a spot he knows is his own, where he can store his things, know where they are, and have them available when he is ready to study.

Expect the best. We make it clear to our kids that we expect them to do their schoolwork completely and on time and at the highest level they are capable of. Not all kids are going to be straight-A students, but each can reach his own potential. Often just by expecting it, we see it accomplished.

We try to promote self-worth, which is a wonderful motivator. If a child is secure in our love, in the family, and in the love of God, he knows he is expected to and capable of performing well.

We set rules and stick to them. Chores and schoolwork are done before playtime, before TV, before anything else. We make few exceptions because we want to instill into our kids' minds our own view of the importance of learning and knowing how to think for themselves.

✺§ August 5 ৹✺

Many people give up on devotions because they see them as New Year's resolutions. Once you've missed, you've broken your resolution, and if you fall behind by three or four days, you'll never get back in the groove. That's one of the reasons we set this book up by dates and encouraged you in the preface to not worry about reading every page. Every once in a while you'll find an entry that is continued from the day before. If you happened to miss the day before, you might want to spend an extra minute or two to go back and review.

Unless you are a superspiritual person, you will probably rank with the majority of people who are not setting aside huge blocks of time each day for their devotions. That doesn't have to be a major problem, and before you label us heretics, hear us out.

The key, in our minds, is to decide and mean it that you know all spiritual instruction and training is good for you, whether or not you have been consistent in the past. If you are in the car and a Bible-teaching program comes on, listen to it, think about it, pray about it. You may have heard none of the previous lessons and won't hear the following, but there is still benefit to be gained. Just as with your personal prayer and Bible study, whether you have missed or will miss in the future, there is still rich treasure there today. Forget the quest for perfection and keep coming back to the Word.

❧ August 6 ☙

In his book *You Are the Message* (Doubleday, 1989), Roger Ailes emphasizes the importance of the first seven seconds in our encounters with strangers. Playing off the adage that first impressions are always best, he says we must concentrate on those initial seconds to evaluate the person and know he is evaluating us.

Ailes arranged for an interview with Charles Manson, the celebrated mass murderer. While setting up the room in the prison, he literally bumped into Manson. Ailes said he found him small, wiry, and mangy. They stared at each other, sizing each other up, in effect determining who was going to take control.

Ailes said he was startled at first, then went on the offensive. He told Manson he was in charge of the interview and that he wanted Manson to follow him. There was a subsequent stare from Manson, but then he backed away, lowered his head, and obeyed.

The same signals we catch and deal with in a first meeting are the signals we give off. It is just as important to know how we come off to others as it is to judge from their eyes, their smiles, and their body language just what we are in for.

By learning to judge others preliminarily, we can learn to give off those signals we want to emit to put others at ease, to make them comfortable, and to earn their respect—important things for someone who wants to evidence Christ to others.

❧ August 7 ❧

How does a couple know when their marriage is in trouble? Usually one partner knows right away, as in our case. Jill was really miserable for years but couldn't convince Pat or even get his attention. It took that buildup and its inevitable explosion to knock him off dead center and see that things were awry with us.

Some couples are in trouble and don't realize it until they find themselves irritated with each other, fantasizing about an affair, or confiding in someone else more than in his or her spouse. A certain amount of disagreement is normal and expected, and it is the expressing of each other's viewpoints without the threat of inflicting pain that can make a marriage grow and mature.

But if you find that the quirks and imperfections you used to accept or even chuckle over now make you fly into a rage or be nasty to your spouse, it's time to admit you have a problem. It's time at least for a talk, and it may be time for counseling.

Many couples avoid counseling because they are afraid to admit they have a problem. They don't want anyone on the pastoral staff to know that "Christian leaders" are struggling. Sadly, they put off getting help until it is too late, and then the whole church and seemingly the whole world knows they have split up.

Be on the lookout for danger spots in your marriage. Keep doing the fun, funny, surprising things that drew you so close when you met, and don't put off getting help when you need it.

❧August 8☙

Pat knows what it's like to live with a perfectionist. But Jill is not so bad that she is unhappy all the time and never gives herself a break. That is the profile of the truly pathological perfectionist, and the person who is burdened that way suffers and makes those around him or her suffer.

Are you a perfectionist? You may need counseling. But if yours is the garden variety perfectionism, maybe you just need a few hints at how to go easier on yourself—and others.

First you need to realize that you have never been perfect, so the goal is ludicrous. The only person who was ever perfect was Jesus, and He suffered anyway. You never have been and never will be, so give it up. Don't get lax and sloppy, just cut yourself some slack. Quit putting yourself down. Treat your-self to something nice.

You are somebody of value in this universe. God loves you. Your family loves you. No one expects you to be superman or superwoman. Treat yourself to something you don't feel you deserve (but don't break your budget doing it).

Then forgive somebody. Most perfectionists hold a grudge against someone who truly offended them, and perhaps it is someone who doesn't deserve to be forgiven. Forgive them anyway. That's what unconditional love and true forgiveness are all about. If you are a Christian, you have been forgiven though you don't deserve it. Share the wealth and enjoy life!

⸸§ August 9 ⸷

Need some creative tips to help keep romance alive? Here are a few things that might keep the spark glowing:

If your spouse is going on a trip, put a note in his luggage for every day he will be gone.

Put rose petals or pieces of candy in a trail from the garage or driveway to the door, then across the room to wherever you will be waiting.

Write all the reasons you love your mate on separate cards and either hide them around the house to be discovered by chance or start him or her with a clue under the pillow that leads to each card and more clues.

The next time you are alone and it is storming out, set up a picnic in the house, near the window.

If all the kids are away some weekend, have a cookout just for the two of you.

If you see wildflowers at the side of the road, stop and make a bouquet for him or her right there.

If you are shopping together, excuse yourself and buy a small gift and a card and present it right there in the store.

Do something you haven't done for years. Go on a sleigh ride or a hayride or go tobogganing.

Surprise your sweetheart with an impromptu date at his or her favorite restaurant.

Bottom line: Make it personal and thoughtful.

❧ August 10 ☙

Parenting is a confusing and contradictory thing. We want to love our children and protect them and hold them dear, yet we want to train them to be independent and get along in this world when the time comes for them to leave home.

The problem lies in timing. A child can't simply be shipped off to college at eighteen, never having been out on his own at all. He can't be expected to maintain a budget or a checking account if he has never been allowed to make his own decisions and mistakes.

Some kids are ready for responsibility at younger ages than others. Some twelve-year-olds can baby-sit. You wouldn't dream of suggesting it to others.

Even more important than that are the bedrock values and self-knowledge we want to instill in our children. Our goal should be to emulate Christ and His unconditional love that both cares for us and allows us to go our own way, always ready to take us back.

No one wants to endure the ordeal of a prodigal son, but it's good to know there is a biblical model of parenting in the New Testament for just that kind of eventuality.

Someone has said that a parent's responsibility is to give children both roots and wings. They need the freedom to test their wings and the confidence to know that they can return where they came from.

❦§ August 11 ?❧

Consistent, regular, disciplined prayer is a rare commodity, even among those of us who call ourselves Christians. As we saw earlier from Elisabeth Elliot, prayer is hard work. But there are reasons we should pray.

God wants our fellowship. He wants us to say with the Psalmist, "As the deer pants for the water brooks, So pants my soul for You, O God" (42:1). The Lord Himself says, "Be still, and know that I am God; I will be exalted among the nations, I will be exalted in the earth!" (Psalm 46:10).

We can't grow unless we get to know God better. We have to stay close to the Source. Our pastor and others have told the story of the man who was hired to paint the white stripe down the middle of the road. The first day he painted ten miles, but each day he produced fewer miles, until on the last day of the week he painted just one mile.

His boss called him in and said, "You started so well, but now you're down to a mile a day."

"Well, boss," the man explained, "you have to remember that every day I'm getting farther and farther from the paint bucket."

We can succeed only if we stay close to the Source. When we pray, we find assistance from God. Psalm 34:15 says, "The eyes of the LORD are on the righteous, And His ears are open to their cry." James 5:16 promises that prayer changes things, and 1 Timothy 2:8 says that prayer is God's will for us.

❧ August 12 ☙

The state of education in this country is poor. When you read the results of surveys of high school seniors that show they don't know where Great Britain is on the map or don't know which half of what century World War II occurred in, you begin to wonder what television has done to our kids' reading and writing skills.

No child is too old to be gradually weaned from television. A cold-turkey withdrawal after years of hours-each-day watching might prove traumatic, but the only way to get a kid to read more is to get him to watch less.

Studies have shown that heavy TV watchers do actually suffer some forms of withdrawal when they quit watching. Eventually, however, they begin to be more conversational, play games with the rest of the family, and start to read.

Have you ever noticed that when people have absolutely nothing else to do, they read? If you doubt that, look around on an airplane when the flight attendants are not demonstrating something and the movie screen is blank. Almost everyone will have his face in a book or magazine.

If you want your kids to read more, read more yourself. Kids still catch our values and priorities, and they will mimic us. Kids of any age still enjoy being read to, depending on the title—yes, even high-schoolers. Make books available. We have thousands of books, but it doesn't take that many to get started. There is a whole new world out there between the book covers.

❦ August 13 ❧

Unrealistic expectations are a hazard to any marriage.

We marry, we say, for better or for worse, but we really don't think about the worse part, do we? We expect our spouse to be the same person who put his best foot forward all during the courting days. We don't expect extra pounds or inches, laziness, crabbiness, selfishness, neglect. We expect to live happily ever after.

In short, we expect too much.

One of the most difficult things spouses expect from each other is extrasensory perception. Yes. We want our minds read. If you don't know why I'm upset, I'm not going to tell you. I'm going to sulk, which is going to make it even more difficult for you to have a clue.

Why do we do this to the one person in the world we say we love more than any other? We don't expect neighbors or friends or associates to read our minds. We tell them what we want, what we don't want, what we are thinking about. But not our spouses; they have to have supernatural powers.

We expect our spouses to know what we want for our birthdays or anniversaries. We drop no hints. We simply assume they should know. They love us and have lived with us for so many years, so what's the problem?

The solution, as usual, is the Golden Rule. Expect less and deliver more, and you will both be happier.

❧ August 14 ❧

What are we communicating to children when we tell them they are our top priorities and then shut them out when we are busy? Ask a youngster what is the most important thing in your life after God and Jesus and see what he says. Most often he will say your work or some project or involvement.

That's natural—nothing to be alarmed about. Sometimes, unless we frequently tell them how important they are to us, children can't tell—even when we are logging many hours a day with them.

An effective response to that answer is, "No! You're wrong! You are way more important to me than that!"

They will act surprised and say, "Really?" They might even disagree and want to argue about it. Then you can say, "You want me to prove it. I'll come and play with you right now." Then, of course, do it.

Now, clearly there are times when we should not be interrupted, but choose those moments carefully or you will again be giving a signal opposite of what you intend to communicate—namely, you are most important to me, but not now.

When you must put off attention to a child, do it with a personal chat. On your lap, eye-to-eye. "Sweetheart, help me. I want to play with you, so let's set a time. I'll finish this [row, recipe, page, list], and then we'll play for half an hour. You go get everything set up."

❧ August 15 ❧

The most gratifying letters are those that come from couples who have not only rekindled their love as a result of one of our books but who have also remarried.

We got one such letter from a couple who had divorced in December 1988 and remarried in August 1989. In the meantime they had heard the story of our rekindled love on "Focus on the Family," and Dr. Ed Wheat's *Love Life for Every Married Couple* had been recommended to the husband around the time of the divorce.

The wife writes, "We were both Christians but had not been attending church or leading very godly lives (no wonder we were divorced!)."

After discovering the books and reading them, she says, "We knew God was bringing us back together, but we were sure struggling! Your book gave us some real direction." After the remarriage, she writes, "[we] have been so blessed ever since. Needless to say, our eight-year-old daughter is quite happy.

"To make a long story short, we have committed our lives to the Lord. We thank the Lord for you, your ministries, and especially your family. We hope to adopt one day, as well."

We are grateful to the Lord that He has used our story to help rekindle other marriages, but we have to say the memories are still painful. We came to the brink of a loss of love, and only God could use it to make something beautiful.

❧ August 16 ❧

Except during the darkest period of our marital problems in 1982, the one thing we have never lost is our sense of humor. It was one of the personality traits we appreciated about each other from the beginning. In fact, before we were married, Pat admits he asked Jill to go out with him on a date that required driving some distance and that Jill was his second choice. His first choice couldn't go.

But we started talking and laughing and enjoying each other so much on that drive that Pat felt comfortable. Our lifetime of love really had its beginning then, and it was because of humor.

We still enjoy seeing the humor behind everyday things. Our kids keep us in stitches, and Pat has collected one-liners for years. We seem to be constantly on the lookout for funny situations and conversations.

One that struck Jill particularly funny happened in Denver when we were on a crowded elevator. There was just enough room for a mother and her children when the doors opened. She herded them on, and then, just before the door closed, led them off again. "Come, kids," she said. "I've changed our minds."

At another venue, we saw a Christian woman we knew give up to another woman her place in the line for the ladies' room. The beneficiary looked startled and then grateful.

"Why, thank you," she said with a grin, heading for the door. "Fair is rare!"

❧§ August 17 ॐ❧

You can imagine that as the parents of thirteen kids, we don't cater to people who put down children. Scripture is clear that Jesus loved children and would not allow even His disciples to prevent them from coming to Him.

And the apostle Paul told Timothy, "Let no one despise your youth, but be an example to the believers in word, in conduct, in love, in spirit, in faith, in purity" (1 Timothy 4:12).

It is true that kids can be exasperating. They don't appreciate all we do for them. They take us for granted, and some kids are even mean to their parents, who love them so much. Henry Ward Beecher said, "We never know the love of the parent until we become parents ourselves."

We have heard Dr. Joseph Stowell, president of the Moody Bible Institute of Chicago, point out that many of God's greatest people began their usefulness as teenagers: Samuel, David, and Mary, for example.

Dr. Stowell adds, "As one of our greatest assets, our youth should be encouraged to claim the cause of Christ for their own. When they do, they may lead the church in vision and idealistic zeal."

We just have to remember, as we train them, that teens need guidelines, no matter how much they resist. They are relieved to have parents who care enough to protect them from their own undisciplined impulses.

❧August 18❧

While we are on the subject of teenagers, it is important to remember that problem teens make up a very small percentage of the population, and there is no reason to assume yours are going to be part of it.

If you have had a warm and loving relationship with lots of communication, there is no reason to expect it to change. Kids need slightly different approaches as they get older. You can't hang on so tightly anymore. They need room to make mistakes. They won't want to be seen with you in public as much as you would like to be seen with them. And they respond better to interaction than to ultimatums.

But don't assume that just because they hit a magic age, they will suddenly be incorrigible. They may want and deserve more rope, and you may want to be more careful than ever about the company they keep, but the teen years can be the most fun and rewarding time of parenting.

A common temptation, especially when a child starts sounding self-confident and quotes naive theories of his friends as gospel, is to argue every statement. Don't do it. He will learn without your criticism who is and is not trustworthy.

Biting your tongue and listening will build his self-esteem. Don't gasp, smirk, or make disparaging noises. Just listen. You will be surprised at how many times he'll say, "But that was a dumb idea, wasn't it?" Just ask why and let *him* tell *you*.

❦August 19❧

Everybody has a gimmick. On the old "Honeymooners" show, Ralph Kramden always had a scheme to get rich. There was an invention, an idea, a can't-miss product, a game show, something that would turn his fortunes around and put him on Easy Street.

Of course he always got his comeuppance by the end of the half hour, but his dream, his goal was a mirage that has fooled people for centuries: the idea that he might somehow get something for nothing.

In tabloids you can read about secrets that could make you a millionaire. If you go for that kind of reading, here's an idea: Forget the millions. Read the story and apply the hints and tips to your relationship, even to your faith. You will find these things are interchangeable and can make a lot of sense when the motive is to get along with others rather than to get rich.

For instance, a common tip is to be persistent. The millionaires, they say, hang in there against all odds. See how you can transfer that principle to your marriage or child rearing?

Believe in your dream. Do you have goals for your spouse and children? Keep your eye on the goal and believe in the worthiness of your quest.

Start small and set realistic targets. Be willing to delegate. Do what you enjoy. See? This is easy. May you be a great spouse, parent, and millionaire!

❧August 20❧

We don't often agree with the advice of columnists in the newspapers. Sometimes their advice is earthy and homey and even right on. But other times it seems they have succumbed to the logic of the world and of the times, making their ethics situational and their truth conditional.

But there was an interesting letter to Ann Landers some years ago in which a man spoke of a request his wife of forty years had made. He said she had sometimes asked him to please come home early.

She didn't say this often, he said. It was mostly on weekends and holidays, but for some reason he usually had something else going. He clarified that he spent a lot of time with his wife, but he always thought that request about being home early was unreasonable or frivolous.

He said he had finally figured out why she had said that. She wasn't just lonely; she was lonely for him. How did he know? He lost her. She had died and he had learned firsthand what loneliness is all about.

He said that now that she is gone, he has found the time to come home early, but there is nobody to come home to. All he wants is what his wife always wanted: someone to do the simple things of life with; someone to care; someone to ask how his day went.

Too many of life's lessons are learned too late to put them into practice. Let's be forewarned.

❧ August 21 ❧

Don Wildmon, the television crusader, calls TV the greatest threat to the existence of our society today. "For the first time in history," he is fond of saying, "man has an instrument through which the masses can be taught effectively, immediately, and effortlessly."

That's a scary way to put it but hard to argue with. Think of what our children are being taught. Wildmon says that by the age of twelve, the average American child will have viewed one hundred thousand violent episodes and seen thirteen thousand persons violently killed. Seventy percent of all allusions to sex will be between people who are not married.

Even more insidious are the sexual connotations of most television advertising. It is difficult for us to even justify letting our sports-minded sons watch pro games because it seems every beer commercial is centered on sex. They know alcohol is bad, but what about all the subliminal sexual messages that go along with the commercials?

We can't emphasize enough the importance of parents being in charge of the TV set. It makes a world of difference if

Dad or Mom is there to give the other view of offensive programming. Some commercials and of course much programming needs to be shut off. But don't do it without an explanation. Get kids to talk about why it is wrong and why we don't want to fill our minds with such trash.

❧ August 22 ☙

Television, we are convinced, is one of the major reasons teenagers find it so difficult to say no to premarital sex. Kids all over face tremendous pressure to give in to sexual temptation. Josh McDowell believes that more than half of evangelical Christian youth are sexually active.

It used to be that the teenager who was sexually promiscuous was ostracized or merely gossiped about. The shame of the fifties was that girls who "got in trouble" rarely got help because they were shunned. Now the stigma is on the pure teen.

It's sad, but it's no wonder. Everything else in our society comes with an "instant" label on it. We have fast food, TV dinners, even mail-order merchandise that is shipped the same day. It used to be if you bought a car you would pick it up a few days later. No more. You can go to a dealer with only good credit and drive a brand-new car home an hour later.

So how do we convince kids that putting off sexual gratification until marriage is the only way to go? Be frank. Be honest. Be open. Be specific. Be practical.

Stop thinking of your teenager as a baby. He may be a baby, but he has a grown-up body and he can be in trouble quickly. Start sex education and warnings early. Be positive. Sex is beautiful and right because it is God's idea. It's fun and it's wonderful, but outside of marriage, sex will ruin a kid's life.

❧August 23❧

We enjoy the great preacher Lehman Strauss whenever we get to hear him, which is usually at Word of Life camp. After he suffered a heart attack, he shared the three lessons he had learned in capsule form: Acceptance, Adjustment, and Attitude.

It was amazing and inspiring that a man as old as Dr. Strauss (who has always looked twenty years younger) could accept his physical impairment, adjust to it, and have a great attitude about it—especially when you consider that he had been taking care of his wife, Elsie, since a stroke confined her to a wheelchair years ago.

He likes to compare the Christian life with God's school, "where we matriculate but never graduate until we die." And he calls the difficult times of life "God's waiting room."

Dr. Strauss is never prouder than when he speaks of his two sons, his grandsons, and his great-grandsons. Then he turns to Elsie in her wheelchair and says, "It all started with her. She led me to the Lord in 1927, and the ripples have been going on ever since."

What a privilege it would be if the Lord tarried and we were able to look back on fifty-plus years of Christian living and ministry. To be grandparents and great-grandparents of the offspring of our precious children!

Think of pointing to a spouse with whom it has been your privilege to live and serve for that long! How we want to redeem the time!

❧ August 24 ❧

Sometimes it is interesting to think of Jesus when He was a child. We are sure our kids would like to be able to get away with what He said to His parents when they lost track of Him for three days. First, we would be so relieved that we would embrace our lost child in tears of joy. Then, if the disappearance had been his fault, he would get the lecture of his life.

That's how the incident began in Luke 2:48–51:

> So when they saw Him, they were amazed; and His mother said to Him, "Son, why have You done this to us? Look, Your father and I have sought You anxiously." And He said to them, "Why is it that you sought Me? Did you not know that I must be about My Father's business?"
>
> But they did not understand the statement which He spoke to them. Then He went down with them and came to Nazareth, and was subject to them, but His mother kept all these things in her heart.

There is a wealth of contemporary truth there if we look close enough. Mary was scolding Him. How could you do this to us? And when He answered, they didn't understand Him! Can't every parent identify with that?

Most important, though, is that we get a glimpse of Jesus as a child. We really hear no more about Him until His public ministry begins eighteen years later, but Luke 2:52 carries those four ways in which He grew and became strong: ". . . in wisdom and stature, and in favor with God and men."

❧ August 25 ❧

Edwin Louis Cole, in his Whitaker House book *Maximized Manhood* (1982), says that five sins kept the children of Israel out of Canaan, the promised land, and that the same five sins are keeping modern Christians from fulfilling God's promises to them today.

The first sin he cites from 1 Corinthians 10 is Lust, which he defines as satisfying self at the expense of God and others—gratification of the flesh. Love is of God and is always giving. Lust is selfish and always wants to get.

Next, says Cole, is Idolatry, a value system we create in which we esteem something more worthy of our devotion than God is. Back then it was a golden calf. Today it could be power, prestige, education, money, business, TV.

Fornication. Every kind of sexual sin. Fornication and adultery are popular everywhere except in the Bible. Men still die in the wilderness, never reaching their promised lands.

Tempting Christ. This is demanding that God do something contrary to His will or inconsistent with His character. Cheating in business and expecting God to honor it is an example.

Murmuring. This in its simplest form is nothing more than complaining, criticizing, faultfinding, rumoring. People murmur about their bosses and then wonder why they don't get promoted. They murmur about the preacher and wonder why their kids don't respond to the Gospel.

God wants us in Canaan, becoming all that He intended.

❧ August 26 ❧

Discouragement attacks everyone, even Christians, and yes, even in times of success. There is a "down" that comes after reaching a goal, winning, achieving, just as there is depression when everything seems to go wrong.

An important thing to realize about discouragement— literally "to lose courage"—is that it is internal. It doesn't really depend on circumstances. If it did, victories and highs would eliminate it. But they don't. In fact, sometimes they seem to initiate it.

But discouragement is not affected by circumstance. It begins from within, and so the inner life is the place to focus when you are ready to start rooting out discouragement. Be careful not to merely try to change your circumstances, because discouragement will find you again.

Trust God, not yourself, to provide. The more we count on our own ingenuity and resources, the less we depend on God. That lack of dependence is again an inner-life factor. Our circumstances will shift from day to day, but God is the constant Provider in our lives.

When you are really discouraged, it is a signal that it may be time to withdraw for a while. The last thing you need is more pressure, more activity. Get to a quiet place, away from the pressure, and spend time in prayer and meditation on the Lord. He can and will fill your soul with hope, healing the inner person.

❦§ August 27 ?❧

Firstborn children often suffer from "new parents" disease. Their parents have never been parents of teens before, and it shows. The child may be fifteen or sixteen, but Mom and Dad still feel overprotective and believe they have a right to know what he's doing every minute, even what he's thinking.

Of course we want to know who his friends and influences are and what he is doing with his time when he is not at home. But part of the growing-up and independence-gaining process is having some privacy and some business that is his alone.

He should not be keeping major things from his parents, of course, but if he is badgered and spied on and robbed of any sense of his private self, he will begin doing just that.

If a teen's mail is read, his drawers rummaged through, or his phone calls listened to, he is going to feel persecuted and stressed. Parents can pull rank and say that his business is their business, but the question is, where and when will it stop? Will he be spied upon and monitored until he leaves home? And then what? Will Mom and Dad call him every day for a report? Or will he just explode with his freedom?

Studies have shown that teens who are trusted and have some privacy actually have better attitudes toward their health and suffer fewer illnesses. (From a study by Dr. Lawrence Fisher, professor of medical psychology, University of California at San Francisco.)

❦§ August 28 ?❧

Ashley Montague, American writer and anthropologist, has said, "When men abandon the upbringing of their children to their wives, a loss is suffered by everyone, but most of all by themselves. For what they lose is the possibility of growth in themselves for being human, which the stimulation of bringing up one's children gives."

Fathers truly involved in bringing up their children get in on wonderful experiences that other fathers miss: the first steps, the first words, the hilarious comments. A friend of ours overheard his six-year-old tell an action-figure toy, "You may die in this mission, but if you go to heaven you can ask Jesus for anything you want, and if it's all right with your mom, He'll give it to ya!"

Pat often leads our devotionals when we are at the beach. One Sunday he spoke on what the ant teaches us from Proverbs 6:6–8: "Go to the ant, you sluggard! Consider her ways and be wise, Which, having no captain, Overseer or ruler, Provides her supplies in the summer, And gathers her food in the harvest."

Back home on Monday night, Karyn was in tears because she had forgotten a project for school—ironically, an ant colony. Pat was able to counsel her that if she had used the foresight, organization, and industry of the very ants she was supposed to study, she would have been prepared.

It was a painful but rich parenting opportunity.

❧August 29 ❧

Jill received this beautiful letter from two dear friends late in 1988:

> Dear Jill,
>   Your parents called us last night to tell us of your four new sons.

> God is going to bless Pat and you so greatly for open-
> ing your hearts to all eight of your special [adopted] chil-
> dren.
> I had goose bumps as your parents were telling us. All
> I could think of is that the two of you rescued eight souls
> from a possible eternity of hell. You have not only pro-
> vided them a home here with you, but you have pro-
> vided all of them the opportunity to spend eternity in
> their heavenly home with God.
> We think it's wonderful. Congratulations.

We hate to admit that many, many responses to our increasing
our family by four were not that gracious. Some people acted
as if they were teasing or kidding, but their looks and body
language were clear. They thought we had lost our minds,
were up to something, or just wanted attention.

Well, attention does come from adopting a passel of children, especially ones from other countries. But it is no motivation and the novelty quickly wears off. Letters from people
who don't question our motives constitute true encouragement.

❧ August 30 ❧

In any parenting relationship, it is important that Mom and
Dad balance each other. Often one is quick-tempered with
the children and the other is lenient. Each can learn from the
other, and the balance is good.

Having regular family devotions is an ideal goal, but any
family will tell you that it is not always possible. Don't despair. Gloria Gaither is one who championed the cause of a

life of devotion, so that when one of her kids would exult about a sunset or a flower or an insect, she would seize the opportunity to give praise to God. That way, spiritual things were not compartmentalized for just church and devotions. Life itself was a devotional.

Of course, there is no substitute for time in the Word and prayer, but make spiritual matters natural and a part of everyday living.

Parents who act the same at home as they do in church or anywhere in public rate high praise from their kids. You often hear stories of people yelling and bickering at each other in the car, then walking into church all smiles and superspiritual. That has to have a negative impact on children.

Try to guide by love rather than by criticism. This is hard for most parents to balance, but the Golden Rule applies. Do you recall your own childhood? Were you motivated more by badgering or by encouragement?

❧ August 31 ❧

Kids have different sets of values than parents do, and that's not all bad. Notre Dame basketball coach John MacLeod remembers when he was coaching the Phoenix Suns and had a big lead on New Jersey at home, about eighteen or nineteen points.

"We blew the lead and lost the game, the ultimate failure. I was really upset. After the game our daughter Kathleen— four or five at the time—said, 'Daddy, I'm sorry about your game, but would you read me *Pinocchio* now?' That put everything in perspective right away."

It isn't that kids don't care about our frustrations; they simply don't understand them and can't imagine why they should interrupt the natural flow of life. In other words, the game is over, but *Pinocchio* is still here waiting to be read.

Kids should be protected from most of the turmoil the adult world endures. They will have their share of it one day. They need not know what we really think of many of the adults they know. We may know something about someone's past that would make him or her a less-than-desirable role model. When our kids say, "We just love so-and-so," it isn't necessary for us to tell all.

Kids grow up quickly enough without being drawn into our unique set of frustrations and hassles. They like to think their parents are able to handle anything that comes along, and when it comes to anything that might impact our children, with God's help we can, can't we?

❧ September 1 ❧

We Protestants are sometimes so averse to the deification of Mary—which we agree is unbiblical—that we sometimes don't study her character enough. Divine she was not. Wonderful she certainly was.

Luke 1:26–38 tells the story of how "in the sixth month the angel Gabriel was sent by God to a city of Galilee named Nazareth, to a virgin betrothed to a man whose name was Joseph, of the house of David. . . . And having come in, the angel said to her, 'Rejoice, highly favored one, the Lord is with you; blessed are you among women!' " The angel told her not to be afraid, "for you have found favor with God."

After hearing the monumental news about her bearing the Christ child, Mary said, "Behold the maidservant of the Lord! Let it be to me according to your word."

What we can glean of Mary's character stands as an outline to anyone seeking to find favor with God.

Mary was humble, in essence a nobody. God entrusted the epiphany of epiphanies to an unknown. Apparently you don't have to have rank or privilege to serve the King.

Mary had faith. She trusted God. She asked how it could be, but she didn't doubt God's ability to do it.

Mary was godly, for she found favor in His sight. And she confirmed the Lord's confidence in her when she made the commitment, "Let it be to me according to your word."

September 2

Is it possible that, after all the whining and griping and soul-searching of both men and women in the equal-rights movement, men like assertive women after all? All we heard during the heyday of this campaign was that men liked women "the old-fashioned way," that men were intimidated by women who knew their own minds and were outspoken.

Now a study says that women who are assertive, even women who take the lead in sexual matters, have more fun and more male support than anyone suspected.

Researchers at Texas A&M University found that a lot of men actually complain about women who *don't* tell men what they want.

In another study, a psychologist found that more than half the women surveyed had asked a man for a first date within the previous twelve months. Surprising was the fact that those women with progressive views of women's roles were no more likely to take the initiative than were traditionally minded women.

Contrary to popular belief, men—regardless of their views

on sex roles—are generally pleased when women either ask them out or hint at the idea, according to the study.

Well, of course you have to wonder how many conservative evangelicals were surveyed. We confess we are still a little stunned when teenage girls call our house wanting to talk to our son. Yes, we are more comfortable with the old ways, though these studies show we are becoming more and more a minority.

❧ September 3 ❧

Gary Collins, host of TV's "Hour Magazine," and Mary Ann Mobley, Miss America 1959, have been married more than twenty years. She says they have never argued. He recalls that twice they argued so forcefully, their then five-year-old daughter worried about them.

The first time, daughter Clancy drew a valentine with two stick-figure people in it, Gary and Mary Ann, and wrote, "Please Don't Argue" beneath it.

The second time she pleaded with them, "Please don't get divorced! You're the only parents in my class who aren't divorced!"

They had not been even close to divorce, but that incident made them swear off arguing in front of their children. Mary Ann says they get along so well because they are opposites in personality but alike on the major issues of life: fidelity, commitment, children, and morals.

She says she takes life and herself too seriously and is shorter-tempered with their kids. He is more even and mellow, calm in crises. Neither is jealous of the other's success, and they trust each other implicitly.

Learning to trust one's spouse is a freeing thing. What a burden to wonder if he or she is being faithful whenever you are out of sight! As Mary Ann has said, "Marry someone you trust, and trust them forever!"

❦§ September 4 ॐ❧

There is a major difference between workaholics and people who love their work. The workaholic thinks he loves his work, but in truth it nearly drives him crazy. He doesn't sleep well, rises early, thinks about the job from the moment he wakes up, pours coffee into himself, races to work, and puts in more hours than anyone. When he is finished, he is not really finished but plans the next day on his way home. If he thinks of something work-related when he gets home, he may dictate a letter, phone his own answering machine at the office, or even call a co-worker. This guy's got it bad.

Some people appear to be workaholics but really have chosen overwork because they are afraid of downtime and intimacy, either with Christ or with others. Work becomes a place to hide from the fear of being transparent and the fear of someone getting to know the real person.

They can handle anything task-oriented, but people dealings and personal relationships send them running for cover. They think if they stay busy enough, no one will see their insecurities.

The worst part about workaholism is that it is a joy robber. Pat is a person who puts in a long, busy day, but he loves it! It brings him fulfillment. He does his job as unto the Lord. The workaholic is nervous, moody, uptight, and miserable, but the man who serves God is happy and blessed.

❧ September 5 ☙

The Twenty-third Psalm has been a song of comfort for God's people throughout the ages. Even in this day of war and turmoil throughout the globe and domestic unrest in North America, that great psalm stands as a balm to the weary soul.

This psalm inspires tranquillity and assurance that puzzles the common man, especially in this age.

"The Lord is my shepherd." What a solace! In John 10:29, Jesus implies that only believers can claim to be His sheep: "My Father, who has given them to Me, is greater than all; and no one is able to snatch them out of My Father's hand."

"I shall not want." How final, how absolute! God gives us everything we need. "And my God shall supply all your need according to His riches in glory by Christ Jesus" (Philippians 4:19).

"He restores my soul." How often we need that! He not only forgives but He also restores. This truth alone should keep us from wanting to sin. How much better it is to be in right relationship with Him than to be chastened or disciplined.

"I will fear no evil." How many can say that today? The older we get, the more people we know who walk through a literal valley of the shadow of death, and no person or home is guaranteed safe anymore. But we don't have to fear evil, because even if it destroys us, we will be with Christ in the heavenlies. Praise the Lord for this precious psalm.

❦§ September 6 ❧❧

A major reason marriages fall into trouble is that one or both of the partners forget the wedding vows. Though these most solemn promises are made before man and God, some consider them just part of a ritual, simply some mumbo jumbo religious talk required to get the ceremony finished.

Of course, nothing could be further from the truth. Whether you used the contemporary "I will keep you only unto myself for as long as we both shall live, or until Christ, who has redeemed us by His blood, returns to take us unto Himself forever" or the more traditional ". . . till death do us part," the vow remains. The "only" modifies "you," not "unto myself."

In other words, some people think the phrase about keeping one only unto himself somehow means doing only that, keeping his wife only unto himself, not keeping her anywhere else. In truth, with the emphasis on "only" placed correctly, it means he will keep only his wife unto himself—and no one else.

When a friend, an acquaintance, or a relative defrauds his spouse, it is fair to remind him (or her, of course) that you were at the ceremony. You heard the promise. He can explain it, rationalize it, bad-mouth his spouse, and excuse it all he wants, but the fact is, he broke his promise. He made himself a liar. He is doing precisely what he promised he would not do.

Calling someone on that usually comes too far after the fact to make a difference, but it can still be effective.

❦§ September 7 ᝥ❧

Another part of modern marriage problems lies in the fact that people don't live up to that other most-important and yet seemingly innocuous vow. In most wedding ceremonies, modern or traditional, there is some mention of sticking with one's mate "for better or for worse, for richer for poorer, in sickness and in health. . . ."

Almost anyone will tell you that in every marriage, trouble arises. It might be financial; it might be health; it might be anything. Whatever form it takes, it is a crucible, and it will make or break the couple. You see people go bankrupt, then a year later divorce. You see people lose a child or have a child stricken with some horrible, lifelong debilitating disease. Within a few years, the pressure on the marriage destroys it.

On the other hand, sometimes you see exactly the opposite results. A couple with a tired, boring, plain, mediocre marriage faces a crisis. Their house burns or they lose their business, maybe even a child. They take refuge in each other, one being strong while the other is weak with grief or remorse, then switching roles. They turn to or back to God.

In a strange way, that "worse," that "poorer," that "sickness," brings out the best in them, makes them remember their vows, points them back toward each other. It is sad when people have to learn lessons the hard way, but sometimes that is the only way God can get through to them. Fortunately, sometimes their marriages and their families end up the better for it.

✺§ September 8 ?✺

It is sometimes difficult for spouses to be each other's best friend. We come to this relationship as opposites in so many ways. Of course there are many exceptions, but generally men are practical, physical, logical, used to camouflaging their emotions, and into sports.

Generally, again let us emphasize *generally*, women are impulsive, psychological, feeling-oriented, used to expressing their moods, and not into sports. You can see the potential for conflict here.

The husband gets his marrying thing out of the way, likes to have a pretty wife who handles the house and the kids, and proceeds to live his life the way he always has. He does what he has to do, doesn't do what he doesn't have to do, keeps his feelings to himself, likes to play, and watches sports whenever he gets the chance. His best friend is another guy, and they do lots of guy things together.

His wife is lonely, depressed, eager to express herself, wants him to be romantic, and would like him to be her best friend and stop being gone so much or always sitting in front of the television.

Can this marriage be saved? Frankly, it will take a lot of work and compromise, but just as frankly, it is *very* typical. In fact, if you are representative of the people who wrote us after reading *Rekindled*, you may see yourself in the above paragraphs.

❧ September 9 ❧

[Continued from yesterday.]

The average couple, as outlined yesterday, needs to make a goal of becoming friends; otherwise, the marriage is headed for trouble. The man needs to become more expressive, more romantic, more sensitive, more self-sacrificing. He needs to tell his wife what he is thinking, spend more time with her, do a little more of what she wants to do and a little less of what he wants to do.

She needs to be sensitive to him as well, a little forgiving when he is not all she hoped he would be, understanding of his needs and wants and pleasures, more self-sacrificing. She needs to do a little more of what he wants to do and a little less of what she wants to do.

It's give and take. It's a man learning to go shopping with his wife occasionally. It's a wife learning enough about sports to be able to enjoy watching a game, or part of a game, with her husband.

Beyond that, here are some practical suggestions:

Maintain your memories. Videotape, make movies, shoot pictures and slides, keep albums, make tape recordings, do whatever is necessary to start banking family memories for quick recall and rehearsal. When times are tough, use these mementos to remind each other what a great thing you have going. Show your mate affection every day. *Every* day.

❧ September 10 ❧

What is maturity?

This is a question any spouse, parent, or kid can ask.

Some people say that maturity, at least psychologically, is

the ability to delay gratification. In other words, if you see two children eating cupcakes and one eats the frosting first while the other saves it till last, you can assume the latter is more mature. He has learned to delay gratification rather than immediately do what he wants to do.

Training kids to work before they play, and training ourselves to do the same, is a good exercise in maturity. High school and college kids who run with their friends and enjoy late-night snacks and movies before a cursory once-over of their studies wind up washing out decent academic careers.

You've seen them. You know them. Perhaps you were one of them. You had great intentions. You were going to take a brief nap after dinner and then carve out four or five hours of good study time. Then it seemed even the slightest distraction would lure you.

The kids are going out for burgers or a show or some other form of recreation. First you sacrifice your nap for it, then the first hour of study, then the second. Then you decide you can forego your homework for one night. That pattern continues until you see others making the honor roll, landing good jobs, getting the promotions, having the great marriages.

❧ September 11 ❧

At the Orlando Magic, we circulate a definition of maturity that goes like this: "Maturity is the capacity to face unpleasantness, frustration, discomfort, and defeat without complaint or collapse. The mature person knows he cannot have everything his own way."

You know people who are both bad losers and bad winners. For some reason immature people have the capacity for both. The bad loser leaves in a huff, makes excuses, or expresses his anger. The bad winner crows and brags and says all those things he doesn't want to hear when he loses.

Someone once said, "Show me a good loser and I'll show you a loser."

We disagree. A good loser can be a real winner. A good loser evidences his maturity by acknowledging and even congratulating the winner. He holds his head high, knowing he has done his best and been defeated, at least that day, by a superior or better-trained or better-prepared foe. Sure, it may have been luck, but prepared people and teams create their own luck.

The mature person is the one who does not always have to decide where the group goes or what it does. He or she is the one who is happy to make others happy and who is ready to get back in the game after a setback.

A mature person is to be followed.

❧September 12❧

The Bible has become precious to us over the years. Jill was raised in a family in which the Book was revered, read, and studied. Her family went to church every Sunday and sat under the solid teaching of the Word.

Pat became a Christian as an adult but soon learned what a source of spiritual life and encouragement the Bible could be. He confesses that early in his walk with Christ, he was not into the Bible as much as he should have been, counting on Sunday-school classes and church services to provide his spiritual food. But once he was challenged to get into the Bible in a systematized way and to start memorizing verses, he was sold on it.

In his reading, Pat has discovered what some great men of history have said about the Bible:

John Quincy Adams said, "I have made it a practice to read the Bible through every year. I usually devote to this reading the first hour after I rise every morning."

Daniel Webster said, "If the Bible does not reach every hamlet, then the pages of a corrupt and licentious literature will."

Woodrow Wilson said, "When you have read the Bible, you will know it is God's Word."

Herbert Hoover said, "There is no book so full of concentrated wisdom as the Bible."

❧ September 13 ❧

What great comfort there is in the knowledge that in our God there is no change, neither shadow of turning (James 1:17). The theologian would use the term *immutability* for the unchanging nature of God. We all know of this attribute, but what does it really mean?

It means that His existence will never change. He is the same yesterday, today, and tomorrow.

It means His purposes don't change. Whatsoever He purposes, it shall stand (Isaiah 14:24). When Balaam the prophet prophesied His plan regarding Israel in Numbers 23:19, he said, "God is not a man, that He should lie . . . has He spoken, and will He not make it good?"

Isaiah 40:8 says, "The grass withers, the flower fades, but the word of our God stands forever." His truth never changes.

Why should it be such a comfort that God never changes? Because He is the only Person in our lives of which that is true. Everyone else seems to be in constant motion and change. People who love us one day don't love us the next. People who are responsible and mature one day are irresponsible and immature the next.

Warranties run out just before products wear out. Lifelong loves fade in disappointment and despair. The one thing, the one Person, the one truth we desperately need to cling to and believe in is that the God of our salvation will never, ever change.

❧ September 14 ☙

Is there a way to divorce-proof a marriage? The first prerequisite is, of course, that both spouses must want just that. If only one partner wants divorce insurance, it will fail.

If you both want to follow God's standard, however, there are indeed ways to make it work. Here is what friends, relatives, acquaintances, and even strangers we have met say about how to keep a marriage together:

Work at understanding each other. It's not easy and it's not automatic. And when you think you know someone, you may not *like* him as much as you *love* him. You must remember that you are just as unique and unlovable at your basest.

Allow each other to be individuals. Be best friends, yes, but give each other room, time, and other interests.

Don't keep secrets from each other or hold grudges.

Respect and tolerate each other.

Love, patience, and understanding can heal pain and smooth the rough spots.

Ignore traditional roles. In other words, men, help with the dishes and take out the trash, scrub a floor, change a diaper.

Women, take the car to be repaired, talk to a repairperson. Doing something about changing sexist roles goes both ways.

Be prepared to meet each other more than halfway. That way you will surely go beyond simply reconciling differences. Making up that way can be lots of fun.

❧ September 15 ☙

Sleep deprivation is one of the trendy new maladies that is a serious health and occupational hazard. Because our bodies *will* function on less sleep than we really need, too many of us push ourselves to do more with less.

Unfortunately, it has been shown that sleep deprivation causes long-term health problems, affects people's reflexes, makes us worse drivers (almost as bad as being under the influence of alcohol), and creates job-related danger and un-productivity.

It used to be believed that even a full night's sleep loss could be made up for by simply getting one solid eight or nine hours sleep the next night. That may still be true, unless the person immediately falls into a pattern of fewer hours of sleep than he really needs each night. Few people can function normally on less than seven hours, and most need eight or even close to nine hours.

When you hear people brag that they have gotten by on four or five hours of sleep for years, look at their eyes. Are they old before their time? Should they really be getting twice what they have gotten away with?

When you have been deprived of sleep, eat a good breakfast, don't take a cold shower, do drive with your window open, stick to your regular routine or get back into it as soon as possible, and force yourself to pay attention to people so you will stay alert.

❧September 16❧

We would do well to pursue godliness with the same dedication and devotion some people pour into their vocations or life's callings.

The story is told of John Audubon, the naturalist, who mastered self-discipline to learn all he could about birds. He sacrificed all manner of creature comforts in exchange for succeeding in his efforts. It was not unusual for him to rise at midnight to slog through swamps and observe the habits of nighthawks or other nocturnal birds.

It is said that Audubon could lie still for hours in the damp darkness, night after night for months, and consider his work a success if he gleaned just one more interesting bit of knowledge about a bird.

One summer he reportedly went every day into a Louisiana bayou to watch and study a waterfowl. He stood motionless in nearly stagnant water up to his neck, trying to look like part of the waterscape. He was surrounded by poisonous water moccasins and alligators, but his friends say that in the end he glowed with satisfaction.

"But what of that?" he has been quoted. "I have the picture of the birds."

To him, his work and its success was worth any sacrifice. What a lesson for us who would be like Jesus! How quickly we give up when we are the least bit inconvenienced!

❧ September 17 ☙

Have you ever wondered how any sane, fair person can honestly look at the evidence surrounding the risen Christ and still not believe?

The tomb is empty, despite the fact that the Romans took every precaution to keep the body from being taken. They knew Jesus had said He would rise from the grave, and though they may not have believed He would, they feared His followers would want to make it appear so.

The stone rolled before the opening of the tomb was sealed with the mark of Caesar, and anyone breaking that seal would be executed.

Sixteen Roman legionnaires, each trained to defend eight square feet with short, revolutionary double-edged swords, were assigned to guard the tomb. While on watch, they were motivated to stay awake on the threat of death. Yet when the stone was rolled away and Jesus rose from the dead, some of the soldiers deserted and others agreed to say they had fallen asleep and that the disciples stole the body.

How could all sixteen have slept at the same time? And how could the unarmed disciples have accomplished this feat? Moving the stone alone would have awakened the troops.

There are many other reasons that should convince a skeptic, but none more than the changed lives of believers, sinners saved by grace.

❧ September 18 ☙

Many people take comfort in the fact that children are resilient, that they bounce back from family, marital, and domestic trouble. The problem is, such resilience is not a fact at all.

Dr. Armand Nicholi, psychiatrist at Harvard Medical School and Massachusetts General Hospital, says he has found that emotional development in children is directly related to the presence of a warm, nurturing, sustained, and continuous interaction with both parents. He adds that "anything that interferes with the vital relationship with either parent can have lasting consequences for the child."

In one study, ninety percent of children from divorced parents said they suffered an acute sense of shock, profound grieving, and irrational fears. Fifty percent felt rejected and abandoned, and three years after the divorce, half the children reported their fathers had stopped seeing them at all.

One-third of the children surveyed feared abandonment by the remaining spouse with what researchers called an "overwhelming intensity."

Thirty-seven percent of the children studied were more dissatisfied and unhappy five years after the divorce than they had been eighteen months after.

So much for the resiliency of children, which is known to be a myth by anyone with the ability to remember his own childhood.

❧ September 19 ❧

One of the things Pat resolved to teach our kids, even before we had kids, was that he is not perfect. Too many kids think their parents have never made mistakes, never did anything stupid or rebellious, never struggled with the same types of temptations they face.

Parents have to scold and cajole and lecture and discipline, but we must never forget to remind our kids that we went through the same things they are going through. They somehow assume that because we are the ones who know what is right and wrong and do the enforcing of the rules, we would never have committed such infractions.

How much better to take a child on your knee after a spanking or having been sent to his room and tell him of a similar event from your own childhood. It will surprise the child without question.

"I remember when my mother spanked me for lying," you might begin.

"*You* lied?"

"Yes, I did."

"And you got spanked for it?"

"You bet I did. And I felt terrible about it. I was glad to get punished, because I felt so guilty. Do you know what I mean?"

There will be a nod and then the inevitable question: "What did you lie about?" Our advice? Go ahead and tell.

❧ September 20 ❧

People who think the solution for a troubled marriage is to buy more things, find a new mate, or have more—or fewer— kids have not considered the logic of the Scriptures.

Proverbs 24:3, 4 says, "Through wisdom a house is built, And by understanding it is established; By knowledge the rooms are filled With all precious and pleasant riches."

Theologians and commentators have many different definitions of wisdom, but clearly in this context it means being able to evaluate something or someone with insight. If we study our mates, really probing to their depths, we will have wisdom to know how to communicate with them and love them.

The *understanding* referred to in verse 3 is a trait that will allow us to see daily hassles of the marriage relationship the way God views any trouble in our lives—as something necessary for our development.

Wouldn't it be wonderful to have every room of your home, and thus your marriage, filled by knowledge? Knowledge is learning, education, understanding. Being filled, in the biblical sense, is to be filled to overflowing. What a picture of a happy marriage!

If there is any question about how this can be accomplished, have no second thoughts. It comes from God. Proverbs 2:6 says, "For the LORD gives wisdom; From His mouth come knowledge and understanding."

❧ September 21 ❧

Playing with their children is one of the most neglected duties of most fathers. We suppose this is true of a lot of mothers too, but somehow they usually seem to find time to read to or play with their kids. It's the dads whose playtime seems so limited, and it's the dads the kids want to play with.

Many modern Christian dads have learned this lesson the hard way, and they know enough to drop what they are doing when their children ask if they can play catch or wrestle, or—depending on the age of the children—even play tag or house or dolls. Yes, dolls. A father doesn't have to sacrifice his masculinity to get on the floor with a little girl and pretend with her dolls. In fact, it can be hilarious if he takes the part of the mother and uses a falsetto voice and perhaps imitates his wife. He shouldn't put her down, of course, but some fun teasing can be educational.

When was the last time *you* initiated the idea of playing? You'll knock your kid's socks off. You are reading or relaxing and your child is nearby. Just say, "Hey, let's play catch." Or even, "Let's play tag." Touch him and say, "You're it," and watch his eyes widen as he tries to catch you.

It won't even hurt to break a rule now and then and let him chase you through the kitchen, where no one is supposed to run. Trust us; if it's your idea and it results in something out of the ordinary—a middle-aged man running or playing dolls—it will create an indelible memory.

❧ September 22 ❧

It is not a sissy thing to love people. Part of what makes life wonderful is the chance to do things for your fellowman simply because you love him. It's not easy and it's not always natural, but loving others is imitative of Christ.

Many people, particularly boys, are worried about appearing weak or sissified, even effeminate, if they show care and concern for others. But just as it is not a sign of weakness for a man to be a professing Christian in a secular work environment, there is nothing but strength shown by the man who cares about other people.

There are many in the business world who have achieved great success while hardly even considering God in their lives. Our kids need to know that being a Christian and letting people know it is not a prerequisite to success, and neither is it a guarantee. But to take your faith into the marketplace, to be a bold and unapologetic believer, will result in great peace of mind. You will be a better person for it and able to work better. You will find love for others in your heart and a special calming strength that will make you a better worker. You won't suffer from guilt for not telling people where you stand.

You will also find strength to stand against temptation, because if people know in advance where you stand, that serves as a hedge. You will want to maintain your reputation.

✑ September 23 ✑

Have you ever noticed God's prescription for an effective senior citizen? Titus 2:1, 2 says, "But as for you, speak the things which are proper for sound doctrine: that the older men be sober, reverent, temperate, sound in faith, in love, in patience."

Sober doesn't simply mean not drunk. It means to be awake and alert and ready. What a difference there is between an elderly man who is sprightly and eager to face each new day, ready for the challenges and new learning opportunities, and the one who wants to nap the day away. Now, perhaps the sleeper has a medical problem, but too often older people just give up and give in to fatigue rather than continuing to eat and exercise sensibly so they have the energy to keep producing with vigor.

Reverent is a bit of a misnomer due to modern translation. The apostle Paul, in writing to Titus, actually used a word that means noble or princely. That's a nice word picture. Imagine an elderly person with class and grace, head held high with dignity, not pride. This is the opposite of silliness or senility.

Temperate describes a person who is not given to extremes. How many older folk do you know who think they have seen and heard everything, know what works and what doesn't, and are never wrong. A temperate senior citizen has a good blend of yesterday and tomorrow in his thinking.

Sound describes the kind of a person we want to be—one with a real knowledge of the true doctrines of faith in Christ.

✍§ September 24 ?✍

Perhaps one of the most misunderstood truths from Scripture has to do with giving to the Lord. We want to be generous. We believe in giving. Frankly we have a problem with what some call the Prosperity Gospel, which in its simplest form says that if you give to God, He will give to you.

The problem we see here is that we are to be imitators of Christ, and the Son of Man often had nowhere to lay His head. He gave His all, everything He was and had, for the Kingdom, and yet He did not prosper. He did not live like a king. He did not even die like a king.

Our rewards for giving are not material, not temporal. They are eternal. Notice how the Bible describes what happens when we give with the right spirit and attitude. Luke 6:38 says, "Give, and it will be given to you: good measure, pressed down, shaken together, and running over will be put into your bosom. For with the same measure that you use, it will be measured back to you."

When we invest in the things of this world, we worry about them. We watch them. We want to gauge their value and worth and growth. But when we give to God, we are freed from worry. He will do with our humble offerings what He will, and it is out of our hands. We will not be exalted or made wealthy in material things, but we will receive an eternal return.

Sacrifice is the essence of giving. The widow's mite is an example to anyone who would give less than his all.

✺§ September 25 ?✺

Insecurity is the disease of the nineties. In fact, it has been the psychological disease of the sixties on up to today. What is the cause for this epidemic of lack of self-worth? People are more educated, talented, gifted, creative, and successful than they have ever been.

Because of modern technology and what we have learned about exercise and diet, people are better-looking than they have ever been. We have underachievers, sure, but we have more and more achievers and even overachievers than ever.

So what is it with all this negativity and lack of self-esteem?

The answer of most psychologists, Christian or secular, lies in the home, the upbringing. The old psychiatrist's joke, "You really hate your mother," is no longer funny. Parents have the ability to make or break their children's adult view of their own worth by what they say and do every day. It is an awesome responsibility.

We have already clarified that we believe it is the responsibility of each individual to *respond* to his upbringing, not to simply live under the weight of it. But we parents put tremendous burdens on our children by the way we talk to them, the "truths" we enter into their memory banks. If we tell them they will never amount to a hill of beans, chances are they will believe us. Let's work at planting only positive messages.

❦§ September 26 ὲ❧

Is it possible that our appearance is as important in our marriages as it is in the outside world? We think so. True, we can hang around in our nightclothes and not lose our "jobs" or places in the family, unlike what would happen if we showed up at work that way. But too many people take advantage of what they think is a "right" in their own homes. They may not bathe or dress if they are not going out for a while, knowing their spouses or kids will understand and roll with it.

When husbands and wives get lax in this area, they run the risk of having other members of their sex look more attractive to their spouses. You would be surprised how many people are attracted to others at work, simply because they have never seen those persons at their worst.

That vision at the office doesn't take into consideration that the attractive person is not much to look at in the morning, may have bad breath, body odor, and ugly, tousled hair. Yet that is our competition.

If for no other reason than the Golden Rule, we should look our best as often as possible for our families. That doesn't mean being dressed and slicked-up all the time, but it does mean always being clean and looking pleasant. Our families already have to endure our moods, illnesses, mistakes, and personality quirks. Let's not subject them to unpleasantness that can be avoided.

❧ September 27 ❧

Want some more tips for keeping your spouse happy with you?

Keep the courting days alive. It's amazing how many people stop dating when they have been married awhile. Going out with each other as often as your budget allows is as fun as when you were dating or even engaged.

You still want to put your best foot forward, but you don't have to weigh every act or word. You can relax and have fun, you can flirt and excite each other, and you can simply talk.

Manners are crucial in a marriage. Isn't it easy to quit saying please and thank you and even those social lubricants such as "What do you think . . ." or "If you don't mind. . . ." Just one spouse getting serious about maintaining politeness can make an impact on the whole family.

Always be on time. This is a minor consideration that goes a long way in showing your spouse how much you care. Chronic lateness is a subtle form of selfishness with its roots in a need to control.

Look to balance your partner's moods. Each of you will be short-tempered sometimes. Work at being kind when your mate is upset. When both of you are angry or inconsiderate or sarcastic at the same time, disaster looms.

❧ September 28 ❧

James 1:19 says, "Therefore, my beloved brethren, let every man be swift to hear, slow to speak, slow to wrath." Now there's a verse with a wealth of counsel!

Becoming a better listener takes diligence and hard work.

Turning over a new leaf, deciding, resolving—none of that gets the job done.

The key is to do it. Listen, don't talk. Clamp those teeth together and don't allow a word out of your mouth. But remember, simply keeping quiet does not mean you are listening. How many times have you held your tongue without listening but just waited for the chance to take advantage of the other person's pause for breath? Proverbs 18:13 says, "He who answers a matter before he hears it, It is folly and shame to him."

Resist the urge to counsel immediately. If your spouse or whoever is pouring out his heart to you is pleading for input, consider it prayerfully and carefully. Ask for time to think and pray about it.

Be sensitive and listen to whether the person really wants advice, because usually he doesn't. He wants sympathy or support or just a listening ear. But he may not want your brilliant ideas.

Husbands are particularly prone to want to solve their wives' problems with a "Why don't you just. . . ." In reality, the complainer just wants to know you care.

❧ September 29 ❧

I had walked life's way with an easy tread,
Had followed where comforts and pleasures led.
Until one day in a quiet place
I met the Master face to face.

With station and rank and wealth for my goal,
Much thought for my body but none for my soul,
I had entered to win in life's mad race,

When I met the Master face to face.
    I had built my castles, had reared them high,
Till their tops had pierced the blue of the sky.
I had sworn to rule with an iron mace
Till I met my Master face to face.

    I met Him and knew Him and blushed to see
That His eyes full with sorrow were fixed on me;
And I faltered and fell at His feet that day,
While my castles melted and vanished away.

    Melted and vanished and in their place
Naught else did I see but the Master's face.
And I cried aloud, "O make me meet
To follow the steps of Thy wounded feet."

    My thought is now for the souls of men,
I have lost my life to find it again,
E'er since that day in a quiet place
I met the Master face to face.

Author Unknown

❧ September 30 ☙

Christians are frequently reminded to pray for the lost, but what does that really mean? If we want to be effective prayer warriors, here are a few things we must do:

Come to prayer with a clean heart. If we harbor sin, God will not hear us (Psalms 66:18 and 24:3–5). However, Psalm 34:15 says, "The eyes of the LORD are on the righteous, And His ears are open to their cry."

Pray with faith. In Matthew 21:21 Jesus is quoted, "I say to you, if you have faith and do not doubt, you will not only do what was done to the fig tree, but also if you say to this mountain, 'Be removed and be cast into the sea,' it will be done."

Remember that the worst of sinners can be saved. Some Christians have a problem with this. They forget that the thief on the cross enjoyed a "deathbed" conversion and that his sins were forgiven in an instant. That may not seem fair to people who have lived most of their lives as believers. God is big enough to forgive and save mass murderers, child molesters, even the lowest of the low.

Pray early. Psalm 63:1 says, "O God, You are my God; Early will I seek You; My soul thirsts for You; My flesh longs for You In a dry and thirsty land Where there is no water." Some of the greatest men of the faith were on their knees every day before they saw anyone.

❧ October 1 ☙

With all the speaking Pat does, it is hard for him to remember what it was like to be petrified to stand before a crowd. Psychologists say that speaking in public is the cause for more fear than anything else in our lives.

While some experts advise practicing a speech thirty or forty times so every word seems comfortable to you, speakers like Pat don't have that much time between appearances. If speaking is not your full-time job, you have other responsibilities that make so much rehearsal time impossible.

Still, Pat advises that no one speak off the cuff. It always shows. Without an outline, even in the form of a few words on an index card, most people tend to ramble. Every speech needs a point, and if you are rambling, you may miss it. And if the speaker misses it, it follows that the audience has no chance.

Pat uses a lot of humor, mostly prepared in advance to fit the audience. But he also listens to what has been said before he steps to the microphone so he can play off what has already gone on and show that he is not married to a script. It is good to toss in other jokes that hit you in these settings, because they are usually fresh and appropriate.

Make eye contact with your listeners. Too many speakers look into space or at their notes or even at their hands. They are nervous, but they appear uninterested and distracted. Show the people they have your interest, and you'll have theirs.

❧ October 2 ❧

You never know what will come from a book. We have written several books, and the reaction to each has been different. By far the most response we have received to one title has been to *Rekindled*, but *Twelve-Part Harmony*, the story of our expanded family, has also generated contacts from many people.

Soon after the book was released, The Adoption Centre got a call from twin evangelists, Boyd and Blaine Cornwell. Jill got back to them and they told her they had been so impressed with the story of our kids that they wanted to come and meet them.

You don't often get responses like that, and neither do you blindly approve such a visit. But Jill sensed they were legitimate and sincere, and after a brief visit by phone, she invited them over to meet the kids.

These two single brothers in their late forties hit it off

famously with our brood, and they spent an afternoon entertaining them. The Cornwells sing, so they taught the kids songs, sang with them, and listened while the kids sang to them.

They've been back since and have become friends of our family. It was not the result we expected from doing a book like that, but it sure has been refreshing and fun. Of course we couldn't allow every reader to come over and get to know the family, but we're sure glad we let the Cornwells. It has given the kids a pair of new friends, and it has taught them about reaching out and being hospitable.

❧ October 3 ❧

Did you know that if you read an hour a day, you would probably read a book a week, or more than fifty a year? Doing that, providing that you carefully select your subject matter, will put you light-years ahead of most people, who manage to read only two to three books a year.

Books are a fabulous learning resource. They hold advantages that other media do not possess. You can move through them at your own pace, speed-reading or carefully reading and re-reading every line. Books broaden your horizons, opening your world to new vistas of information from every part of the universe and from every century.

We love and collect books. Our personal library has so many thousands of titles that we had to go through and organize them with the Dewey decimal system. We want our kids to see us reading and to know of our appreciation for books so they will become readers too.

You can pick a subject and read all the latest information

about it, as Pat decided to do some years ago with books on the Civil War, or you can simply compile and schedule books to read on any subject that interests you.

Libraries have become more user-friendly over the years, allowing longer lending times and easily renewing books when necessary. So don't let finances or negative library experiences of the past get in your way. Get into books.

⮲§ October 4 ⮳

While we are on the subject of reading, here are some ideas for getting the most from what you ingest from the printed page:

Read with pen in hand. Educators tell us that we remember twice what we write as compared with what we simply hear or read. Even if you never look at the note again, the fact that you have jotted it will make more of a mark on your memory.

Read with a dictionary nearby. Resist the temptation to pass over words you don't recognize. This is the fastest way we know to increase your vocabulary. Do you know what a *prototype* is? No, it's not a fancy, foot-oriented typewriter. Look it up. Use it in conversation.

Read with memory in mind. Scripture is not the only writing profitable for memorization. If you hit upon a great quote or speech from the past, perhaps even some beautifully written prose or a poem, commit it to memory. Memorization is a study and learning aid that will enhance your powers of concentration and retention.

Join a reading or book club. It's great fun to sit with members of like mind once a week or so and discuss a great piece of literature you are all reading at once. You'll be amazed at the different interpretations and insights that come from each reader. Also, there's nothing like the feeling of camaraderie when someone sees what you see in a specific passage.

❧ October 5 ❧

Parents who are afraid to be too strict for fear of "losing" their children should read the information in a study conducted by Dr. Stanley Coopersmith, associate professor of psychology at the University of California.

He researched more than seventeen hundred middle-class boys and their families, following them from preteen years through early adulthood. Dr. Coopersmith came to some surprising conclusions after distinguishing the high self-esteem men from the low. The high self-esteem boys were more loved and appreciated at home, and they were also from families where the parents were strict and enforced discipline.

The low self-esteem group tended to come from families in which discipline was inconsistent and unfair and made the parents look as if they didn't care. There is a certain dynamic in fair, consistent, enforced discipline that proves to children we truly love them and care about them and that they are important enough to us to keep us involved in their lives.

There must be balance, however. Obviously, a merely strict home will not always turn out well-adjusted kids. The most effective and productive homes in Dr. Coopersmith's study were those where the kids, though carefully monitored by their parents, also felt they had a voice and would be heard democratically in some fair fashion. Treated with love and fairness, these boys flourished as high self-esteem adults.

❧October 6❧

Second Chronicles 16:9 says that "the eyes of the LORD run to and fro throughout the whole earth, to show Himself strong on behalf of those whose heart is loyal to Him." In the New American Standard Bible this verse is rendered, ". . . that He may strongly support those whose heart is completely His."

The great nineteenth-century evangelist Dwight L. Moody once heard Henry Varley say, "The world has yet to see what God could do through a man wholly consecrated to Him."

Moody vowed, "By the grace of God, I'll be that man."

God is still searching for men and women like that. What does He find in your town, in your home, in your heart? Do you drop in to church once or twice a week, go to a Christian concert, read your Bible occasionally, and tell yourself you are sold out to Christ?

Luke 9:23 quotes Jesus, "If anyone desires to come after Me, let him deny himself, and take up his cross daily, and follow Me." In John 8:31 he says, "If you abide in My word, you are My disciples indeed."

Mark says of Jesus, ". . . in the morning, having risen a long while before daylight, He went out and departed to a solitary place; and there He prayed" (Mark 1:35). Is that your practice?

We have a long way to go from our easy evangelical lives to modeling the character of Jesus. God still searches to and fro.

❧October 7❧

Studies show that both a son's and a daughter's most basic feelings about their sexuality are related to their interaction with their father, not their mother. Of course, lots of interaction between kids and *both* parents is crucial to their balanced development, but this generally accepted truth about fathers cannot be ignored.

For years, people on the other side of the homosexual issue have attempted to give the lie to the argument that loving, affectionate, touching, attentive fathers produce heterosexual males while uncaring, aloof, macho, inattentive, and sometimes nonexistent fathers are more likely to produce homosexual males.

We are not in a position to argue the issue of whether homosexuals are born or made (we believe the latter, of course), but more and more studies are showing that homosexual men have a disproportionate history of dysfunctional father figures. They did not get enough physical or verbal love, not enough attention in discipline and playtime, and they grew up missing or resenting their fathers.

How this translates into homosexual mind-sets and practices, we don't know. A wonderfully saved former homosexual told a friend of ours that his reaction to his first homosexual experience was gratitude to his partner, not for the sex but for making him feel cared for, something his father had never been able to accomplish. A lesson for dads.

❧ October 8 ❧

A new technique is allowing husbands and wives to really communicate with each other for the first time in years. It is called "word pictures" and is simply an imitation of much of the way Scripture is portrayed. Jesus used word pictures every time He told a parable.

Rather than just harping on each other or arguing and bickering all the time, spouses can use word pictures to let one another know what is really on their minds.

For instance, if a husband dreads going home after work because his wife is always on his case about some chore he has forgotten or things she needs done around the house, he might normally either retreat and ignore her or he might get into an argument with her.

The wife, on the other hand, might resent the kind of day her husband gets to have. While she is slaving away and trying to keep track of the kids, he's eating business lunches at fancy restaurants, meeting with high-powered people, and making important decisions.

If this couple can get away by themselves and tell each other how they feel in word pictures (i. e., the man says he feels like a whipped puppy after competing all day and coming home to a stern taskmistress, and the wife says she feels as if she and the family are getting what is left of him, leftovers every day) they will begin to really hear—and see—each other.

❧ October 9 ☙

We recently heard a speaker list the ten things bosses hate in their employees, according to a five-year study at Georgia State University. Avoiding these pet peeves might result in your getting that raise you want. Adopting them will surely hold you back.

1. Procrastination.
2. Passing the buck.
3. Saying you know how to do something and then

messing it up. This causes more problems than it solves, even though you are eager to please.

4. Showing no initiative. Bosses can't stand people who do only enough to get by, not putting out a little extra to excel, for example, clerks who stand around waiting for customers to approach.

5. Not delivering. Bosses feel cheated when assignments come back sloppy or unfinished.

6. Incompetence. Trying to fill a job beyond your ability causes problems above and below you.

7. Spreading rumors. Gossip results in dissension and distrust.

8. Going over the boss's head. A sign of overambition.

9. Engaging in too much chitchatting. The workplace is for work, not for socializing.

10. Laziness. A good worker can coast occasionally, but inactivity will drive the boss crazy.

❧ October 10 ❧

God's timing is always perfect.

A couple of our kids were complaining that we were not being fair. When they did something wrong, we made them run. All the kids run every day, but for certain infractions, we add a mile. They were griping. It was unfair enough that we asked each to handle his share of the household chores, but this running for punishment was *really* unfair.

We are grateful to be able to provide our kids a nice, big home on a lake, with a pool, a basketball court, and all kinds of activities. But we feel we would be lax in our responsibilities if we didn't require a certain amount of cooperation and involvement from each child.

But here is where God's timing comes in. We were just going through this trauma of being accused of unfair parenting (though the extra mile is good for their bodies as well as for their behavior) when our daily family devotional was opened to a page on just that subject.

It was entitled, "My Teammate Dropped the Ball and Coach Yelled at Me!" It was based on 1 Peter 2 and was written by Elliot Johnson. Johnson made the point that life isn't fair. Suffering is not brought on by God because He hates us. He has a purpose in it.

Romans 8:29 says, "For whom He foreknew, He also predestined to be conformed to the image of His Son. . . ."

❧ October 11 ❧

Oklahoma businessman Gene Warr developed a list to help people make decisions in questionable matters. It was cited in *Honesty, Morality and Conscience* by Dr. Jerry White, director of The Navigators (NavPress, 1979):

1. Does the Bible say it is wrong? (John 14:21; 1 Samuel 15:22).
2. Will it hurt my body? (1 Corinthians 6:19, 20).
3. Will it hurt my mind? (Philippians 4:8).
4. Will it enslave me? (1 Corinthians 6:12).
5. Is it good stewardship? (1 Corinthians 4:2).
6. Will it glorify God? (1 Corinthians 10:31; Philippians 1:20).

7. Will it profit and edify others? (Hebrews 10:24; 1 Corinthians 10:33).

8. Will it help me to serve? (1 Corinthians 9:19, 10:23, 24).

9. Is it worth imitating? (1 Corinthians 11:1; Philippians 4:9).

10. Will it cause others to stumble? (1 Corinthians 8:9; Romans 14:21).

11. Is it the best? (Philippians 1:9, 10).

If you can answer all those questions positively and still do whatever it is you were wondering about, you should have little trouble living with the decision!

❧ October 12 ❧

One of our favorite radio preachers is Dr. John F. MacArthur, Jr., pastor of the Grace Community Church of the Valley, Panorama City, California. Dr. MacArthur is not only a good speaker and pastor but he is also an outstanding theologian and author of dozens of works.

Dr. MacArthur cites two basic biblical principles that he says state the divine pattern for the family:

First, the family members are to mutually submit to one another, and second, there has to be authority and submission.

He says that in the most famous of all submission verses, Ephesians 5:22 ("Wives, submit to your own husbands, as to the Lord"), the verb *submit* does not appear in the original manuscript. It is only implied. Therefore, Dr. MacArthur believes that Paul was saying everyone—not just the wives—is to practice submission.

In Ephesians 5:25, Paul tells husbands to love their wives as Christ loved the church. In other words, be prepared to die for her, the ultimate act of submission. Paul also tells children to obey their parents; again, submission.

In 1 Corinthians 11:3, Paul writes, "But I want you to know that the head of every man is Christ, the head of woman is man, and the head of Christ is God." The same kind of structure is necessary in marriage.

More on this tomorrow.

❧ October 13 ❧

That Paul says God is the head of Christ has caused confusion for believers for years. Does it mean God is superior to Christ? Dr. MacArthur says no, based on John 10:30, where Jesus says, "I and My Father are one." So, God the Father is the head of Christ in function only, not in essence or nature.

The same is true in the family. The wife, with no loss of dignity, takes the place of submission to the headship of her husband. He is not to subject her. She is to submit herself.

The husband is not to rule over his wife but to love her. A husband's supreme concern should be his wife's holiness and virtue, according to Ephesians 5:26, 27: "That He might sanctify and cleanse it with the washing of water by the word, that He might present it to Himself a glorious church, not having spot or wrinkle or any such thing, but that it should be holy and without blemish."

A husband should care for his wife as he would care for himself, supplying everything she needs, according to Ephesians 5:29, 30: "For no one ever hated his own flesh, but nourishes and cherishes it, just as the Lord does the church. For we are members of His body, of His flesh and of His bones."

Ephesians 5:31 says that "a man shall leave his father and mother and be joined to his wife, and the two shall become one flesh."

Marriage is an unbreakable, indivisible union.

❦ October 14 ❧

Blaise Pascal, seventeenth-century French thinker, mathematician, and scientist, was not only a prodigy in his scientific areas but is also known for having profoundly influenced generations of philosophers and theologians. Consider this insightful observation:

> The Christian religion teaches men these two truths: that there is a God whom men can know, and there is a corruption in their natures which renders them unworthy of Him. It is equally important for man to know both these points; and it is equally dangerous for man to know God without knowing his own wretchedness, and to know his own wretchedness without knowing a redeemer who can free him from it. The knowledge of only one of these points gives rise either to the pride of the philosophers, who have known God and not their own wretchedness, or to the despair of atheists, who know their own wretchedness but not the redeemer.

A friend of ours was challenged by an atheist to "convert to atheism. It will cure all your psychoses and neuroses."

Our friend said, "No. You people don't get enough holidays."

Well, of course there are other than humorous reasons to stay away from atheism. Even agnosticism is more intellectually honest. But as Pascal says, it is crucial for us to know both that there is a God and that we are loved even though we are unworthy.

❧ October 15 ❧

Pat went to speak at a fund-raiser and while there he met the director of the organization. What Pat intended as merely casual small talk resulted in some real insight. He asked the man how things were going.

"Well, frankly, I'm on my way to see my son in a drug rehab center after this meeting."

In the course of the conversation, the man said he and his wife were separated and their family was falling apart.

"What caused it?" Pat asked. "If you had to point to three things, what would they be?"

The man thought for a moment and came up with these reasons:

1. "I was not the disciplinarian. My wife was. After a busy day at work, I didn't want to be bothered with that. I just wanted to sit in front of the TV and relax."

2. "My wife and I were not communicating. We didn't support each other, and we argued in front of the children, which made them the same kind of people we are."

3. "I was a classic 'feeling stuffer.' I stuffed my feelings deep inside, but they wouldn't stay there for long. They were like a volcano, and when I blew, they spewed out."

This was similar to the malady Pat suffered from for years, but we now see the value of getting things out on the table and not letting them bubble beneath the surface, waiting to explode.

❧ October 16 ❧

Ephesians 4:11–15 says:

> He [Christ] Himself gave some to be apostles, some prophets, some evangelists, and some pastors and teachers, for the equipping of the saints for the work of ministry, for the edifying of the body of Christ, till we all come to the unity of the faith and the knowledge of the Son of God, to a perfect man, to the measure of the stature of the fullness of Christ; that we should no longer be children, tossed to and fro and carried about with every wind of doctrine, by the trickery of men, in the cunning craftiness by which they lie in wait to deceive, but, speaking the truth in love, may grow up in all things into Him who is the head. . . .

Jesus calls us to a commitment that should produce in us changes in our attitude, behavior, and character. These changes, of course, should be for the better, resulting in maturity. And how will we know when we are becoming mature?

When we develop self-control, holding our passions and desires in check.

When we are able to control our tempers and can settle differences without violence.

When we evidence patience, willing to pass up immediate pleasure for long-term gain.

When we can face unpleasantness, frustration, discomfort, and defeat without complaint or collapse.

When we are humble and can admit our mistakes.

❧ October 17 ☙

Maturity is also evidenced by the ability to keep from saying, "I told you so."

It is seen in dependability, keeping one's word, coming through crisis. Immature people make excuses. They are the confused, the disorganized. Their lives are a jumble of broken promises, former friends, unfinished business, and good intentions.

The mature person knows that people are unreasonable, illogical, and self-centered and loves them anyway. He knows that if you do good, people will accuse you of selfish motives, but he does good anyway.

He knows that if he is successful he will win false friends and true enemies, but he succeeds anyway. The good he does today will be forgotten tomorrow, but he does good anyway. He knows that honesty and frankness make him vulnerable, but he is honest and frank anyway.

People favor underdogs but follow only top dogs. Fight for some underdogs anyway.

What you spend years building may be destroyed overnight. Build anyway.

People who really need help might attack you if you help them. Help them anyway.

Give the world the best you have, and you may get kicked in the teeth. Give the world your best anyway.

❧§October 18?❧

It seems that almost every day we get some kind of response to our book *Rekindled*, the story of the rebirth of our marriage. Unfortunately, because we have written and spoken on that subject, the general perception is that we have this marriage thing aced out. Nothing could be further from the truth.

We have to work at it and work at it hard every day. We still face issues that become problems, and we are constantly working toward new and better ways of resolving our differences. We are not Mr. and Mrs. Perfect, and though we know more than we ever have and should have more insight than ever on husband-wife relationships, we are still working on ours.

When Bill Bright introduced his wife in public as charming and witty and wonderful and special, Pat got a jab in the ribs. When was the last time he complimented his wife in public?

Come to think of it, when was the last time Pat brought Jill breakfast in bed?

There are major differences in our personalities. If Pat has to drive to Gainesville, he lowers his head, points the car toward that city, and gets there as quickly as is legal and safe. Jill would pack a picnic lunch, notice the cloud formations, and point out the beautiful farm animals to the children.

Now if we have to go to Gainesville together . . . well, you can see we couldn't trade off driving. We're still working on a few things.

❧ October 19 ❧

Herb Score, the great Cleveland Indians pitcher and then broadcaster, says he has carried the following poem, author unknown, since he was in high school. "The meaning to me," he said, "is that we must make the best of the ability God has given us. We have to do the things that are right rather than those that make us look good or popular. When all is said and done and we put our head on the pillow each night, it's just us and God, and we don't fool either one."

The Man in the Glass

When you get what you want in your struggle for self and the world makes you king for a day, just go to the mirror and look at yourself, and see what that man has to say.

For it isn't your father or mother or wife whose judgment upon you must pass. The fellow whose verdict counts most in your life is the one staring back from the glass.

You may be like Jack Horner and chisel a plum and think you're a wonderful guy. But the man in the glass says you're only a bum if you can't look him straight in the eye.

He's the fellow to please—never mind all the rest, for he's with you clear to the end. And you've passed your most dangerous, difficult test if the man in the glass is your friend.

You may fool the whole world down the pathway of years and get pats on the back as you pass. But your final reward will be heartache and tears if you've cheated the man in the glass.

❦§ October 20 ᘒ❧

People who don't have a clue as to who they are or why they are here should take a look at someone who knew the answers to both those questions. The apostle Paul had no doubt of his reason for being.

In Titus 1:1 he describes himself as "Paul, a servant of God and an apostle of Jesus Christ, according to the faith of God's elect and the acknowledgment of the truth which is according to godliness."

He was a servant of God, a slave. Christ was Lord of his life, and when we make Christ Lord of our lives, we become slaves. That sounds negative, but it doesn't have to be. There is great freedom in this kind of bondage.

Dr. Robert A. Cook, former president and now chancellor of The King's College, Briarcliff Manor, New York, used to say, "A slave has no opinions. He gives no orders; he takes orders. He has no plan; somebody plans for him. He has no property; somebody else owns everything that pertains to him. He doesn't have the power even over his life. He has no tomorrows, only today and his master. That's a slave."

If God is the Master, let us willingly be the slaves! The apostles were asked by what power they did their works, and they said, "We are His." When you belong to Jesus, identity is established and you are assured. You have to worry no longer. You belong to Him.

❦§ October 21 ᘒ❧

Someone once told Zig Ziglar, sales motivation expert and author, that a person should go into marriage with his eyes wide-open and stay in the marriage with his eyes half-shut. In other words, make it a point to not notice your mate's faults and peculiarities.

Majoring on your mate's minor faults is like wasting your time at the sideshows and missing the main events at the circus. Too many people spend too much time majoring on the minors. A good rule is to train yourself to think when you are upset.

If your wife lets the inventory run out on one of your favorite snacks, instead of crabbing at her, think. Remember that she has to put up with your dirty socks somehow rarely finding their way to the hamper.

And if your husband leaves drawers or doors open, don't humiliate him by demanding that he come back right this instant and shut them. Just do it. Make a joke about it later. Tease him. Tell him you'll work harder at remembering to keep him supplied with his favorite foods if he'll remember to shut the cupboard door when he's finished rummaging for them. Think. Remember that he puts up with your faults too.

If you are both making this a daily practice, you will be surprised to see the improvements from both sides. It's when we get criticized and harped on that we dig in our heels and stop growing.

❧ October 22 ☙

You would be hard-pressed to find someone who wouldn't admit to wanting to be happy. God wants us to enjoy our salvation, so if we are Christians and not happy, something is wrong.

Of course, happiness is not silliness or giddiness or an insistence on grinning even when tragedy has befallen us. But there is a deep joy in knowing our sins have been forgiven and that our eternal destiny has been assured. So now what? Can we pursue happiness?

Yes.

First, do something to serve someone else. Psychiatrists and psychologists have said that people, even those deep in depression, can rally when they get their minds off themselves and their troubles and start doing for others.

Don't be upset when troubles hit. Job 5:17 says, "Behold, happy is the man whom God corrects; Therefore do not despise the chastening of the Almighty." Hebrews 12:6 adds, "For whom the LORD loves He chastens, And scourges every son whom He receives."

Dwell in the safety of the Lord. Deuteronomy 33:29 says, "Happy are you, O Israel! Who is like you, a people saved by the LORD, The shield of your help And the sword of your majesty! Your enemies shall submit to you, And you shall tread down their high places."

Clearly we are to be happy if for no other reason than that we have been chosen and saved by God.

❧ October 23 ❧

A sign of the times is that some corporations offer their employees insurance coverage for marriage and family counseling. They have learned that an employee who brings his marital or family strife to the office is a less productive worker.

The biggest problem in most families, of course, is a schedule too tightly packed. The healthy family makes time for every member. Husbands and wives may need to schedule their times together. It is not a bad idea to have a time budget, just like a financial budget, to make sure every child in the family gets his fair share of attention.

We have for years been trying to put the lie to the old myth about quality time versus quantity time. Kids need us when they need us, and all the time we spend with them is quality in their eyes. We can't simply see and deal with them only when they fit into our schedules.

Maintain parental authority—and flexibility. We are in charge, but it's all right to ask kids what they feel is a good curfew and what they suggest as a consequence if they violate it. If the suggestion is outlandish, overrule it. If it is acceptable, accept it and see the satisfaction in your child's glowing eyes.

Divide up family responsibilities. This is the only way we can survive, but even normal-size families will strengthen themselves with this approach.

❧ October 24 ❧

Our kids provide some of our lightest moments during the day. Little Michael, our youngest, was pleading for a violin, probably the most difficult instrument to play.

"You've got to learn how to play the piano first," we told him.

Michael said, "I already learned how to do that. Grandma taught me that a long time ago."

Friends of our were teaching their five-year-old daughter about the twelve tribes of Israel. She asked, "Are the Williams a nation? They all have different moms." Well, there *are* twelve of them!

Jill had the kids at Busch Gardens and one of the workers

said, "Ma'am, can I ask you a question? Why do all these kids call you Mom?"

"Because I am."

Pat likes to tell of the clerk at the grocery store who asked, "Are these all your children, or is this a picnic?"

He said, "They're all ours, and believe me, it's no picnic."

❧ October 25 ❧

The Bible has as many dramatic things to say about the tongue as about anything. Proverbs 18:21 says that death and life are in the power of the tongue, and Proverbs 12:18 says that reckless words pierce like "a sword, But the tongue of the wise promotes health."

Positive feedback is a wonderful motivator, a fact not lost on the secular world of business. Some years ago a small book was released called *The One Minute Manager* (Kenneth Blanchard and Spencer Johnson, Morrow, 1982). In short, it advised praising one's subordinates.

It became a best-seller, probably because its advice was biblical, whether or not the author intended it to be. Jesus was One who specialized in positive verbal strokes. He often told people, "Your faith has made you whole."

Even Jesus Himself received praise from His own Father when, upon the occasion of His baptism (Luke 3:22), "the Holy Spirit descended in bodily form like a dove upon Him, and a voice came from heaven which said, 'You are My beloved Son; in You I am well pleased.' "

Experts in this area agree that to be most effective, verbal praise should be quick, pointed, and genuine. It's not enough to tell someone he's doing "a great job." Better to say, "That report you just gave was really educational. I learned from it and liked it. I especially appreciated the statistics on sales, and you did good work."

❦§ October 26 ❧❥

We used to love to listen to the mellifluous voice of the late, great radio Bible teacher J. Vernon McGee.

Dr. McGee once pointed to Philippians 4, where Paul tells of the four essential elements that produce the power for Christian living:

The source—Joy.

The secret—Prayer.

The sanctuary—Thinking upon Christ.

The satisfaction—Living in Christ.

He said that Philippians 4:8 could be labeled the briefest biography of the Lord Jesus Christ in the Scriptures: "Finally, brethren, whatever things are true, whatever things are noble, whatever things are just, whatever things are pure, whatever things are lovely, whatever things are of good report, if there is any virtue and if there is anything praiseworthy—meditate on these things."

Jesus is defined by all the attributes in that verse! If we think or meditate on truth, nobility, justice, purity, loveliness, good report, virtue, and praiseworthiness, we are thinking about Jesus!

Dr. McGee added, in his inimitable way, that Jesus was not only the Truth and told the truth but that He was also the bureau of standards for truth. Dr. McGee said that moments spent in the Bible kept Christians stable in their thinking.

❧ October 27 ❧

One day last year a woman showed up at the offices of the Orlando Magic and demanded to talk to Pat. She had four kids in tow and told the receptionist she—and they—were prepared to sleep in the reception area until he was free to talk to her.

As Pat suspected, she had been a reader of *Rekindled*. "My husband has left me and the kids," she said. "Now what do I do?"

She explained that she had tried to reason with him by phone. She wanted to tell him that she would do anything to get him back. She would change, turn over a new leaf, whatever it took.

Pat breathed a silent prayer for wisdom, knowing it wasn't wise to counsel a woman but assuming that in his office, with his colleagues close by, he could be quick and to the point. He chose to counsel her on the benefits of tough love, as made popular by Dr. James Dobson.

"The more you chase, whine, beg, cry, and plead, the further away you'll drive him," Pat said. "The one who needs the relationship the least controls it. You stay strong, confident, and self-respectful, be winsome, exciting, positive, and pursue your own interests, and you'll find yourself attractive and he'll be curious to know what's happened to you. Tell him he married you of his own free will, and he left of his own will. If and when he wants to come back, it will be his choice. And lose twenty-five pounds."

That last may have hurt, but she left excited and determined.

❧ October 28 ☙

A favorite TV moment for us—and they are rare in a household where TV is under strict control—was the U.S. Olympic hockey gold medal victory over the Soviet Union at Lake Placid in 1980. Al Michaels shouting during the waning seconds, "Do you believe in miracles? Yes!" will go down in sports broadcast history.

But the most touching scene on the ice at the end of that momentous game was goalie Jim Craig scanning the crowd and mouthing, "Where's my father? Where's my father?"

The young man skated around, draped in the American flag, wanting to share this moment of moments with his dad. It was revealed later that his mother had recently died of cancer. This win was for her and for Dad, and he wanted his dad with him to savor it.

What are we saying when we ask where our Father is? Are we asking because we want to share some sweet event with Him or because it seems as if He has abandoned us?

What about when He is searching the hordes for us? Where are we? Where have we been?

Even more than we long for sweet communion with our Heavenly Father, He longs to communicate with us. Our desire is echoed by the Psalmist: "As the deer pants for the water brooks, So pants my soul for You, O God" (Psalm 42:1).

May we never have to hear, as Adam did, our God imploring, "Where are you?" (Genesis 3:9).

❦§ October 29 ?❧

We learned a valuable lesson from the experience of a friend. She had been in a terrible automobile accident and had broken all four limbs. She was in excruciating pain and was healing so slowly that she was deeply depressed.

When people came to visit her, she at first assumed they wanted her to be honest and straightforward about her progress. They would ask how she was feeling or how she was doing or what was her prognosis. She would tell them. "It's very difficult. The pain is horrible, even with the painkillers. It's going to be a long mending process, and I'm exhausted by it already."

Strangely, she noticed that people would literally, physically begin to back away from her. They might still pray with and for her and say encouraging words with a smile. But they moved away, and soon, sooner than she expected, they felt led to leave.

She tried an experiment. The next time someone visited and asked how she was doing, she said, "Great, under the circumstances. I'm going to beat this, with God's help, and I plan to be back in the swing of things as soon as I can."

You guessed it. Her visitor moved closer to the bed. Touched her face. Stayed for a long time.

What a lesson! Same person, same injuries, same prognosis, but evidence of a different attitude. Positivity draws people; negativity pushes them away.

❧ October 30 ❧

We are strong advocates of loving and communicating with kids to help build their sense of family and self-esteem, but there are other elements of child rearing that are just as important.

Kids who become successful are ones who have been encouraged to do their best. They need to be challenged and pushed—with support—into unfamiliar territory. Kids need to learn that mistakes are opportunities for growth and do not threaten the love, approval, and acceptance of their parents. Kids like success, and once they have enjoyed it, they'll be back for more.

It is important to set goals that are reachable, not ones that will discourage and frustrate them. Some kids need to be asked, "Can you do this?" Some need to be told, "You can do it." Learn what motivates your children.

Parents of successful children expect to be respected, then they earn it by respecting their children. It is too easy to fall into the trap of demanding rather than commanding respect. You can say children should respect you because you are older and in authority and are, after all, the parent. But will they really respect you if you listen judgmentally or invade their privacy or put down their emotions?

The toughest and most important thing a parent does for a successful kid is to let him go. Perhaps we'll address that topic in a future book when our oldest has left home. We're not ready yet.

❦ October 31 ❧

Sadly, on this point about trying to raise successful kids, of the parents who responded to an advice columnist's question, "Would you have children again if you had it to do over?" more than half said no. Admittedly, the question begs the wrong answer. Nonetheless, the survey touched a nerve. Parents were frustrated, upset, disappointed. They felt let down by their kids and would not have gone through the hassle had they known in advance.

Maybe when they were raising their kids, these parents should have used this filtering device on their activities:

1. If it's right, enjoy it.
2. If it's wrong, you know what to do. Don't do it.
3. If you don't know whether it's right or wrong, it's probably wrong, so refer to number two.

Those simple, enforced rules might save a lot of parents a lot of grief. They must understand that kids, though they may not even realize it, want limits. They want to be protected from their own sometimes ridiculous impulses.

A visiting foreign dignitary once said, "Never in my travels have I seen *parents* obey their *children* as much as in America."

❦ November 1 ❧

Pat was speaking to a women's group about Dr. Dobson's "red thread" theory: Every child has a red thread running through his personality that will make him a standout at one skill or ability or another.

The women were with Pat, nodding, appearing eager to get home and find the area in each of their kids that would give those children a slight advantage in life.

"Now," Pat said, "get your pencils ready because I'm about to tell you the one special skill you must have in order to find that red thread."

The crowd rustled for scratch paper, pens, and pencils.

"You've got to be able to drive," he said. "Yes, you must be able to drive a car."

He was speaking tongue in cheek only to a point. "If you have the ability to drive back and forth eighty thousand times to dance class, art school, swim meets, play practice, soccer, baseball, basketball, and music lessons, your kid has a chance to discover his red thread."

Pat clarified that not only do all those activities go into helping a child discover his gifts but that the drive time also allows lots of interacting between parent and child. A woman later told Pat that she agreed, but she couldn't get her husband to leave the TV to take her kids on even one trip to an activity. "I'll keep doing it myself," she said.

❧ November 2 ❧

Despite all the activities our kids are involved in—and with twelve, you can imagine something is cooking every day—Jill sometimes worries that as a family, we are really not having enough fun.

Between school and church and athletics and drama and dance, it seems we are simply running here and there, picking up kids, dropping off kids, and watching a plethora of games and performances. Each kid enjoys his or her individual endeavor, of course, but is the family having enough fun together?

Sooooo . . . we looked for ways to have fun that didn't involved competition. One Sunday we left right after church for a wonderful state park where we enjoyed walking tours, streams, woods, a picnic, and hide-and-seek. Three of the kids fell in the water and came up laughing.

The point was that we dropped all other activities, planned and unplanned, and did something together, as a family, that the kids and we could remember. We really did have fun, and the kids still talk about it.

Pat's former pastor and longtime acquaintance, Dr. George Sweeting (former pastor of Moody Memorial Church, then president and now chancellor of the Moody Bible Institute of Chicago), has said that his interaction with his grandchildren is different than with his own sons when they were growing up. "We spend less time driving them places and more time talking with them."

❧ November 3 ❧

Research by The Institute of Athletic Motivation shows eleven attitudes that are vital for success in sports. We were struck by how adaptable these findings are to any endeavor:

1. Desire. Dedicated athletes have a strong desire to improve, to compete, and to win.
2. Aggressiveness. Winners make things happen, thriving on competition.
3. Determination. This is the refusal to quit, the persistence to try and try again.

4. Responsibility. Winners admit errors and will not blame others or make excuses.
5. Leadership. Successful athletes like to influence others and take control of situations.
6. Self-confidence. Winners never doubt their own ability.
7. Emotional control. Top athletes deliver peak performance regardless of the circumstances.
8. Mental toughness. Winners accept strong criticism and rigorous training from demanding coaches.
9. Coachability. Winners respect both the coach and the coaching process, accepting and following advice.
10. Conscientiousness. True stars put the welfare of the team first and don't bend the rules to suit themselves.
11. Trust. Trusting athletes communicate and cooperate better with their teammates and coaches.

❦ November 4 ❧

Because of our personal interest in international adoption, we always look for interesting stories about this exciting endeavor. We recently heard one such story from Dr. Virginia Bailey of Children's Services International, an organization that helped with the arrival of Stephen and Thomas.

Dr. Bailey tells of the World War II orphans from European Russia (and there were many, for twenty million Soviets died in the war), who were evacuated out of the war zone from Moscow to Tashkent in the Uzbek Republic.

When the trains arrived with the children aboard, the people of Tashkent took them into their homes and reared them as their own children.

Every Soviet city remembers World War II with a memorial in a central location. In Tashkent, the people chose to remember the war with a monument honoring the adoption of thousands of children by Uzbek families.

The monument specifically honors the Shamakhmudov family, who adopted fifteen children, as representative of the adopting families. Perhaps the only adoption monument in the world, it stands in a central location in Tashkent on a large square in front of the new concert hall.

We have traveled to many countries and have enjoyed countless tourist attractions and wonders, but we look forward to the day when we can see that inspiring monument.

❧ November 5 ❧

Luke 8:22–24 tells the familiar story of Jesus and the disciples in a storm:

> Now it happened, on a certain day, that He got into a boat with His disciples. And He said to them, "Let us go over to the other side of the lake." And they launched out. But as they sailed He fell asleep. And a windstorm came down on the lake, and they were filling with water, and were in jeopardy. And they came to Him and awoke Him, saying, "Master, Master, we are perishing!"

One night, not long after our twin Koreans, Stephen and Thomas, had joined the family, Pat read them that story from a Bible picture book. The little guys lay wide-eyed in their beds, staring at the pictures and trying to understand Pat's words.

Pat slowed, wondering if they were grasping the story. Then Stephen pointed to the faces of the disciples.

"*Musowo*," he whispered. [Afraid.]

Thomas pointed to Jesus' face.

"*Ana musowo*," he said softly. [Not afraid.]

Pat was thrilled that the message was getting through and happy to read on: "Then He arose and rebuked the wind and the raging of the water. And they ceased, and there was a calm. . . . And they were afraid, and marveled, saying to one another, 'Who can this be? For He commands even the winds and water, and they obey Him!' " (Luke 8:24, 25).

❧ November 6 ☙

Have you ever wondered why God allows pain, trials, even failure in our lives?

According to Scripture, it could be to determine the strength of our faith, or to humble us, lest we think we are stronger than we are. Certainly trials will wean us from worldliness and teach us of heaven's resources, making us set our affections on things above.

Hebrews 12:7–10 says:

> If you endure chastening, God deals with you as with sons; for what son is there whom a father does not chasten? But if you are without chastening, of which all have become partakers, then you are illegitimate and not sons. Furthermore, we have had human fathers who corrected us, and we paid them respect. Shall we not much more

readily be in subjection to the Father of spirits and live? For they indeed for a few days chastened us as seemed best to them, but He for our profit, that we may be partakers of His holiness.

So, God allows trials to chasten us and to develop our endurance. This spurs maturity to greater usefulness. Trials will test the genuineness of our faith and strengthen us to spiritual maturity.

Through trials we are made able to help others in their difficult times. The way we respond can teach us the value of the blessings of God. Psalm 63:3 says, "Because Your lovingkindness is better than life, My lips shall praise You."

❧ November 7 ☙

Here are five ways to turn trouble into triumph:

1. Have a joyful attitude. James 1:2 says, "My brethren, count it all joy when you fall into various trials." That takes determination and forethought, training ourselves to have Spirit-controlled minds.

2. Have an understanding mind. James 1:3 goes on, "Knowing that the testing of your faith produces patience." Testing builds endurance that equips us for even greater service.

3. Have a submissive will. James 1:4 says, "But let patience have its perfect work, that you may be perfect and complete, lacking nothing." In other words, we are not to fight trouble. We are to be grateful. God has a purpose in it for us. Psalm 135:6 says, "Whatever the LORD pleases He does, In heaven and in earth, In the seas and in all deep places."

4. Have a believing heart. James 1:5, 6: "If any of you lacks wisdom, let him ask of God, who gives to all liberally and without reproach, and it will be given to him. But let him ask in faith, with no doubting, for he who doubts is like a wave of the sea driven and tossed by the wind."

5. Have a humble spirit. Trials strip us down to what is really important.

Our true trust must be in eternal riches.

❧ November 8 ☙

The late Ozzie Nelson of "Ozzie and Harriet" TV fame told the story of a little friend of his son David who came to spend a weekend with the Nelsons. Walter was a cute and active kid, and shortly after he arrived, Ozzie, Rick, and Dave were out in the yard with him, throwing around a football.

"You've got a pretty good arm," Walter told Ozzie. "You throw that football pretty well. But you should see my dad throw it."

The next day, at Sunday dinner, Ozzie was carving the meat when Walter spoke up again. "You carve that meat really well, sir," he told Ozzie, smiling. "But not quite as good as my dad does it."

When the visit was over and Walter's mother showed up to drive him home, Ozzie met her at the door. They exchanged pleasantries and he told her what a good boy Walter had been. "I'd sure like to meet your husband," Ozzie said. "He sounds like one great guy!"

"It sounds as if Walter has been talking about his father again," she said, whispering. "He was three when his dad was killed."

That boy had an ideal father inside him, one who could do no wrong but did everything well. In fact, he did everything better than anyone else. How like our relationship with our Heavenly Father! Only for us it's no delusion. It's real.

✺§ November 9 ?✺

We visit Word of Life Camp in Schroon Lake, New York, frequently. We have always been impressed by the legacy of Jack Wyrtzen and his family and staff at that wonderful ministry to the Christian home.

One summer, Pat was talking with musician Don Wyrtzen and Pastor Dave Wyrtzen, two of Jack's sons, and they told him that thirty-two Wyrtzens had returned for a reunion. All thirty-two of them were actively serving the Lord in some capacity.

Pat asked if the sons could list what their parents did to lay a foundation for such a sterling record.

They listed four things:

1. Their father modeled the Christian life before the family.
2. Both parents evidenced the reality of Jesus in their lives each day.
3. The grace of God was—and is still—at work.
4. The Word of God was viewed and used as an anchor in the home.

What a message and what a heritage! While we don't expect all our children to wind up in full-time Christian service—after all, we aren't either—our hope and prayer is that they will love Christ with all their hearts and will want to be active, contributing members of local evangelical churches, eager to share their faith.

❧ November 10 ❧

We hear from a lot of people who say they are not into the Bible because they don't understand it. Frankly, that's not a good excuse anymore. Sure, when all we had to choose from was the King James Version, some might have been able to thumb their noses at that beautiful language and claim it was too much work. But now, with a translation for every taste, there is no excuse for anyone to avoid the Bible.

Only believers can truly understand the Scriptures. First Corinthians 2:11, 14 says, ". . . no one knows the things of God except the Spirit of God. . . . But the natural man does not receive the things of the Spirit of God, for they are foolishness to him; nor can he know them, because they are spiritually discerned."

And the person who would understand the Bible must be diligent and committed. The study of Scripture is hard work, according to 2 Timothy 2:15: "Be diligent to present yourself approved to God, a worker who does not need to be ashamed, rightly dividing the word of truth."

The Bible student must also have a great desire to be holy and righteous, willing to let God purify his life. He must be Spirit-controlled* and come to the Scripture in an attitude of prayer.

*1 John 2:20 says, "But you have an anointing from the Holy One, and you know all things."

❧ November 11 ❦

With two-thirds of our children adoptees (at this writing), we find ourselves especially sensitive to stories of families who take in orphans. One such comes from Gary Smith, whom Pat knew as a Philadelphia sports columnist some years ago.

Smith became a special contributor to *Sports Illustrated*, and his work took him to Bolivia for a story. He had just been married, so he took his wife, Sally, along for a honeymoon. They decided to stay awhile. Smith taught English at an orphanage and Sally worked as a volunteer in the pediatric ward of a local hospital.

One day a six-month-old girl was admitted. Gabriela had been abandoned and had developed many ailments. Sally fed her and worked with her, but otherwise Gabri was pretty much left unattended in a crib. She was listless and seemed to have no curiosity.

After six months, no one had claimed her. The Smiths talked it over and decided, "Let's go for it." When they first brought her home to their one-bedroom apartment, she was fourteen months old and couldn't crawl. Within a couple of weeks she seemed to come alive and her personality burst forth. She became a healthy, happy, smiling child.

❧ November 12 ❦

After being arrested for painting graffiti on Abraham Lincoln's tomb in Springfield, Illinois, five teenagers explained that they had acted out of boredom. The three sixteen-year-old boys and two fifteen-year-old girls also knocked over thirty-three grave markers in Oak Ridge Cemetery, also, they said, because they were bored.

Baby-sitters come early to see the kids, to swim, whatever, because they're bored.

A housecleaner showed up two hours early. She was bored.

An NBA team owner from another city told Pat he was going to get more personally involved with his team, "because I'm bored."

When, a week after school was out, one of our kids asked Jill what there was to do—he was bored—Pat had heard enough. He enrolled one boy in a basketball camp one week and a baseball camp the next and made plans for all the kids for all the remaining weeks of the summer. He told the boys he never wanted to hear "I'm bored!" again.

Jill fought the problem with a family library card. She does not want our children to grow up feeling that we, or anyone else, owe them entertainment. We even offer small incentives for reading a certain number of books.

There still are times when there's "nothing to do." Jill's advice? Do nothing. Whatever happened to just sitting and daydreaming awhile? Everyone needs time for that.

❧November 13 ❧

One cure for boredom we do not allow is television. It is no baby-sitter, and it is not interactive. The mind is not engaged so much as neutralized.

For the thirty-three or so hours a week that the average five-year-old spends in front of the television set, he is deprived of his most important learning tool: the ability to ask questions and receive answers.

TV stimulates antischool and antireading biases in children. It's like a steady diet of educational dessert. Kids can sit and watch other kids their age answer ridiculously easy or meaningless questions (such as pop singers' latest record titles) and win the right to spill goop on someone from the other team.

While books open in children feelings of empathy toward victims, TV so overpowers them with images of violence that it tends to desensitize them.

Television is addictive. Studies have shown that people who try to give up TV cold turkey actually suffer from certain forms of withdrawal: edginess, moodiness, depression, even sadness.

TV commercials may be the most insidious influence on children. Thousands of messages a year indicate to them there is no problem that can't be solved by purchasing a product. This trivializes life and impresses upon a defenseless mind that the answer to life is making enough money to anesthetize yourself from pain.

❦ November 14 ❧

There are all kinds of ways to cut down on television watching. Try whichever of these you think might make sense in your own situation.

Monitor the set. Set a time limit per day or even set a policy of weekends only. Certainly don't allow TV watching before chores and homework are done, and even then never allow someone to watch just for the sake of watching. None of this turning it on to see what is on and flipping through all the channels to find something. Have a plan and a purpose. Yes, you can watch something just for its entertainment value or simply because you think it's funny, but don't get hooked on the next program and the next.

Try a system where family members "buy" TV time by doing certain chores or by reading books.

Limit yourself on the number of TV sets you will allow in the home. None in the bedrooms. In fact, maybe the best set should be in the basement or even the garage, where viewing is not such a pleasure.

Watch with your children so you know what is going on and can counteract any bad morals or philosophy that would otherwise go unchallenged.

If your set needs repair, ignore it for a while. A set that is not easy to watch is more trouble than it is worth. It might be an easy way to start withdrawing for good.

❧ November 15 ☙

In September 1988, Bob played the role of a kid (typecasting!) in a TV spot to help the Orlando Magic sell ten thousand season tickets. He did a backyard basketball scene with a man who played his father.

Later, Pat asked Bob how it went.

"Fine, but it was really hard to be a son with a pretend father."

That was a stark message. The last thing any kid wants is a pretend father. And the last thing any father should want is to be seen as that by his kids.

Bob's teacher challenged him, in front of the whole class, to a push-up contest. Bob was psyched. He loves a challenge, particularly a physical one. Pat has a hard time getting Bob to do a lot of push-ups, but teachers are able to get responses parents can't always get.

Bob immediately dropped to the floor and did seventy push-ups. The teacher did seventy-one.

Bob told Pat later, "I'm going to work and get up to a hundred and then challenge him. Except this time, *I'm* going last."

That reminded Pat of a sit-up contest at the beach where Thomas and two of our other kids competed to see who could do the most. Thomas, who a year before had been unable to do even *1*, won with 520, 170 more than the second-place kid.

❧ November 16 ❧

Would you believe exercise can play a part in ruining a marriage? It had a role in our problems ten years ago.

Exercise can be addictive, just like almost anything else that makes you feel good. Some people who exercise too much actually have low self-esteem and try to make up for it by concentrating for hours on their physical health to keep from dealing with their emotions.

That was not Pat's problem, but the same hassle resulted. Jill felt Pat was on top of his professional, spiritual, and physical life but was neglecting her and the kids. The difficulty was that if he had been addicted to drugs or alcohol, she would have had all the understanding and sympathy she wanted from friends and family. But how do you complain about a husband who is at the top of his profession, memorizes a verse of Scripture a day, studies his Bible an hour a day, and runs several miles?

Experts advise telling your overexercising spouse that you

feel hurt and neglected. In our case, it took a little more drama than a heart-to-heart talk, but the result was the same. Pat learned that a person who runs more than a modest amount each week is running for things other than cardiovascular strength. He changed the priorities in his life, getting his marriage and family where they belonged, and our life hasn't been the same since.

❧ November 17 ❧

One of our favorite people in the world is Dr. J.—Julius Erving—and not simply because he was one of the best players in the history of basketball. Dr. J. is an outstanding Christian and a consummate gentleman. He is one famous man who has never lost his sense of everyone's importance. He has a unique ability to talk to people and make them feel special, as evidenced in this incident:

A man named Larry McFadden and his two sons went to a celebrity gold tournament in Winston-Salem, North Carolina, where the boys spotted Doc. The boys ran to him and the ten-year-old said, "Hey, Dr. J., do you know Larry McFadden?"

As Doc signed autographs for them he thought. He meets so many people. "The name sounds familiar," he said. "I'm not sure."

The kid, thinking so much of his own father that he assumed everyone in the world knew him, said, "Well, we're his boys!"

Doc looked up and noticed their father pointing the camera at him. "Larry McFadden!" he said. "I want my picture taken with Larry McFadden's boys!"

You can bet those boys never forgot that day. Their dad sure hasn't. Contrast that to the way too many superstars feel put-upon by their fans. Sure, there are some excesses, and people should consider stars' privacy and time with their families. But, like Dr. J., stars should realize that making people feel special is a small return for the lives they have been blessed with.

November 18

Sometimes we don't get time to ourselves until well after dark when all the kids are finally in bed.

One night at ten we strolled the neighborhood hand in hand, enjoying the quiet breezes.

As we turned a corner, we saw a woman hunched over a plant, a flashlight in her hand.

Noticing us, she said, "Come over here and see this." We didn't know what to think, but she looked harmless.

In the faint glow of her flashlight, we saw beautiful flowers blooming, coming out of their casings slowly but surely. She said they were called night bloomers. Her husband said the flower blooms one night a year and that's all. It will be "locked up tight as a turkey neck in the morning. The buds will fall off and never bloom again."

That sounded like something that would preach. How many Christians do you know who had a wonderful first love of Christ and blossomed big and beautifully one time? Then the daylight of life intruded, their blossoms fell away, and they were never to be heard from again. At least until next year's revival or evangelistic crusade.

The flowers we saw were indeed beautiful while they

lasted. But who wants to check them every night to see if that is the night they'll bloom? How much lovelier are those flowers—and Christians—that bloom regularly over the long haul.

❧November 19❧

One of the reasons we care so much about the company our kids keep is that we believe no one is morally neutral. They may think they are. They may insist they are. But everyone we meet has the potential to influence us for good or for bad, and we had better learn to be able to tell the difference.

Proverbs 13:20 says, "He who walks with wise men will be wise, But the companion of fools will be destroyed."

For some reason you seldom hear that a good man has influenced bad ones. On a one-to-one basis, yes, we sometimes lead people to Christ. But when it's you against the gang or the group, eventually they hold sway.

Proverbs 1:10 says, "My son, if sinners entice you, Do not consent."

The Proverbs are full of advice about whom to avoid.

Proverbs 20:19 warns, "He who goes about as a talebearer reveals secrets; Therefore do not associate with one who flatters with his lips."

Proverbs 22:24, 25 advises, "Make no friendship with an angry man, And with a furious man do not go, Lest you learn his ways And set a snare for your soul."

Proverbs 29:3 says, "Whoever loves wisdom makes his father rejoice, But a companion of harlots wastes his wealth."

And Pat and Jill Williams say, read Proverbs and choose your friends—and your kids' friends—with godly fear.

❧November 20❧

There is something special about a boy's relationship with his dad. Some kids act totally different around their dads than they do when they are with anyone else. Others evidence no difference. Both can be signs of respect and acceptance.

They say that Shaquille O'Neal, the great young Louisiana State University basketball center (a seven-footer) is as obedient as a private around his father. There's good reason: his dad is a drill sergeant in the army, six feet, five inches tall and 280 pounds.

An LSU teammate says that Shaquille is all yessir/nosir around his dad, "so you can see how he got so tough and disciplined."

When he was in junior high school in Germany—when his father was stationed there—he got into a lot of fights. "I had such a bad temper," Shaquille says, "that I almost got thrown out of school." He adds that his dad eventually cured him of that, wearing him out with a paddle.

Many believed Shaquille O'Neal could have played NBA ball when he was a sophomore in college, and by the time you read this, he may be in the NBA. It will be more than talent that gets him there, because talented collegiate players are a dime a dozen.

It's attitude that an NBA club looks for, someone willing to work hard and be disciplined, someone who was raised well. If he happens to be seven feet tall, so much the better.

❧November 21❧

What a wonderful metaphor we see of Jesus in John 10 when He refers to Himself as the Shepherd of the sheep!

In John 10:4 Jesus says of the shepherd, "And when he brings out his own sheep, he goes before them; and the sheep follow him, for they know his voice." Then Jesus says, in verses 7 and 8, "I am the door of the sheep. All who ever came before Me are thieves and robbers, but the sheep did not hear them."

In verse 11, He adds, "I am the good shepherd. The good shepherd gives His life for the sheep. In verses 14 and 15: "I know My sheep, and am known by My own. As the Father knows Me, even so I know the Father; and I lay down My life for the sheep."

How we wish our children truly knew our voices! We think they do. We know they should. But we still can call the same child four or five times and get no response. When we end up shouting, the child responds as if we have really cut him by hollering.

It is frustrating to call one of your own children, one who should know every nuance of your voice, and get no response. How often do we put God through this parental turmoil? He knows us. He knows our frames and remembers that we are dust, yet we must grieve Him when we don't respond to His voice.

The next time you call for one of your children and you are pretty sure he heard you, think of whether you always answer when your Heavenly Father calls you.

❧ November 22 ☙

You can never hear, see, or read enough tips on having a healthy marriage, so here are a few more:

Try "mirroring" as a listening technique. Nearly every list

of matrimonial tips includes something on communicating better, listening better. Mirroring is a way to accomplish that. When your spouse says he would rather do something different from the usual for your anniversary this year, something other than going out to dinner, for instance, rather than assuming you know what he means, mirror back to him what you thought you heard.

"You mean you'd rather do something a little more exotic, get away, spend a little more?" Because if he does, you are going to remind him of some unpaid bills.

But he says, "No, actually, the opposite. I'd like to just take a walk, have a picnic, and relax that day."

So, he wanted a *cheaper* way to celebrate and was indeed thinking of the budget after all. How much better that you didn't immediately fly into a diatribe about spending, causing him to go on the defensive and get mad.

Another tip is to tell your partner what he or she is doing right. It's easy to make a list of pet peeves and irritations. We've been storing and harboring those for so long, we'd need a legal pad to do them justice. But think now about the other side of the coin. What *is* your mate doing right? Show him your list and be ready to reward him.

❧ November 23 ☙

The difference between our marriage now and ten years ago is obvious and visible to our friends. Here is a paragraph from a letter Pat received from a friend:

> Jill was most delightful and [my wife] was very much impressed with her charm, candor, and, most important,

being real. You've obviously made much progress [since the marriage crisis].

When I arrived at the dinner, my view of Jill was unobstructed. Her eyes, looking at a person across the room—you—told the whole story. They said, "I love, admire, and respect him."

She radiated that message and it was a brief but memorable experience. I congratulate you on earning that look, that love.

May God bless you and Jill as you toil in His vineyard.

There's nothing like knowing that a relationship has been not merely salvaged but also resurrected, born anew. We have clarified before that we are not overconfident and never want to take each other for granted again.

But even that resolve gives us a sense of security about our love and our future. We both know now that it takes work and dedication and commitment. The joy that has returned to our household, our partnership, and our family has made it more than worthwhile to make the effort to fix it with God's help.

❧ November 24 ☙

Maybe the Thanksgiving season is the time to give a gift this year. We know gift-giving is usually reserved for another holiday, but think about it.

Half the world is too hungry today to think about being thankful, let alone to really be thankful. Today more people will go hungry than at any other time in history.

Famous people have commented on the problem. The ancient Roman, Seneca, said, "A hungry people is unreasonable, unjust, and unmerciful."

Albert Einstein said, "An empty stomach is not a good political advisor."

Adlai Stevenson said, "A hungry man is not a free man."

Woodrow Wilson said, "No one can worship God or love his neighbor on an empty stomach."

So can you think of someone to give a gift to on Thanksgiving this year? Is anyone you know hungry? Maybe not, but you know where to find them. Someone from your church, or even a local social agency, can point you in the right direction.

Involve the kids. Give them the experience of seeing grateful, hungry eyes, a smile of appreciation when a meal is delivered. Kids think they are making memories of exciting games or concerts or vacations, but when they have been personally involved in seeing that a less fortunate person is having a better Thanksgiving, they will truly never forget it.

✎§ November 25 ව✎

Save those precious notes your children occasionally write you. The day comes when they stop doing that, and you only hope they will start up again after they have had their own children.

Here's one we received from Karyn when she was eight, complete, unabridged, and uncorrected:

> Dear Mom and Dad,
> I love you very much!!!!!!!
> Dad, keep working hard on that team!!!
> Mom, keep Michael out of trouble!!!
> I'm working hard in school, very hard! I did all my
> English, and I did it very well. I did my math, and I did

it very well. I did my tape booklet, and I did it the best of all! I did my critical thinking very, very well!

Now, back to the note. I'm doing very well on everything. We're making a booklet about spelling, and it's coming along good so far, very good!

Today in jim we did mats and handstands and head stands. All of it was fun. I got to demenstrate the stands.

I did very well in school today, and I had fun. I did all my work dilegently and had fun doing it.

Well, I hope I'm on time today. Yes, I hope!

Well, love you both very much!!!!!

By by,

Love, Karyn

❧ November 26 ❧

We appreciate so much John MacArthur's outline of the basic things the Bible claims for itself. Here's a quick overview of it, as we heard it, to the best of our recollection.

The Bible claims to be:

Inerrant (Proverbs 30:5, 6: "Every word of God is pure; He is a shield to those who put their trust in Him. Do not add to His words, Lest He reprove you, and you be found a liar").

Infallible (Psalm 19:7: "The law of the LORD is perfect, converting the soul; The testimony of the LORD is sure, making wise the simple").

Complete (Revelation 22:19: "And if anyone takes away from the words of the book of this prophecy, God shall take away his part from the Book of Life, from the holy city, and from the things which are written in this book").

Authoritative (Isaiah 1:2: "Hear, O heavens, and give ear, O earth! For the LORD has spoken."

Sufficient (2 Timothy 3:16, 17: "All Scripture is given by inspiration of God, and is profitable for doctrine, for reproof, for correction, for instruction in righteousness, that the man of God may be complete, thoroughly equipped for every good work").

Effective (Isaiah 55:11: "So shall My word be that goes forth from My mouth; It shall not return to Me void, But it shall accomplish what I please, And it shall prosper in the thing for which I sent it").

❧ November 27 ☙

Pat likes to ask the family a question at mealtime and get responses from everyone. His question at breakfast one morning was, "If you could ask God to do one thing for you, what would it be?"

David, our eldest Filipino and quite a baseball player, said, "Beat the Blue Jays tonight."

Our hearts sank. It wasn't going to happen. The Blue Jays had won the first half of the season and were undefeated. The Cards, on which David played, hadn't come close to winning a game.

That night we watched in awe as the Cards did the impossible. They built a small lead and then played better than they ever had before, holding off the Blue Jays to win 4-3.

David was thrilled. "Dad," he said, "I asked God and He did it."

He was excited to know that God was alive and involved in every aspect of our lives.

We don't encourage our kids to ask for athletic victories,

but we do try to teach them to ask God to help them do their best and glorify Him.

But neither do we want to pooh-pooh the work of God in the small areas of our lives. It is not beyond our faith to think that God cared about the outcome of that one game for the sake of those little ball players who had endured a half season of frustration.

❧ November 28 ☙

Our dear friend and brother in Christ Wendell Kempton has paraphrased 1 Corinthians 13:4ff like this:

Love is extraordinarily patient.
Love glories in being kind.
Love is not envious.
Love is not proud.
Love is not ostentatious or showy.
Love doesn't push itself into the limelight.
Love maintains its cool under pressure.
Love is optimistic and looks at people in the best light.
Love never runs upstairs or runs down people.
Love will not and cannot find satisfaction in that which is
    wrong.
Love covers, shelters, and protects its object in all things.
Love searches for what is good and gives the benefit of the
    doubt.
Love is full of expectation.*

*Psalm 34:12: "Who is the man who desires life, And loves many days, that he may see good?"

Love endures through good times and bad.
Love never fails, fades, or falls away.

❧ November 29 ☙

A few years ago, Pat was pleased to get a chance to talk to George Beverly Shea, Billy Graham's great soloist, at an evangelistic crusade in Syracuse.

The singer, who had just turned eighty, seemed to enjoy hearing the story of how Pat felt confirmation of his love for Jill and knew he would marry her, all while Bev Shea sang on the radio, "I'd Rather Have Jesus" (but I'll settle for Jill).

Shea was overwhelmed and mentioned the story later on the platform. He told Pat that he had an older brother, Whitney, eighty-five, in Kissimmee, Florida, whom he called once a week for "wisdom and good counsel."

Pat was impressed that even at his age, Mr. Shea would consult his older brother.

A couple of days later, Stephen and Thomas celebrated their two-year anniversary with our family. At breakfast, Pat asked them to name the number-one thing they liked about being here.

Stephen answered quickly: "That you guys love me."

We hope when our kids are old, if we are still around, they'll still come to us for advice and guidance, and they'll be as good friends of each other as Bev and Whitney Shea were in their eighties.

That is something impossible to legislate and difficult to predict, but we want our kids to be good friends forever.

❧ November 30 ☙

Though we know we must face it soon, it's hard for us to fathom the pain of letting our firstborn go. It won't be long before Jim leaves us for college and whatever else his future holds. He will still be with us between school years and at holidays, of course, but the concept of his living with us full-time will be over.

That's the way it should be. We've seen the pain of adult children coming back to live with their parents. Though it seems handy at the time and the parents are glad to have them back, it never seems to work out for the long term.

Jim knows he will always have a special place in our hearts and will always be welcome in our home. When he comes back to visit as a collegian, he'll be a guest of honor, as he and his family will be for years to come.

When Pat called big-league catcher Bob Boone to congratulate him on having surpassed Al Lopez for catching more games than anyone in history, he reached Bob's wife, Sue. Their son Brett was in his first year at Southern Cal then, and Sue shared her pain at letting him go. Still, she summarized beautifully what we are looking forward to: "As a Christian, my job has been to prepare him for this. It's hard, but I have to let him go. He's in the Lord's hands. And now I just hope the Lord has a Christian girl he's preparing to zap Brett."

❧ December 1 ☙

Since marrying a beauty queen who has always been self-conscious and insecure about her looks (Jill was first runner-up to Miss Illinois in 1972), Pat has been fascinated by how beautiful women feel about their images. If you have always envied the gorgeous people, consider these shocking statements:

Elizabeth Taylor: "I've never thought of myself as beautiful." Donna Mills: "I hate my mouth. It's small and it's crooked." Lauren Hutton: "My nose is uneven." Linda Ronstadt: "I look awful in photographs." Suzanne Somers: "My legs are too thin." Kristy McNichol: "My lips are too fat."

Jane Fonda: "There are days when I feel I should pack it in, that I am a complete fraud, that I don't deserve any of the accolades I've received." Linda Evans: "I'm too big up top and too small down below. I have to be careful what I wear or I look like an upside down pyramid." Valerie Bertinelli: "I get thoughts like, *I used to be pretty, what's going on? I'm not aging well.*"

Chris Evert: "To this day I remember being thirteen and wondering how I could compete with all the beautiful girls without spending five million dollars on plastic surgery." Connie Chung: "I look like a refugee when I get up in the morning." Deborah Norville: "There are people who are far prettier." Vanna White: "There are lots of prettier girls in Hollywood." Dr. Joyce Brothers: "Women tend to think of themselves as less attractive than they are; men view themselves as more attractive."

❧ December 2 ❧

The question of the night at the dinner table once in December 1988 was, "If you could have dinner with anyone in the world, who would you pick?"

Jill chose Roger Whitaker. She loves the singer's voice and how he renders a song, especially, "You Are the Wind Beneath My Wings."

Pat chose Ted Williams, one of the greatest pure hitters in the history of baseball, a star famous when Pat was growing up.

Bob chose Orel Hershiser, the Dodger pitching great who had just come off a season in which he had won twenty-three games, pitched fifty-nine consecutive scoreless innings, been selected MVP of the National League Championship Series and the World Series, and won the Cy Young award.

Jim chose his coach at school. Not a famous man. You wouldn't even know his name. But that showed us the power of authority, teachers, and coaches in a boy's life. Coaches have the power to impact a child more than almost anyone else. They can implant memories that will never fade.

Most important, those memories can be good or bad. Jim happened to respect and admire his coach and would have chosen him as his dinner partner. But coaches can also be bad examples.

People with the unique opportunity to impact kids this way, even as volunteer Little League coaches, should take note.

❧December 3☙

Just as Dr. Joyce Brothers said that men and women have different views of their own attractiveness, so do they differ on their views of love.

For women, experts say intimacy is the most important aspect of true love. They love to make their men feel special.

They tend to want to nurture their lovers. Closeness and compassion are important to them.

For men, sexual arousal is an important part of love, but being tender and expressive when they communicate is difficult. They want to be nurtured and adored, but they see giving and sharing as weaknesses.

Men and women also view commitment differently. Women seem more eager to commit emotionally faster and complain that it seems to take a man forever to make a commitment. Men aren't nearly as afraid of supporting a wife and family as they are of emotional dependency and the pain of ending a relationship.

A woman wants a man to make an early emotional attachment so she won't feel as if she's being used. A man wants to be accepted as a man, to get some indication from a woman that they will eventually be close. Only then will he feel free to become emotionally involved.

The reason so many relationships end early is that men and women come to the encounter with such different views and expectations. Welcome to reality!

❧ December 4 ❧

Pat's question of the day at breakfast a couple of years ago went to ten of the kids and was, "What will you most remember about your father in thirty years?"

Thomas: "Taking me to the field to play baseball."

Michael: "Hugging and kissing me when you put me to bed."

David: "Helping me to play basketball."

Sammy: "Tickling me when you put me to bed."

Andrea: "Giving me hugs."

Stephen: "Taking me to the Doyle Baseball School."

Sarah: "Taking me to swim meets."

Karyn: "Taking me to my dance classes."

Brian: "Taking me to get an ice-cream cone on my birthday."

Peter: "Making me do push-ups."

So much for Dad's spiritual involvement in the kids' lives! In truth, we hope these memories will grow and develop and change over the years as the kids grow up. Peter's push-up memory is probably a negative now, but when he's a big, strong, quick, successful high school, college, or even pro athlete, he'll thank Pat for that prodding.

Like Karyn, one of Pat's memories of *her* will be taking her to dance classes, now five nights a week as she has turned a corner and committed to dance. He'll never forget the sign above the mirrors in the studio that tells chatty little preteen girls: "Shut up and dance!"

❧ December 5 ❧

Singer/songwriter/composer/performer/producer/publisher Bill Gaither is also a big professional basketball aficionado. In fact, it was talking with Bill about booming cities that helped draw Pat to Orlando. Bill has always liked the town and had seen its potential.

Knowing that Bill is a thinker, in a phone conversation with him a couple of years ago, Pat asked him what two things were foremost in his mind right then.

Gaither said first, "We have sung about it, written about it, and spoken it, but now that our kids are grown we can say the

Gospel works in raising kids. It's a tough world out there, but we see that our kids are well-adjusted, not perfect but learning and striving as they should be. Our kids saw how their mom and dad tried to work things out as we thought the Lord wanted us to, trying to keep our priorities straight, being home with them or taking them on the road with us, being back for our own church every Sunday, that kind of thing."

And second, he said, "I believe the decade of the nineties will be the decade of men once again accepting their biblical, God-given roles of leadership in the home, the church, and the community."

Bill is one who believes in the valuable contributions of the women in his family and his work, but he is calling for men to get back into the spiritual picture.

❧ December 6 ❧

Kids say the cutest things.

When Michael was five, he was riding home from church on Jill's lap in the van. He looked into the outside rearview mirror, turned, and whispered to Jill, "Isn't that how Jesus is going to come back?"

"Huh?"

He said, "Watch me." He stared into the mirror for several seconds, then blinked. "Isn't that how Jesus is going to come for us? That fast? In the blinking of an eye?"

That is the same kid who suffered one morning with a sore neck and told his sister, "Karyn, don't sit too close to me. I don't want to give you a stiff neck."

On the one hand, both of those stories are funny, and of

course stiff necks are not contagious. But the stories also show Michael's spiritual and personal sensitivity.

Another of our favorite funny stories is of the time a friend of Karyn joined us for dinner. As usual, Pat had his question for the meal.

He asked, "What do you think you'll be doing exactly fifteen years from right now?"

The kids all thought of their dreamed-for professions: lawyer, scientist, ball player. But Karyn's friend replied, "Fifteen years from right now? I'll probably be eating dinner!"

❧ December 7 ☙

Parents should handle their children's sex education themselves. We are not saying there is anything wrong with a high school class on the biology and physiology of reproduction, but by the time our kids get to that point, we want them to know the basics.

Most important is that they learn sex is beautiful and right and fun and proper and rewarding because it was God's idea. He set it within the context of marriage, and any sexual activity outside of that is also outside His will and leads to chaos.

So many parents are nervous about talking to their kids about this most important aspect of adult life that they often allow them to pick up their information from friends or worse sources. This leads to warped views of men and women and the idea that sex is somehow dirty or sinful and Christians engage in sex only for procreation. There is still the notion in some circles that sex is *the* original sin.

If our kids learn the specifics of the beauty of sex from us, they take into their dating and courtship relationships a much healthier view of it. They will understand the value of waiting and of protecting their and their partner's virginity and how honoring to God it is to enter the marriage bed in purity.

Sex education should be a normal part of living. Questions should be answered as they arise, not only in a secret, private place or a classroom. Kids should know by example, not just by lecture, that sex is a normal, wonderful part of life.

❧ December 8 ☙

While we are on the subject of sex, how about a few tips for adults?

It is important to remember that making love doesn't always mean having sex. There are a lot of ways to make emotional love. Talking to one another, sharing intimate thoughts and moments, is a great way to show love.

To a man, sex is risky business. When he makes an overture to his wife, he is asking for acceptance, and rejection is difficult. Of course, it's his place to begin the process early, not treating his wife like a piece of furniture all day and then expecting her to be an animal in bed. But the wife needs to understand his vulnerability too.

When he has made his approach at the wrong time, it is crucial to word the reaction as a postponement, not a cancellation or a rejection. The wife might even suggest a later day and time so he won't feel he is being rejected.

Variety is the spice of life, but novelty quickly wears off. Always wanting to do something different and unique in the area of sex can insult your partner. If your sex life becomes monotonous, remember and talk about what attracted you to your spouse in the first place.

Taking time for real intimacy will lead to lovemaking that is truly that: more than sex, more than gymnastics, but truly the making and showing of love.

❧ December 9 ☙

During the summer of 1989 we had the unique privilege of having a foreign guest in our home. Thomas is a French student, Jim's age, who fit right in with our family. He and Jimmy got along great, and we tried to do all the touristy things that people come to Orlando for (all the theme parks and attractions).

We couldn't have asked for a better student to match our family and our life-style. Thomas was just wonderful and appreciated all the things we did with him and for him.

We called the French Thomas "T" to differentiate him from our own Thomas. When it was time for us to take T to the airport, we all cried and said how much we would like to do this again.

It was a sad time as we watched T's plane lift off. When we got home, Jill immediately wrote his mother to tell her what a fine son she had and what a great addition he had been to our family that summer. She thanked T's mother for allowing him to come. She told her we loved him and how well he had blended in with our big family and the frenetic pace.

T's mother penned a poignant letter in broken English. One sentence said, "Now I know I do not speak into a desert."

Isn't that how we sometimes feel? We would say we feel as if we are talking to a brick wall. She wondered if she had spoken into a desert until she heard that her son had done just fine.

❧ December 10 ❧

Many otherwise happy marriages run into turmoil during the retirement years. It is a good idea to plan for those unique stresses now.

The toughest times come to those couples who have not spent a lot of time together over the years. They may have been busy with jobs and kids and other responsibilities, and now both are home together for extended periods for the first time.

Routines are interrupted. Maybe one wants to watch one show on TV and the other something else. Maybe one has a habit of meeting friends and now the other feels left out or wants to tag along.

Often one winds up caring for the other physically, which is all part of "for better or for worse, in sickness and in health" but is nonetheless stressful. Too frequently, the wife winds up as nursemaid to her husband, yet she may not be a vision of health either. She may be tired and ill herself, and now she is confined to the home because of him.

These are things best discussed while both partners are still active and healthy. What *will* we do in that situation? Determine who will spell the serving partner so he or she can get some relief.

Also, the best time to get used to being with each other for long stretches is before it is mandatory. Plan more and more vacations together and get to know each other again.

❧ December 11 ❧

Sometimes you get letters from friends that just make you want to scream. A few years ago, Jill got one from an old friend that made her cry. Here are some excerpts:

> My desire is for our marriage to be centered on Christ. Men seem to have a hard time putting God first and their wives second. You can put the books under their noses, but you can't make them read. I wish my husband would study *Love Life* . . . as much as he studies his job. I wish he would study the Bible as much as he studies his job.
>
> Please, if you have time, pray. I sometimes wish I were single again. At least I could go to church and be spiritually fed and sing in the choir. My hubby is a Christian, I have no doubt, but his priorities are way off and he's not willing to put Christ first.
>
> I want so much for him to memorize Scripture and for us to have Bible study together. I want to come and visit you for a while, but he says it is too far. There is no more fun or spontaneity left in my life.
>
> We have moved into a five-bedroom house. But as they say, a house is not a home. The spirit in a relationship is a home.

What a sad letter! Who wants to have all the things in life that people strive for and have an unhappy marriage? This friend will be miserable until her husband rearranges his priorities.

❧ December 12 ❧

Why is it that kids are quicker than adults to forgive?

A few summers ago, when Bob was younger and more sensitive to criticism, Pat was driving him to a 9:00 A.M. baseball practice. Bob also brought along his stuff for a noon soccer match. After baseball practice, he changed into his soccer stuff in the car and discovered a huge knot in the laces of one of his soccer shoes.

As kids will do, he pulled it tighter trying to get it loose, and now he needed Dad's help. It was so lodged that even Pat couldn't free it. Not one for patience with such things, Pat exploded and yelled at Bob for not having his equipment ready in advance, for making the knot worse before asking for help, all that. Bob wound up crying and left the car for the soccer game in his white baseball shoes.

Pat felt terrible and followed him to the field. He called Bob over and apologized for losing his temper. Bob did not respond.

In the game Bob scored his first two goals of the season and played the best game of his life. Afterward, Pat hugged him and told him how proud he was of him.

"Will you forgive me for yelling at you, Bobby?"

Bobby looked at Pat. "Oh, I already did."

That was probably why he was free to play so well. We learned never to be too proud to admit that you are wrong.

❧ December 13 ❧

The differences between men and women are clearly reflected in Pat and Jill. Pat likes events, happenings, attractions, things to do and see. Jill cherishes relationships, quiet moments, romance.

When we spent a romantic weekend in Key West a few years ago, we both had a great time but for different reasons. As we took a walk a week later, reminiscing about it, Jill said, "You know what my favorite thing was?"

Pat is the question man. He loves asking them and tallying the answers. He loves a quiz. He took a shot.

"The sunsets."

"Nope."

"Visiting the Hemingway house."

"Nope."

"The dinners."

"Nope."

"I give up."

"My favorite thing," she said, "was watching the movie together on TV, just lying in bed holding hands."

Pat probably would rather have been on the phone or watching a ball game, but this had been a weekend for Jill. And certainly if he thought he could have provided her a wonderful memory simply by lying in bed, holding her hand, and watching a TV movie, he could have done that at home. (Just kidding.)

❧§ December 14 ?❧

We are nonsmokers and nondrinkers, and not just because we attend a Baptist church. We agree with most evangelicals who say that smoking and drinking are bad for the body and would violate 1 Corinthians 6:19: "Or do you not know that your body is the temple of the Holy Spirit who is in you, whom you have from God, and you are not your own?"

We are not saying, of course, that a person who smokes or drinks cannot be a Christian. Nor are we saying that smoking or drinking are that much worse for the body than gluttony or lack of exercise. But Christians are to be moderate in all things, and there is enough evidence linking alcohol to traffic deaths and domestic violence alone to make anyone a teetotaler.

As for smoking, again, more than enough research has shown the devastating effects of even secondhand smoke on people, especially infants, to make most people want to quit.

We went to a Johnny Mathis concert a few years ago and were standing nearby when he signed an album cover for an adoring fan. He was pleasant and wonderful to her, but after he had written "Best Wishes" and signed his name on the picture that showed him with a cigarette, he circled the cigarette and added with his pen, "Don't smoke."

Whether he had already quit or was simply trying to counteract his bad example, we don't know. But it was impressive that he cared enough to give that warning.

❧ December 15 ❧

Pat and Jim (then thirteen) had an hour's drive from the beach to school, so Pat asked him what his goals were, "say from now until Thanksgiving?"

Not everyone is as organized or as goal-oriented as Pat, and Jim said, "I don't know."

"Okay," Pat said, "let's talk about them and write them down. Start with school. What do you want to accomplish there over the next few months?"

"I want to make the honor roll."

"Write it down. Now what will it take to do that?"

"Thirty more minutes of hard study a day."

"Write it down. What about sports?"

"I want to start on the soccer team. If I jog twenty minutes and sprint ten minutes and do three sets of twenty-five push-ups and one hundred sit-ups every day, I'll make it. To start on the basketball team I need to dribble for twenty minutes a day and shoot for thirty minutes."

"How about spiritually?"

"I want to read my Bible and pray five minutes a day and memorize a verse a week."

He also set goals of earning money for a surfboard by doing jobs and spending five minutes alone each day with a different member of the family.

He seemed enthused to be more organized and know what his goals were.

❧ December 16 ❧

When unheard-of Scott Simpson came out of nowhere to win the 1987 U.S. Open golf championship, the media were not ready for or comfortable with his story. He had won more than a million and a half dollars on the tour in nine years but had never finished higher than a tie for thirteen in a major championship.

Now he had dramatically beaten Tom Watson and was surrounded by pens and microphones that didn't really want to record what he had to say. He gave the glory to God. He believed he could not have won the Open without God's help, and he wasn't about to let the subject rest.

He said he had been cranky and irritable during the days leading up to the Open and had been especially upset with his play at the Westchester Classic the week before, where he had lost his temper.

After a Bible study with fellow Professional Golfers Association members, he decided he would remain calm and in control, regardless what happened in the Open.

"I wasn't concerned with winning or losing," he told reporters. "I am a Christian and that is the most important thing in my life. It really helped when the pressure was on. I was determined to do the best I could do, regardless what happened. I had made a commitment to the Lord not to get angry and do the best I could. It was a real comfort to me. Now my priorities will be the same: God, family, and golf, in that order."

❦ December 17 ❧

It doesn't seem that long ago we were at the beach with eight kids, all going off to do their own things. Jill wept.

Pat said, "Jillo, they're all growing up."

Jill said, "I don't like it. I want some more babies."

We got more babies. Five of them. We don't know when it will stop. We know the need will never end, so there will be troubled children out there somewhere who will need us.

It hasn't been all rosy. Some people are stunned when they find out one of our boys stole some money from Jill's purse, took a little brother and two bikes, and ran away for thirty-one hours. He had threatened the other kids with bodily harm if they told. We had every law-enforcement agency we could think of out looking for them.

When Jill discovered they had left on their own and had not been kidnapped, she was relieved. Angry, but not scared. The older boy was a kid who had lived on his own on the streets. It was a monumentally selfish and stupid thing to run away, but she did not worry about his safety.

His reason? He didn't like having to do chores or run miles when he didn't do them. We know it's hard to understand how a kid could resent a few household chores in exchange for "the good life." But troubled, orphaned kids bring with them the baggage of their former lives. It's all part of the bargain of adopting.

❧December 18❧

We've been reading a lot lately about the Orient and about how its children seem to do so well academically. Part of this is environment and mind-set. As eight of our children are Asian, we like to keep up on what is happening there and what the current thinking is about children from there.

Larry Burkett, noted Christian financial expert, says there are four principles of Japan's success that we need to teach our children:

First is respect for authority. Somehow it seems we have lost that in this country.

Second is the sharing of responsibility. Others first. It is the old adage, "It's amazing how much can be accomplished by someone who doesn't care who gets the credit."

Third is a reward for quality. The Japanese do not reward quantity unless the quality is also there.

Fourth is dedication to society. We are all part of a unit. This is crucial in families, especially large ones.

Other Japanese secrets, according to our reading, include the fact that to Japanese women, child rearing is highly prestigious. The education of the children is their number-one priority.

Something not as admirable about Japanese culture is that the fathers are as bad as ours when it comes to getting involved with their children.

❧December 19❧

When you read the New Testament, you get the distinct impression that Jesus knew of the human tendency to worry and be anxious about the things of our lives. In John 14:1–3,

He actually commands that we not let things bother us so much:

> Let not your heart be troubled; you believe in God, believe also in Me. In My Father's house are many mansions; if it were not so, I would have told you. I go to prepare a place for you. And if I go and prepare a place for you, I will come again and receive you to Myself; that where I am, there you may be also.

When Jesus tells His disciples there are many mansions in His Father's house, it seems He is assuring them there will be room for everyone, so they need not worry about even that.

He also tells them He is not only going to prepare the place but He will also return. Unless we are willing to call God a liar, Jesus is coming again!

Later in that same chapter comes one of the most famous and divisive verses in Christendom, John 14:6: "Jesus said to him, 'I am the way, the truth, and the life. No one comes to the Father except through Me.' "

That verse is divisive because people would like to believe there are a lot of ways to God. But for the Christian, this is another verse of comfort. If our trust is in Him, we have guaranteed our futures with the only real answer ever provided.

❧ December 20 ☙

When Karyn was heavily into gymnastics, we once ran into a U.S. Olympic medalist at Brown's Gym in Orlando. Brandy Johnson had won a medal in Korea as a teenager and then retired from the sport at eighteen.

Karyn was thrilled to meet her, of course, and got an autograph. Pat took the opportunity to find out what her family life was like and what made her tick. He wanted to know the secret to her success.

Brandy told Pat she had grown up in Tallahassee but her family had sent her to Orlando so she could get the coaching she needed for international competition. She and her mother had come by themselves at first, but her father couldn't stand being that far from her most of the time.

Eventually, he quit his career in Tallahassee and found a job in Orlando so the family could be together. That is a true picture of parental sacrifice for the sake of finding and encouraging that red thread in a child's life. A good parent makes sacrifices.

Pat saw the pride and joy in Brandy's eyes when she related that "Daddy just couldn't stand it anymore," and she knew what he couldn't stand was being away from his daughter.

It was probably that kind of love and support that went into making Brandy the athlete she was—one who could concentrate fully on her sport because she was secure at home.

❦ December 21 ❧

Did you know that there are at least six conditions for answered prayer?

First is that the prayer has to be offered in the name of Jesus. In John 16:23, 24 He says, ". . . Most assuredly, I say to you, whatever you ask the Father in My name He will give you. Until now you have asked nothing in My name. Ask, and you will receive, that your joy may be full."

Second, it must always be offered for the glory of God, not

for our own motives. James 4:3 says, "You ask and do not receive, because you ask amiss, that you may spend it on your pleasures."

Third, answered prayer comes from a heart that does not harbor known sin. "If I regard iniquity in my heart, The Lord will not hear" (Psalm 66:18).

Fourth, such prayer is offered from a heart that is both forgiven and forgiving. Mark 11:25 says, "And whenever you stand praying, if you have anything against anyone, forgive him, that your Father in heaven may also forgive you your trespasses."

Fifth, we must always pray with faith. Matthew 21:22 promises, "And all things, whatever you ask in prayer, believing, you will receive."

Sixth, such prayer must be backed up by a life of obedience. First John 3:22 says, "And whatever we ask we receive from Him, because we keep His commandments and do those things that are pleasing in His sight."

❧ December 22 ❧

We have wondered why we lose certain personality traits and character qualities as we get older. Perhaps this is the reason Jesus said we have to become as little children to enter into the Kingdom of heaven.

We know everyone is born in sin and no one is inherently good, but children sometimes have an innocence and others-orientation about them that seems unique to their age.

They seem to have fewer inhibitions about loving people. They seem to need friends, cultivate them, and enjoy them more than adults do. We all need friends, but children are often better at making them than grown-ups are.

Kids have a need to know, which too many adults have lost. Remember when you wanted to drink in everything life had to teach you? Nowadays people learn what they have to and try to make a living. The wonder of learning has been lost on too many of us middle-agers.

Kids are more open-minded than adults. Having an open mind doesn't mean giving up your convictions or even your preferences, but it does mean rethinking prejudices and opening yourself to others' ideas.

Optimism. Aren't kids more optimistic? They truly believe things will get better, things will work out. They bounce back easier from defeat and are not blown away by one loss. We still have a lot to learn from kids.

❧ December 23 ❧

The Williams family loves animals of all kinds. If Jill had her way, she would probably have one—or two—of each kind in the backyard. But we have friendly neighbors and would like to keep it that way.

We love to see animals at the zoo and read about them in books from the library. One fascinating thing we have learned is that wolves mate for life. In the winter the cold makes them form packs, but the rest of the year they separate into family units.

Studies seem to show that the male wolf loves his mate and works and sacrifices along with her to care for the young. Wolf mates are separated only by death.

Fortunately, there are human husbands who are willing to

sacrifice to love their mates. In the Chinese language the character that means *man* and the character that means *woman* are brought together to form a character that means *good*.

They mean what God said when He brought man and woman together for the first time. Genesis 1:31 says that "God saw everything that He had made, and indeed it was very good."

In the view of many people, including us, it is the couple, working together, that makes all the difference. Marriage is the second most important thing to God in creation, so those of us who are married should commit ourselves to staying together and making it the beautiful and wonderful gift God Himself intended it to be.

❧ December 24 ❧

A favorite Christmas story of ours is one that Macel Falwell, Jerry's wife, tells. It centers on the Christmas of 1961.

The Falwells are a close family and always celebrate the holidays together. Mrs. Falwell's parents, two sisters, and brother were all at the Falwell home that year.

Earlier in the year, Macel had asked Jerry what he wanted for Christmas. "I'd really like a baby," he had said.

When the doctor told Macel in September that she was pregnant, she told no one, not even her family. She wanted the announcement to be her gift to Jerry alone on Christmas Day.

After they had opened all their gifts, Macel told Jerry she had another gift for him and called him into the next room. When they were alone, she took both his hands in hers and looked at him lovingly. "Jerry," she said, "we're going to have a baby."

He was so stunned he didn't believe her at first. "Prove it to me!" he said.

She showed him a book on pregnancy. "The doctor gave me this."

He laughed. "You could have bought that. Show me something that really proves it." He wanted it to be true so badly.

Macel found a prescription the doctor had written her for morning sickness. That did the trick and Jerry Falwell stood there with tears rolling down his cheeks. Jerry, Jr., was born the following June, on Father's Day of 1962.

❧ December 25 ❧

Merry Christmas!

And on this day, think of this: Scripture is clear that the second Person of the triune Godhead, Jehovah God, who became Jesus the Christ, was the One who created the world.

Jesus created the animals who stood in the stable near His manger cradle. He created the grass that became the hay. He created man and woman; Joseph and Mary were descendants of Adam and Eve, as we all are.

He created the womb from which He was born. Jesus created the tree from which the wood was taken to make a cross where He would hang for the sins of the world.

So as you celebrate Christmas this year, remember Philippians 2:5–11:

> Let this mind be in you which was also in Christ Jesus,
> who, being in the form of God, did not consider it rob-

bery to be equal with God, but made Himself of no reputation, taking the form of a servant, and coming in the likeness of men. And being found in appearance as a man, He humbled Himself and became obedient to the point of death, even the death of the cross. Therefore God also has highly exalted Him and given Him the name which is above every name, that at the name of Jesus every knee should bow, of those in heaven, and of those on earth, and of those under the earth, and that every tongue should confess that Jesus Christ is Lord, to the glory of God the Father.

❧ December 26 ☙

We are the kind of parents who like to be very involved in our children's education, and we recommend it. We have had good and bad experiences, and we get as involved as we need to, regardless. Once, when we were not happy with the school they were in and couldn't effect changes, we home-schooled our kids for a while until we could find spots in good Christian schools for each of them.

We try to let our kids know from the first day of school each year that their success is important to us. We care enough to get to know the teachers and administrators, and we keep up with each child's progress, homework, and behavior.

One thing we try to avoid is being put in the position of being a pawn, moved back and forth between the teacher and our child. It would be easy for a kid to use parent against teacher, and vice versa, when he knows how much each cares about his progress.

It is not easy, but we like to see our children's work. That's twelve sets of papers every day, but we want to be able to give praise where it is due and help where it is needed. When kids think you have just glanced at the top page and tossed the rest, they wonder—and rightfully so—if you really care what they are doing.

Another important duty for parents of students is to let kids bounce their ideas off you. Be careful not to overreact, because often children will try to shock you with outrageous suggestions. They are just testing the waters.

❧ December 27 ❧

Pat spoke on *Rekindled* at a management club in Cocoa Beach a few years ago. Afterward, a mother with a young son and a teenage daughter approached him. The mother's marriage had failed, she said, but she wanted to apply the right principles—the Bless, Edify, Share, and Touch therapy—to her children.

Pat encouraged her and promised to pray for her, noticing that the daughter was in tears. She was not in a mood to say why, but Pat could only assume that our story had spawned in her memories of how her parents had once been or at least how she always wished they would be. She had to have been longing for a real family with a dad at home.

Contrast that to the father who told Jill that because he travels a lot, he has made it a practice to call his wife when he gets to the airport. She can tell him of any crisis or happening at home so he can think about it during his drive time and is able to deal with it in wisdom when he arrives. That way he's not hit with problems as soon as he walks in and is careful not to try to apply a quick fix or fly off the handle.

Outside a church in Orlando we saw a sign that said, "The Opposite of Love Is Indifference."

Ask ten people on the street to tell you the opposite of love, and they'll say "hate." But anyone who has been in a bad marriage where a spouse moved from struggling to indifference knows the truth of the statement on the church sign.

❦ December 28 ❧

Dr. James Dobson has always said there are two most important messages that must be communicated clearly and repeatedly to a child, especially during his first four years:

First is the concept—Dobson calls it a beacon or a guiding light—that the child is loved by his parents more than he can possibly understand. Say, "You are precious to me and I thank God every day that He gave you to me to raise."

Second is that "because I love, I must teach you to obey me. That is the only way I can take care of you and protect you from things that might hurt you."

Dr. Dobson recommends that parents read to children Ephesians 6:1, "Children, obey your parents in the Lord, for this is right."

Most important is that parents develop their own philosophies of how to raise children. Obviously, also early in their development, children need to know the basics of your faith. They receive Christ at surprisingly early ages these days, and as you know, we have no problem with that. They need not be theologians and understand all the nuances of doctrine. They simply need to understand that their sins have separated them from God but Jesus has made a way of escape.

Most children who receive Christ have experiences later when they decide for themselves to live for the Lord and not exercise an inherited faith. What a joy to see them do that!

❦ December 29 ❧

Jill had been disciplining the boys and had to raise her voice. Pat said to Bob, "You know, men are different from women."

"Yeah, I know," Bob said. "Women are always mad."

Well, women aren't *always* mad, but it does seem that the day-to-day frustrations of raising kids usually takes its toll more on Mom than on Dad.

When Jill is feeling particularly sorry for herself, however, she reminds herself of stories like the following that make our life seem a lot easier:

According to a *Chicago Tribune* story in June 1987, Dorothy Johnson was a widowed mother of four grown children, working in a factory and looking forward to an easier life as she approached fifty in 1969. A co-worker pleaded for her help. His daughter had given birth to triplets out of wedlock, and the young father had disappeared.

When Dorothy saw the babies in their three tiny cribs, she prayed that God would help her raise them and see them graduate from high school. When they were eight, she legally adopted them, and between working full-time and being a mother, she indeed saw them through high school graduation.

At the adoption proceeding, the judge asked one of the girls if she knew what adoption was. "Yes," she said, "it's when you come out of a lady's stomach and she doesn't want you so they give you to a mom who does. Aren't we lucky?" They sure were.

❧ December 30 ❧

Even after having stayed with us all the way through this year, are you still afraid your marriage is lackluster? As we have tried to clarify, we don't have any easy answers. We still struggle. We still have to work hard. We both change every day, and so does our marriage.

Remember never to deny there is a problem. Get it on the table and start devising a solution. If either of you has a problem, the marriage has a problem, and it needs to be fixed.

Shake off any dull routine. If you are bored because you do the same things the same way all the time, it is up to you to change. If you always have your date night on the same night of the week, switch it. Go somewhere else. Make it lunch instead of dinner—anything to change the environment.

Try trading household chores. In our house, the kids change them all the time, drawing for certain jobs and trading for others. We've considered letting Pat do the cooking one day while Jill does his work, just so each can gain a new appreciation for what the other does.

Do something nice for your spouse every day. It doesn't have to be elaborate or require hours of preparation, just something that will remind him or her that you are still in love. Pat brings Jill fresh-squeezed orange juice in bed every day.

Regardless of what you choose to do, do it with a heart of love and most likely it will not go unrewarded.

❧ December 31 ❧

Better than the advice of any expert are the truths and principles for raising children found in the Word of God. As we close out this year and look forward to the next, consider the concepts found in Ephesians 6:2–4: " 'Honor your father and mother,' which is the first commandment with promise: 'that it may be well with you and you may live long on the earth.' And you, fathers, do not provoke your children to wrath, but bring them up in the training and admonition of the Lord."

We must teach children to obey authority and to honor their parents. We must accept them as they are. We must give them ourselves, including our love, our discipline, our security.

We need to allow them freedom to make mistakes. They need to see our trust and our acceptance of them, no matter what.

Unconditional love is the bottom line in parent-child relationships, and it is so difficult for parents because it is not a human capacity. Unconditional love is a divine characteristic that can be exercised only by a person who has Christ living in him.

Let God do the loving of your children through you. He is better at it, has more experience, and has the resources of the universe at His fingertips.

Happy New Year!